Hold the Enlightenment

Hold the

VILLARD Ⓥ NEW YORK

Enlightenment

Tim Cahill

"Hold the Enlightenment" previously appeared in *Yoga Journal;* "Bug Scream,"
"The Platypus Hunter," "Fire and Ice and Everything Nice," "The Caravan of
White Gold," "The Terrible Land," "The House of Boots," "This Teeming Ark,"
"Near Massacre Ranch," "Fubsy Hors D'oeuvres," "Gorillas in Our Schools," "The
Entranced Duck," "Castle and More Castles," "Culinary Schadenfreude,"
"Swimming with Great White Sharks," "Atlatl Bob's Splendid Lack of Simple
Sanity," "Fully Unprepared," "Evilfish," "Collision Course," "The Big Muddy,"
"Professor Cahill's Travel 101," "My Brother, the Pot Dealer," "Dirty Money,"
"Panic," and "Trusty and Grace" all appeared in *Outside* magazine, sometimes in
a slightly different form and often under a different title; "The Search for the
Caspian Tiger," "Powder Keg," "The World's Most Dangerous Friend," and
"The Cowpersons of Tanzania" all appeared in *Men's Journal,* sometimes in a
slightly different form and, in one case, under a different title; "Stutter" appeared
in *Modern Maturity.*

Library of Congress Cataloging-in-Publication Data

Cahill, Tim.
Hold the enlightenment / Tim Cahill.
p.   cm.
ISBN 0-375-50766-3
I. Title.

PS3553.A365 H65 2002
813'.54—dc21   2002074263

Villard Books website address: www.villard.com

Printed in the United States of America on acid-free paper

2 3 4 5 6 7 8 9

FIRST EDITION

Book design by Joseph Rutt

To Rollie Bestor and Phil Cibik

Acknowledgments

Thanks to Larry Burke and everyone at *Outside,* both past and present. I am always proud to appear in the magazine and to work with editors like Hal Espen.

Todd Jones at *Yoga Journal* let me have an awful lot of fun, and the readers didn't cancel their subscriptions in droves, or so he said. Maybe he's just being nice.

Mark Cohen at *Men's Journal* could get it done even when the volume got a little high. Sid Evans edited a prizewinning story under great pressure. Thanks also to John Wood at *Modern Maturity.*

And an all-embracing thank you to Mark Bryant, who edited stories of mine at both *Outside* and *Men's Journal.* The finest compliment any writer can give to any editor is the one I offer you here: Mark, I'd work for you again in a heartbeat.

Contents

Unattractive to the Opposite Sex:
An Introduction

Introductions, I feel, in my mean-spirited way, are an appropriate forum to even the score, settle old debts, avenge insults, spew a lot of invective, and basically have fun decimating the wicked or the undiscriminating. Unfortunately, I am currently living in a hell of insufficient aggravation. Critics have generally been kind, or if not precisely kind, then at least fair. In fact, two of the stories in this collection were selected to be included in the *Best American Travel Writing* books: "This Teeming Ark," in 2000, and "Powder Keg," which appeared under the title "Volcano Alley Is Ticking," in 2001.

The truth is, I actually had to look for someone to kick around here. Happily, after a quick root through my files, I found Hal Clifford, a columnist for the *Aspen Times*. Hal published his interview with me and, in what I suspect was meant to be a humorous aside, he suggested that I was "unattractive to the opposite sex." Somehow I had not been aware of this previously. I wondered how Hal knew.

Another fellow, a newspaper critic, noted that in a previous collection, I had included a piece written for *Modern Maturity*, the magazine of the American Association of Retired Persons, and from that concluded that I was "getting tired." It is probably for that reason I've included the only piece I've written for *Modern Maturity* of late. I'm not so tired that I mind drawing fire from imbeciles. On the other hand, the article in question is very short indeed, and its very brevity may supply munitions to the moron.

Similarly, I haven't been vigorous or virtuous enough to thank the hundreds of people who have written me letters over the years, and I'll do it here, all in a lump. Thank you. Really. I'm glad you liked the books, your letters truly do brighten my day, and I'm sincerely sorry that I haven't written back. It's not you. I never write back. I do, however, spend a lot of time feeling guilty about not responding to all the well-written missives. Somebody writing to a writer works on the letter and that is obvious. To do even half as well as you in reply, I'd have to work on it too, and, hey, that's what I do for a living. I'm not a guy who writes letters, as my mother reminds me from time to time.

This doesn't mean I don't think about what people say. A perceptive reader noted that the conclusion of the story "Castle and More Castles" echoed a thought expressed by the late poet and scientist Loren Eiseley, in his collection *Star Thrower*. Eiseley is a favorite of mine and I've quoted him twice in this book, once in "Evilfish" and once in "Professor Cahill's Travel 101." I can't very well argue that I am unfamiliar with the work, and the idea expressed at the end of the castle story is indeed very similar to one penned by Eiseley. Well, okay, it's almost identical.

So I spent days reading Eisely then rereading my own work, and wondering whether I unconsciously swiped the idea or whether such concepts might occur to folks of parallel sentiments contemplating a similar set of conditions.

What I mean to say here is that the letters do not fall on deaf ears, or, more appropriately I suppose, on blind eyes. I read them. I think about them. Some, like the Eiseley letter, challenge me for days.

And I really do intend to answer them. Really. I put them in a large file box that is placed on a prominent shelf in my office. The box is labeled "Correspondence 2002," or whatever the year happens to be. Every time I see the file, which is every day that I work in my office, I feel exceedingly guilty and know that I am not a good person. Generally, almost always in early January, I seal up the box, add the word "Unanswered" to the label, and carry it out to my garage. I have yearly file boxes—"Unanswered

Correspondence"—from almost three decades out there. There is no room for my truck anymore, only for the rows upon rows of boxes, mute accusations, piled high over my head. Sometimes I have nightmares about them: angry boxes on a mission of vengeance.

So, to decades' worth of letter writers, many thanks and my sincere apologies.

And as long as I'm thanking folks, I would like to mention those anonymous people who have brightened the darkest portion of my life: the time spent on airplanes. Occasionally, I walk down the aisle and someone is actually reading one of my books. Sometimes, that person will laugh aloud, and I want to glance over her shoulder and see what it was that got her. Which piece, what part? I enter the rest room knowing, beyond a shadow of a doubt, that I am the God of Humor.

But that's not so. I'm reminded of that every time I do a vanity search on the Internet and discover a site where ordinary folks—as opposed to big-deal journalists—review books. Most people say nice things, but sometimes there are warnings, and quite appropriate ones at that: this guy, the reviewers say of me, is certainly worth reading but he is not as funny as Dave Barry. True, but nobody is as funny as Dave Barry. Except for P. J. O'Rourke. Nobody is as funny as P.J. Or Bill Bryson, for that matter. Or, well, there are a lot of writers who are funnier than I am. The sad fact is that I seldom set out to be funny at all. It just happens and it always surprises me when it does.

On those rare occasions when I have actually tried to be funny, I've failed. Miserably. Witness the story "Panic," which is about a hairy-chested adventure guy—me—with the worst case of stage fright in television history. Now, that is funny on the face of it, but the essay was not a knee-slapper and turned out to be about mortality, chaos, the organizing principle of story, and one tiny redemption. (I'm serious: The story was recently anthologized in *A Man's Guide to Simple Abundance,* which is full of enlightening and redemptive essays. My presence there has a sort of a sore-thumb resonance.)

Longtime readers may recognize an adventure or two from previous books. The climbing aspect of "Panic" is a prime example. As the years close in on me—I'm in my mid-fifties as I write this—it occurs to me that I ought at least to *try* to figure out what it all means. I doubt that I will, but my thoughts on enlightenment altogether can be found in the first story in this book.

"Stutter," a small piece from *Modern Maturity* about the guide Grant Thompson, is partially about a bad fall I took climbing in the Queen Charlotte Islands, as is "Fully Unprepared," which is also about the death of a loved one. I've written about that trip, but never about the full extent of the injuries I suffered, the fact that I literally couldn't walk for months, and the operation that got me back on my feet. The story is a contemplation of mortality.

Of course, this collection does have some basic episodes of adventure—diving with great white sharks in South Africa, for instance—but many of the dangerous obstacles here are human. This is new. Part of my job, as I see it, is to get to the most remote and inaccessible places on earth. It used to be easy to find such places, but now adventure-travel tour packages take people all over the earth, even to the summit of Everest. What the guides can't do is take folks to areas that are politically unstable and they can't do this because they can't get insurance.

These days, "remote" is defined as far away plus armaments, and factions, and ancient enmities. To truly get "Out There," as the column I write is called, I often feel I'm being funneled into places where people point guns at you. The Cold War is over, and there are places in the former Soviet Union—and elsewhere—that have been pretty much closed to this day. Tribal enmities flare, warlords rule, and if you want to get farther than the end of the road, you have to get by the line of guns. The weapons are most evident here in stories such as "The Search for the Caspian Tiger," "The Caravan of White Gold," and "The World's Most Dangerous Friend."

Attentive readers will note that certain of my friends, people I've written about in the past, make multiple appearances in the book: Matt Smith is here, along with my pals Joel Rogers, Atlatl Bob

Perkins, Linnea Larson, Nick Nichols, Michael Fay, Cynthia Moses, and Grant Thompson.

Occasionally, a reader more anal than I writes to ask why I don't organize my collections in some fashion—all deserts in this section, for instance, and forests in that, arctic ice here, animal stories there. And what about some sinew of connection between the pieces? Once again, I've read those letters, and contemplated them, and in this collection, I played around with the order of the stories, such as it is. It seemed entirely artificial to me. The stories are not arranged chronologically, but they are a fairly representative sampling of my life. Looking at them, I feel as if time has folded in on itself, and that my various travels have the chaotic logic of a pinball in urgent play. What can I say? I have a low threshold of boredom and this is the way I live my life.

If there is any organizing principle at work here, it is emotional, though, Lord knows, the stories can be read one at a time and in any order without damage to the intended construct. But let me be among the many to warn you: not all the stories are funny. I want to make you laugh, sure, but I also want to make you cry. I used to tell my students in writing seminars that if you can do that—make 'em laugh and make 'em cry in the same work—then you've created the "illusion of depth." I've been thinking about that lately and am willing to amend my thought: I now believe the profundity is genuine and not illusory.

Not that there's a lot of deep thinking in, say, the opening piece, "Hold the Enlightenment," an account of a yoga retreat I endured (and enjoyed) in Jamaica. In fact, as I reread the story, it seems to be a wholesale rejection of wisdom, insight, and understanding altogether. Enlightenment, as I try to explain, is a poor career path for a writer.

The last essay here, "Trusty and Grace," is a personal piece that echoes biblical psalms, involves canine flatulence right up there in the first paragraph, and, in the end, made me, the author, cry. I had no idea that it would do that. I first read the story aloud, live, on National Public Radio. When I got toward the end, I choked up, stumbled on the words "brave little girl," swallowed, and then faltered again on "brave woman." My eyes smarted, my voice broke. My carefully cultivated reputation as your typically insensitive guy went up in flames. You'll see me trying to retrieve that status throughout this book.

In any case, whatever the emotional weight of any of these essays, the prose in each has been honed to the best of my ability and is meant to be attractive to members of all sexes. I suppose psychologists would call that overcompensation.

Tim Cahill
Montana
December 2001

Hold the Enlightenment

Hold the Enlightenment

I am not a yoga kinda guy. Yoga people are sensitive, aware, largely sober, slender, double-jointed, humorless vegans who are concerned with their own spiritual welfare and don't hesitate to tell you about it. They are spiritually intense and consequently enormously boring in the manner of folks who, in their own self-absorption, feel you ought be alerted as to the quantity and texture of their last bowel movement.

Or so I used to think.

But there I was, taking my first yoga class, in an open-sided bar/restaurant while, a few hundred feet below, the Caribbean Sea exploded off the high coral cliffs of Negril, Jamaica. I was doing some position, an asana, that was something like what I'd call a wrestler's bridge: it required balancing on my head and hands up top, and the soles of my feet below. Hotel employees had removed tables and chairs from the restaurant for this class, and, because I was apprehensive, I'd positioned myself in the area where I felt most comfortable, which is to say, next to the bar. In the field of my vision, I could see an upside-down line of several bottles of rum, and, above them, a black-and-white picture of Bob Marley, the patron saint of Jamaican reggae. There is a picture of Bob Marley in every single bar in Jamaica. I know: I've done the research. One of Marley's best songs has a line that goes "Every little thing, is going to be all right." That, I decided, was my mantra.

I'm a writer, of sorts. My job, such as it is, requires me to travel to remote countries, where I have, in the past few decades, covered the drug/guerrilla war in Colombia, investigated the murder of an American in the jungles of Peru, dived with great white sharks off the coast of South Africa, and sat negotiating my fate with Tuareg warlords in the southern Sahara. Pretty hairy-chested stuff, but the truth is, I was a little scared about meeting all the yoga folks in Jamaica. There's a lot of testosterone involved in what I do. I assumed that yoga people would perceive me as some sort of throwback: a Neolithic macho, and an abyss of awareness.

Well, everybody wants to be liked, and I deeply feared the scorn of the assembled yogis and yoginis. The books I read before coming to Jamaica had calmed me somewhat: yoga, I learned, is not a religion, and you can take from it what you will. Go only for the physical benefits: fine, yoga doesn't have a problem with that. Use it for stress relief and meditation: sure, okay. Or a person might opt for a total yoga lifestyle, which includes diet, meditation, and the search for enlightenment. Take from it what you will: yoga, according to the books, doesn't give a rat's ass.

But I assumed that people who would choose to spend their vacations doing four hours of yoga a day would be lifestyle folks, the kind of weenies who might sneer at my own rather soiled lifestyle. I feared my classmates would be holier than thou, or, in any case, holier than I, which is pretty much a slam dunk.

In fact, my classmates—a couple of dozen of them—did not appear at all the way I thought yoga people were supposed to look. The men were not little weenie guys, for one thing, and there were several of them there—I only say this out of journalistic integrity— who probably could have taken me at arm wrestling. The women— whose ages spanned a couple of generations—were not hippie burnouts and acid crawlbacks. None wore patchouli oil, and an extraordinary number of them were highly attractive. The rest were just conventionally good-looking. Don't misunderstand: I was with my wife, and I am not single and looking. But if I were, I'd take yoga classes, if only to meet chicks.

Our instructors were John Schumacher, founder and director of Unity Woods, a studio with locations throughout the East, and Barbara Benagh of Boston's Yoga Studio. We had started the class by introducing ourselves and talking about our experience with yoga. Several of the students had studied for twenty years or more. My wife and I were the only total beginners, but, when my turn came, I told the assembled yogis, "I haven't done any yoga physically, but I've read three entire books and figure I know everything there is to know about it."

There was a brief moment of silence, and I thought, yep, humorless. And then the class burst into laughter. Not a lot of it. It wasn't that good a joke. I looked up at Bob Marley and thought: Every little thing, is going to be all right.

The books in question had been sent to me by Todd Jones of *Yoga Journal,* who had asked me to write a story about my first yoga class. Todd said he was looking for "a view of our little subculture from the outside." That seemed fair enough, and I asked him if he could mail me some introductory texts.

He sent yoga books appropriately addressed to dummies and idiots, along with Erich Schiffmann's *Yoga: The Spirit and Practice of Moving into Stillness,* which I found well written but a bit on the ethereal side, at least for me. I figured yoga kinda guys might get a lot out of it.

What I was able to glean from all this material was that the poses, or asanas, were developed thousands of years ago to give people control over their bodies. Such control is essentially for yogic meditation. The purpose and goal of meditation is the bliss of eventual enlightenment. That stopped me cold. Enlightenment? No sir, whoa Nellie. None of that whoop-de-do for me, thank you very much.

The Enlightened Masters I have read are invariably incomprehensible and the Masters themselves are entirely incapable of constructing a single coherent English sentence. I'm not discussing someone like Eric Schiffmann, who is actually very good. What I'm talking about here is Flat Out Enlightenment, which is mostly unintelligible gibberish and reads to me like someone swimming through a thick custard of delirium. And don't think I don't know my Enlightened Masters. I've been to ashrams in India, power spots, and convergence points and "vortices" in California and Colorado and New Mexico. I have spent time chatting to a woman with many, many followers who lives near my home in Montana and who channels Enlightened Masters all day long as if making calls on a cellular phone.

The link between them all—the convergence people, the gurus, the Enlightened—is that, in their written materials anyway, they don't make any sense at all. For that reason they all are self-published, which is to say, they themselves pay someone else to publish the work in question. As a professional writer, I prefer the opposite strategy, in which the publisher pays you. Enlightenment, my reading suggested, is an exceedingly poor career path for a writer.

Oh, I knew bliss and enlightenment aren't often achieved. It said as much in each of the books I read. One strives toward the light. Okay, I'd buy that, sure, but what if I turned out to be one of those guys who just happens to "get it" straight away? What if I was an anomaly? I'd crank out a few asanas, sit cross-legged, thinking-but-not-thinking, and all of a sudden, flash-bang, I'd see it all: the meaning of life, my own connection to the cosmos, and the blinding curve of energy that is the pulsing soul of universal consciousness itself, and I'd know, beyond the shadow of a doubt, that at that moment, I was completely and irrevocably screwed.

Enlightened people are dead meat in the publishing industry. I'd lose my jobs, such as they are. My mortgage would go unpaid, my wife would leave me, and I'd wander the earth in ragged clothes, informing the less spiritually fortunate of a consciousness above and beyond. Perhaps those people might give me a few coins with which I could buy a scrap of bread. This is to say that, in my mind, enlightenment and homelessness are synonymous situations.

I called Todd Jones back at *Yoga Journal* and said I'd take the course, but I intended to resist enlightenment. And if, through some cruel trick of fate, I did become enlightened, I was going to go out there to Berkeley, California, and kick his ass.

So, there I was, three days into the yoga vacation, with twelve big hours of yoga under my belt. I had feared, on the whole, that yoga might be too light a workout for me: a bunch of sissy stuff about standing on one leg for a couple of breaths. I typically run (or plod) two miles a day, occasionally lift weights, and stretch assiduously. I had called Todd Jones before I left and asked if he couldn't get me into one of the more sweaty disciplines, some kind of power yoga.

"If I put you, as an absolute beginner, in an ashtanga class for a week," Todd said mildly, "you really would kick my ass."

He was right about that. I was able to do many of the asanas, but it had never occurred to me that once you attained the position, it was necessary to keep working through it. It never got any easier. If you did it right, you were always working at the very edge of what you could do. In a typical four-hour day, I felt I'd gotten a pretty good physical workout, and each would have been a lot more effective if I could have done some of the more advanced work we typically did late in the session. Todd Jones was right about ahstanga.

I was standing at the bar after an afternoon class, having a beer and a cigarette, when John Schumacher stopped by for a chat. I was wearing a T-shirt I had bought from John, who runs the Unity Woods Yoga Center. The shirt featured a large triangle whose legs read: "serenity," "awareness," "health."

"I suppose," I said, "I'm a bad advertisement for Unity Woods."

"Not at all," John said. "We'll just add the words 'not applicable.' "

There were several people at the bar, and though some undoubtedly lived a yoga lifestyle, others did not. No one talked about Obstacles Along the Path. There were even a few smokers, and several who drank alcohol, though hardly in the quantities I find refreshing. A "yoga vacation," I was told, is different than a "yoga retreat," where I might have felt considerably more out of place.

In the class, there was a guy who taught stress reduction at various corporations, an engineer who'd worked in the Middle East, among other places, and a woman who'd been to India several times and studied with a man named Inyengar, who, I knew from my reading, was considered hot stuff and one of the modern masters.

There was a psychiatrist there, and we talked a little about my preconceptions. "Exactly," the doctor said. "I don't tell people I practice yoga for that reason. Some people automatically think it means you also do crystal healing or some such."

The stress-reduction guy told a yoga story that made me laugh. "I was at a convention in one of those big hotels. I check in, strip naked, and start on my yoga. So I'm doing a headstand, and the door opens. There was a mix-up at reception and they'd given someone else my key. The guy says, 'whoops,' and closes the door. All I ever saw was his shoes. All he ever saw, I'm sure, was, well, what he could see from his level. I spent three days looking at people's shoes, wondering which guy it was. He probably figured I was some strange kind of pervert."

"Ignorant people think that about yoga," I said, from the perspective of a twelve-hour-old yogi.

I spoke with the woman who'd studied with Inyengar. Her husband told me about the time he accidentally poured out her cake batter before an important party. "I thought it was a dirty dish," he explained. His wife discovered the transgression just after her yoga class, and didn't yell at him very much at all. "I decided then and there that I'd encourage her to take all the yoga she wanted," he said.

The instructors had diametrically opposed styles of teaching. John Schumacher, who has studied with Inyengar several times, was about precision. I was amazed that he could stand there, tell me exactly what I was feeling, and then suggest a certain shift of balance that made the asana more steady, more exact, more difficult but somehow more comfortable. The right way felt right. The wrong way did not.

Barbara Benagh, on the other hand, tended to use visualization. I was not the only student who didn't know exactly where she was going. You'd be sitting cross-legged, imagining roots sprouting out of your butt, or some such, and then she'd have you twist just so, move the other arm, extend the right leg, and suddenly you were up in a complex position you never imagined you could do.

Barbara's overall strategy for the week, it seemed, was to guide the students through a plan to get energy running back and forth from the groin to the back through what she called the lumbar bridge. This may not be entirely correct: I sometimes lost the thread of what Barbara was saying late in the class, either because I couldn't feel what she meant physically, or because the concepts were too advanced for me. People who had been studying yoga for several years, however, like Inverted Naked Man, told me that they'd been working on those very concepts for the last year and that they were in the midst of a kind of mental and physical breakthrough, thanks to Barbara.

While Barbara and John had been teaching together at this "yoga vacation" for over fifteen years, they were quite dissimilar in other ways. Barbara, for instance, loved marathon-length mountain biking sessions, and she was an avid swimmer, racking up as much as a mile a day before teaching class. John, on the other hand, felt yoga, done consistently, was all a person needed to stay in good shape.

"Well," I said, over dinner with the both of them one night, "you've gotta do some cardiovascular stuff, running or whatever."

John didn't think so. Yogic breathing, properly practiced, was all a person needed. He himself had recently had his cardiovascular system tested and he'd scored pretty much off the scale. He never ran. "I think all that stuff about keeping the heart rate at such and such for so many minutes is a real caveman way of doing it."

Well, yeah, I thought, if you're John Schumacher, maybe you can keep your heart healthy through a combination of breathing and asanas. I wasn't John Schumacher and I was going to just keep plodding along in my own Neolithic fashion, but I'd throw in a couple of hours of yoga a week as well. I had discovered that it made me feel good.

Unexpectedly, my wife and I became friendly with several of our classmates. That was my biggest surprise. There was a singular lack of sanctimony among the assembled students. And, indeed, several of us made plans to return next year. My preconceptions about yoga people had been pretty well demolished, but I wasn't able to absorb the whole discipline and philosophy in a single week. I resolved to work hard on my asanas, then come back next year, and make the lot of them look like pissants.

Given that state of mind, I suppose it hardly needs to be said that

I successfully avoided enlightenment. Happily, I suffered not a single stab of awareness, though I fear that if I keep this up for any length of time, I may have some difficulties with serenity. That's something I'm going to have to work on, this creeping and insidious tranquillity. I'm a nail-biting, chain-smoking, hard-drinking deadline junkie. That's my life. I love it, and I worry a lot about the curse of incipient equanimity. In my worst moments of serene composure, I assure myself that, even though I am currently practicing yoga, enlightenment is a long shot and I'm not going to get there. For that reason alone, I tell myself, every little thing is going to be all right.

The Search for the
Caspian Tiger

I was sitting in the Owl, a small bar in a small town in Montana, when I was lifted bodily from the stool—no small feat—and kissed exuberantly on both my cheeks. "Doctor C," Tommy the Turk said by way of greeting. He was a barrel-chested man, bald as a billiard ball, and he wore a wool-woven blue and white cap, like a yarmulke. I assumed that he was back from one Central Asian war or another. People who know these deadly disputes and these places know Thomas Goltz. He is a war correspondent of certain distinction and has received invitations to share his knowledge of shadowy wars in obscure places from prestigious universities, various institutions, and the CIA. "I've got a quest for you, Doctor," Tommy said.

He showed me a clipping from the London *Sunday Express*. The lead sentence said that high in the mountains of Turkey "could lie a secret which will stun scientists: the return from the dead of a lost species." The article quoted a Dr. Guven Eken, of the Society for the Protection of Nature: "The Caspian tiger is considered to be extinct but in South East Turkey, local hunters claim to have seen tigers in the mountains."

We toasted Tommy's safe arrival back in Montana and discussed the idea of searching for the ghost tiger. As I recall, this involved many toasts. The next morning I woke up with some fuzzy recollection about an agreement to go to Turkey and search for the Caspian tiger with Tommy the Turk, a guy famous for covering wars. Was that a good idea? Would we get shot at? And what the hell did I know about tigers?

One week later, to the day, Tommy and I were in Istanbul, along with photographer Rob Howard, nicknamed—for reasons impervious to investigative reporting—the Duck. We were sitting at a café overlooking the Bosporus and talking with Dr. Guven Eken, who had been quoted in the *Sunday Express*. He was an Art Garfunkel–looking guy who confessed that he had never actually been to the southeastern part of Turkey, didn't know anything at all about tigers, and didn't really actually have the names of any hunters who'd seen one. He'd only heard rumors. *The guy had only heard rumors.*

So now we were tracking *rumors* of a ghost tiger.

Dr. Eken sought to dissuade us altogether. The southeastern part of the country was "sensitive," and "security" was a problem.

The security situation, in a nutshell—Tommy knew it well—involves a long-running Kurdish insurrection. There are 25 million Kurds living in five different countries, including the southeast of Turkey. The Kurds are said to be the largest ethnic group in the world without a homeland. But there is a homeland, of sorts. Northern Iraq is a de facto, unrecognized Kurdish statelet, and has been ever since the U.S.-NATO no-fly zone was imposed over the region after the Gulf War. The two ruling Kurdish groups there are largely sympathetic to the United States. A third group—operating in both Turkey and northern Iraq—is the Kurdish Workers Party, the PKK, a Marxist-Leninist organization which has been at war with Turkey since 1986. It had been largely defanged since the arrest of its leader, Abdullah Ocalan, in February of 1999. Ocalan, called Apo, was facing execution, and had recently spoken out against violence. But pockets of resistance still existed, especially in remote, mountainous, little-inhabited areas of the country, like the southeast, where there were skirmishes now and again. The day before our meeting with Dr. Eken, for instance, there had been an article in the paper: two insurrectionists had been killed by soldiers in a prolonged gun battle near the border with Iraq outside the town of Shemdinli. It was Tommy's impression that things were winding down in the southeast and that we could talk our way through most military checkpoints.

Dr. Eken said we ought to talk to the Society for the Protection of Nature's big-mammal man, Emry Can, in Ankara. The Caspian tiger, I knew, once ranged from southern Russia through Afghanistan to Iran, Iraq, Azerbaijan, and Turkey. The last one was shot in the southeastern Turkish town of Uludere in 1970. A big creature—males measure nine feet from the tip of the tail to the nose and weigh in excess of five hundred pounds—it looked very much like the classic Bengal tiger, with khaki-colored skin and black stripes on its legs. In the winter, it got a lot furrier than your basic Bengal.

The Romans used to capture them on the banks of the Tigris in Turkey and take them to Rome for their circuses. And that is how the animal got its name: the Tigris cat, *Pantera tiger*. It is, I think, a good thing the big cats weren't found on the Euphrates, or there'd be a magnificent animal with a very silly name: Euphrator.

The rest of our brief stay in Istanbul involved sitting around in innumerable offices smoking lots of cigarettes while Tommy talked about tigers in exchange for press passes and letters of introduction. Foreign journalists we met along the way assured us that we probably couldn't get to certain towns in the southeast, notably Shemdinli, which was one of the last redoubts of the disintegrating remnants of the PKK.

Mostly, we were given to understand by our fellow journalists that the military didn't want to see another "cuddly Kurd/terrible Turk" story: a piece about how the military oppressed these proud tribal people, who were not allowed to speak their own language, or wear their own distinctive style of dress. Only last month, we were told, an American TV crew and a British one had been expelled from the area.

We took the night train down to the capital city of Ankara, and sat in a dozen more offices while people smoked thousands of cigarettes. We obtained letters from the appropriate officials stating that our mission was a tiger search; we talked to the head of the

Hunting and Wildlife Directory of the Forestry Department, who said he'd send a representative to travel with us. So we'd have a minder.

We talked with Emry Can, the big-mammal expert at the Society for the Protection of Nature, who interrogated us fiercely—he thought we were hunters, looking to knock off the last tiger. He himself had not been to the southeast, but was planning an expedition "next year, or perhaps the year after." Scientists, he suggested, will tell you that the species needs five hundred animals for a viable breeding population, but it was Emry Can's opinion that the Caspian tiger could survive with a breeding population as low as fifty individuals.

Anything we might find, he said—tracks called pug marks, even confirmed sightings—would be of great significance. Unfortunately, he had no idea where we might start our search.

And so, with no destination firmly in mind, we flew to the major town in the southeast, Van, on the shores of Lake Van, the largest freshwater lake in Turkey. Traveling with Tommy, I discovered, involved all manner of minor and major confrontations. Like Cuban toilet paper, Tommy the Turk doesn't take shit off anyone. For instance, the man has to have his coffee in the morning. He carries his own ground beans and coffee press, but when he asked for hot water at one hotel, the room clerk refused to fetch a pot. It was Ramadan, the Islamic holy month of fasting from daybreak until sundown. The fast includes water, and indeed, some pious Muslims do not even swallow their own saliva but spit into a hankie all day long. No way the clerk was going to get hot water for a bunch of infidels.

"How dare you," Tommy raged in fluent Turkish. "Did not the Prophet, peace be upon him, declare that travelers were specifically exempted from the fast? Did not the Prophet, peace be upon him, also say that . . ." And so on, for about half a dozen scriptural points until he had spiritually shamed this poor son of a bitch into getting us a pot of hot water.

Tommy grew up in Fargo, North Dakota, has a master's in Middle Eastern studies, speaks fluent Turkish and passable Arabic along with Russian, Kurd, German, and a handful of other languages. He is also the author and editor of the *Insight Guide to Turkey*. Over the last decade or so, he has spent a lot of time dodging bullets in various war zones. His *Azerbaijan Diary* is the definitive book on the conflict there, and he is currently writing a memoir about the war in Chechnya. With his Turkish wrestler's build and shaven head, he can pass for a local in Turkey, and my man eats snotty room clerks for breakfast.

In Van, we met Saim Guclu, the chief engineer of the National Forest Eastern Anatolia. Saim provided a vehicle: a small Nissan truck with an extended cab and Forestry Department decals on the doors. He was a big, jolly man in his early sixties, at a guess, with a white mustache. His driver's name could be translated as "Mr. Security." He was a quiet fellow in a sport coat. Neither man struck me as an intelligence officer. On the other hand, they wanted $300 a day for the car if we took pictures in any national parks.

Saim seemed to be what he claimed to be: a forestry official. He said: "I am ashamed to admit that I have never been to Uludere, where the last tiger was shot. I have never been to Shemdinli. We have done no inventory of the animals in these places. Of course, our department has only existed since 1994. Your presence here is very helpful to me, you see. We now have our permission to do something we should have done years ago." Saim had pored over books and documents in the Forestry Department, looking for information on the Caspian tiger, and there was virtually nothing there.

We shared what we knew. There are eight subspecies of tiger, and three of them are considered extinct: the Balinese tiger, the Javanese tiger, and the Caspian tiger, *Pantera tigris virgata*. No data is available on its prey, gestation period, or rate of cub mortality. Both Saim and I had discovered that the Caspian tiger was the second largest subspecies: only the endangered Siberian tiger was bigger. Aside from that, we were both guessing about everything. Most tigers have a territory of ten to twenty miles, though this depends on the available food. Perhaps the Caspian tiger might eat wild pig and wild goat. It might live as long as most wild tigers: ten to fifteen years, and eat, oh, forty pounds of meat at a sitting.

I was developing an overwhelming fondness for the forgotten and ignored ghost creature. Often Saim, a knowledgeable and well-read scholar, deferred to me in discussions about the tiger's possible range and prey. There was so little credible research available that it didn't take much, or so it seemed, to become something of an expert on the Caspian tiger.

"If we find evidence that the tiger exists," Saim said, "it will be a great thing not only for Turkey but for all the world. Wildlife doesn't belong to any one country."

"How dare you," Tommy was saying to the soldier at one of the many military checkpoints at a snowy pass along the winding two-lane paved road to Uludere. We were riding along with Saim in the Forestry Department car, with Mr. Security at the wheel.

The soldier had just said, "Why don't you stay home? Why come here and stir up trouble?" He meant: We don't want to read any more cuddly Kurd/terrible Turk stories in the foreign media.

Tommy said, "How dare you speak to me in that tone of voice, before you know who I am and what my mission is?" This gave the soldier pause. In these situations, and at this point, Tommy usually trotted out the papers and passes and letters we'd smoked so many cigarettes to obtain. He explained about the tiger, and this conversation generally settled down into some friendly banter and invariably led to an invitation to take tea. We found ourselves smoking more cigarettes and laughing about one thing or another. My name, for instance, was a matter of great hilarity. In Turkey no one is named Tim, but many are called Timur in honor of the fourteenth-century Mongol who conquered Persia, southern Russia, and Turkey. He was known for his deeds of cruelty: in India, for instance, he is said to have killed eighty thousand in Delhi alone. Historic mass murder was looked upon with a degree of respect. It was my last name that was the problem. Cahill is pronounced "Djaheel" in Turkish and means, I regret to report, "ignorant." So Tommy and the soldiers sat around drinking tea and smoking cigarettes and handing my passport from one to the other and laughing out loud at my very name. Timur the Ignorant: it was like being called "Atilla the Dope."

The road dropped down out of the snow into flatter land and ran parallel to the border of Iraq until we reached the turnoff to Uludere. The narrow two-lane wound its way up a green, flowing creek lined with white-bark poplars, and we passed an abandoned village of quaint stone houses, all of them missing a wall or simply leveled by artillery fire. "We don't know who did this," Saim said. "The PKK or the military. Whoever: let Allah strike them blind."

And then we were in Uludere proper. Homes on the outskirts were made of river rock and looked almost medieval, but the downtown was filled with newer, poured-concrete shops, and the streets were crowded with unemployed men. They were mostly Kurds: tall, generally slender people with imposing, hawklike faces.

We stepped out of the car and were immediately surrounded by dozens of people, mostly men, all of them answering our questions at full volume and at the same time. No one knew the man who had shot the tiger in 1970, but there was a fellow who shot one in the sixties. He was dead. Forty years ago, the paved road we'd driven had been a mule trail. Uludere was now a big town. No one had heard anything about tigers for years.

An old man said there had been lots of tigers about in the early sixties. He heard them at night, while he tended his sheep. They made a sound a little like the whinny of a horse, like the bray of a donkey. Not the hee-haw sound: the "ahhhh" sound they make. Someone else said the animal was so heavy it took three men to carry a dead one; that its track looked like that of a domestic cat, but bigger, with the talons as long as a man's index finger. The big cat, he said, seemed to "seize" the snow: when the pads of its paws flexed, it left a little snowball in the middle of the track.

We had been talking with the men for about ten minutes when the subgovernor of the province arrived along with several cops. This self-inflated little turd threatened to confiscate our film and "detain" us until he could ascertain for sure the nature of our business in Uludere. Saim, the Duck, and I retreated to the truck behind a solid wall of Tommy talk while Mr. Security fired up the engine. A cop put his hand on Tommy's shoulder, but he shook it off, jumped into the truck, and said, "Go, go, go."

Back in Van, we were out of ideas. But it was a nice, sunny day and we drove to a dock about twenty-five miles outside of Van and hired a boat to take us to the old Armenian church of Akdamar Island.

We'd heard rumors of a Loch Ness–type monster in the lake and asked the boatman, Recp Avci, about it. "There are no monsters," he said, "but there are some very large snakes." I assume he meant eels. "I have never seen one. My father did: he said it was as big around as a fifty-five-gallon oil drum and as long as this boat." The boat appeared to be forty-five feet long.

"But," Saim said, "you are describing a monster."

The island was rugged and rocky and it rose out of the clear blue waters of Lake Van like a shattered sculpture. The church, built in 915 by the Armenian king I. Gagig, was surrounded by almond trees, the branches bare and gnarled in the winter sun, and looked like a combination cathedral and mosque, a central dome set on four axes in the Byzantine style. The lower walls were covered over in bas-relief. There were depictions of a naked man and woman in a garden, and another of the same man and woman eating something that looked like an apple. There was a knight on horseback spearing something that looked very much like the Lake Van monster. Another sculpture showed a man being tossed from an open boat into the mouth of what could, once again, only be the Lake Van monster.

More to the point, there were tigers all over the walls. After the Armenians were driven from the church by the Turks, the place had become a mosque. The Muslims had painted animals around the upper dome: goats and wolves and, once again, tigers. Lots of tigers.

I sat in the sun, looking out across the lake at the shining, snow-clad mountains and thought: "At least, in historical times, there were tigers here." Also apparently present were Saint George, Adam and Eve, along with Jonah and the Lake Van monster.

That night, we walked through the maze of cobblestone alleyways off the main street of Van and finally found a shop where they could resole one of Tommy's boots. The cobbler, Mustafa, talked as he worked. He had never seen a tiger, or any evidence of one, around Lake Van and he hunted birds in the mountains quite often. Still, Mustafa said, if we liked, he could call the most avid hunter he knew and invite him down to the shop to talk. Halim was a man of fifty-six, a Jack Palance look-alike with long arms and hands the size of canned hams. He agreed that there were no tigers anywhere nearby, and hadn't been for many years. He had heard rumors about tiger sightings to the east, however. We should talk to his hunting partner, a baker named Hamiz Kaya.

"Where does Hamiz Kaya live?" Tommy asked.

"Shemdinli," Halim said.

We drove southeast, passing from checkpoint to checkpoint, and moving ever deeper into the mountains. The road took us over a pass in what might have been the Swiss Alps, with the snow several feet deep. Far below, a narrow valley stretched out as far as the eye could see, and at its farthest extent, hard up against the mountains rising abruptly behind, was the little town of Shemdinli. Tiger town, terror town, take your pick.

We drove down the main street, an amalgam of two- and three-story buildings of the type that collapse during earthquakes. Small patches of sooty gray snow lay in the street. We parked next to the bakery, and asked if Hamiz Kaya, the bread maker, was there. Once again, we were surrounded by townspeople, a dozen or more of them: tall, slender men with hawkish faces wearing baggy pants and cummerbunds. Kurds.

Were we here to talk about the terror? they wanted to know, and we said, no, we were here to talk about tigers. We had read reports that there had been several recent sightings. Hunters, the paper said, had seen the animal in these mountains.

"Then they lie," one man shouted. "No one hunts here." The dangers, men on all sides explained, were simply too great. The mountain trails were mined. A hunter could be mistaken for a terrorist and shot by the military; or he might be mistaken for a military commando and shot by the terrorists. Since the insurrection began in 1984, more than thirty thousand people had been killed. "No one hunts here," a man insisted.

"I have been in the mountains," said a distinguished-looking older man wearing a wool sport coat over a pink sweater.

Musa Iren, seventy-two, said he had seen a tiger in the mountains not far away, near Yaylapinar. That was eight years ago, and he had tracked it through the snow for two days.

"Do they make a sound?" Tommy asked.

"Like a donkey," Musa said. He made an "ahhhh" sort of sound.

"Describe the tracks."

"The tracks were like that of a cat, but as big as my hand, and the talons were as long as my index finger," Musa said. Tommy and I passed a significant look.

"Anything else?"

"Yes," Musa said, "when the tiger walks, he 'seizes' the snow and leaves a small ball of packed snow in the middle of the track."

"This is true," said another older man named Cirkin, who said he shot a tiger, also near Yaylapinar, forty years ago. It required thirteen rounds from a shotgun to kill the animal, and it took three men to carry it.

"These animals are not extinct," Musa said. "I guarantee you they are up there. Not just one or two, but many."

There was some general scoffing about this. Another man came to Musa's aid: "Because no one hunts—it is sixteen years now—the animals are coming back. Even here, near town, we see more bears and wild goats and wolves and wild pigs. Why not tigers?"

There were now fifty or sixty men gathered about, all shouting out their opinions, mostly negative. "Listen to me," Musa said, "you know the village of Ormancik, the little forest, on the border with Iraq? Four years ago a man of that village, Haji Ak, killed a tiger. He brought me the skin, and I had it in my shop for two years. I could not sell it and gave it back to him."

I was, I think, wildly excited as I wrote place names in my notebook—Yaylapinar, Ormancik, Otakar. At precisely that moment, of course, we were arrested by the police.

Tommy the Turk refused to get in the cop car because he wanted to begin this whole interrogation process by exerting some measure of control. "We'll walk, thanks," he said, as if the cop was a pal who'd just offered him a ride. The crowd had melted away, and we trudged slowly behind the police car as it moved past a green army tank and down a steep hill toward a two-story cement bunker that was the police station.

Inside the gray unpainted cement building was a maze of corridors, with cops coming and going every which way, but down the largest and longest hallway, there was a central office where a man in a stylish suit sat behind an imposing wooden desk. This had to be the chief, and Tommy bulled past the cop who had detained us, rapped once on the open door, and strode into the chief's office. "Please tell me exactly what is going on here," he said in Turkish. Better to be the complaining party than a meek detainee.

"We need to know," the chief said in near perfect English, "what you are doing in our town." The name plaque on his desk read: Mustafa Sahin.

The chief was a sucker for Tommy talk, and we left with his own personal phone number in case there was any more trouble. He had also called the commanding military officer of the province, Colonel Eshrem.

There was, it seemed, a military checkpoint at the gravel road on the edge of town, the road that led to Yaylapinar and Otakar and Ormancik: tiger country, or so we had been led to believe. We needed to talk to the colonel to pass, and were escorted to the army post and then through a leather-padded wooden door studded with brass tacks, and then a second padded door, like a kind of air lock.

Certain military and police officials we had met regarded our mission as a highly laughable cover story for some nefarious activity or another, but the colonel not only believed us, he thought the search for the Caspian tiger was a worthy goal. He was a man given to folksy aphorisms: "You search for the tiger," he said. "We say time spent searching for treasures lost is never time wasted."

Unfortunately, the colonel could not allow us to travel down the gravel road to Yaylapinar and especially not to Ormancik. That was where the two PKK insurgents had been shot a week ago. The PKK was all over the area, and there would be a military strike against them within a week.

Still, the colonel thought it would be a grand thing if tigers still existed, here, in the midst of war. There was, he said, thinking aloud, a military exercise the next day. Several village guards, armed Kurds loyal to the government, would be meeting in Yaylapinar. "So, you could get to Yaylapinar," the colonel said. He didn't think we'd be in much danger.

"And tonight," the colonel said, "you will please be my guests. Sleep here, in the barracks."

And so I spent a night in a Turkish military barracks, which, I know, sounds like a fantasy out of a John Rechy book. In fact, we were given private rooms set aside for visiting officers and they were better than those in any hotel we'd seen: two beds to a room, clean sheets, a hot shower, and a sit-down toilet that actually flushed.

The next morning, we were finally on our way, searching for the tiger . . . with a military escort. There were two trucks, one of them full of uniformed soldiers, and the other inexplicably empty. An armored personnel carrier brought up the rear. We rode in a Jeep Cherokee with a Captain Milbray as the convoy made its way along a road cut into the side of a ridiculously steep slope. There was a river far below, and burned-out military vehicles littered the banks.

In these mountains, or so the colonel had said, some trails are so narrow, the slopes so steep, that a mule cannot turn and back up. People embarking on such a section of trail signal one another with whistles, because you do not want to meet another traveler coming your way. This circumstance would involve a negotiation about whose mule must take the long fall.

Our gravel and dirt road was not that narrow, but it was tight enough that the story had the ring of truth. The river bottoms were at perhaps three thousand feet, while several of the mountains rose to eight thousand. The valleys themselves were intensely

V shaped, as if Allah had hacked them out of the high ground with one great whack of his mighty ax. There was only a thin sliver of sky visible between the slopes above. It was the first time I'd ever felt claustrophobic in the mountains.

Captain Milbray didn't buy our tiger story, not even a little bit. "I've been out in these mountains for four years," he said. "I've seen bears and wild goats and wild pigs, but never a tiger. And none of my men has ever seen one."

"Have you ever looked for one?" I asked.

"No," the captain said. "Well, two days ago I shot one. But I ate it. Even the skin."

"What a good joke, Captain," Tommy said.

Presently, the road branched off to Yaylapinar. We stopped for a moment, and suddenly over a dozen heavily armed Kurds and several soldiers appeared out of nowhere. They came pouring down the slopes at a dead run, the Kurds in tribal dress—baggy pants and turbans and cummerbunds—and armed with knives, grenades, and automatic weapons. We were surrounded by armed men in the space of thirty seconds, and even though I knew they were with us, it was an acutely menacing display. This is how fast it can happen to you out here, I thought. And then the Kurds and the soldiers piled into the empty truck and we were moving into another V-shaped valley on our way to Yaylapinar.

The road dropped into the valley of the Pison River. There were patches of snow on green grass, and cows grazed in the fields. The town itself consisted of perhaps forty houses, and dozens of people surrounded us as we stepped out of the Jeep. Someone put out white plastic lawn chairs. Tommy and I interviewed a man named Zulfir, who had shot a tiger, a female, perhaps ten years ago. "The mark of this animal," Zulfir said, "is that when he walks, he seizes the snow. The talons are as long as my first finger."

Other men were butting in now, talking about tigers in the old days, and now Captain Milbray seemed to be caught up in the interview.

"When you shot the tiger," he said to Zulfir, "was it before or after your military service? Before or after your first child was born?" In this manner we ascertained that the tiger had been shot not ten years ago, but more like forty.

Captain Milbray was no longer mocking us. "Why," he asked Zulfir, "did you shoot the tiger?"

"In those days, he who shot a tiger was a hero."

"These are not those days," the captain said. "Today, he who shoots a tiger is my enemy. I will see that he goes to jail."

As quick as that. I found the captain's conversion rather inspiring.

We went to another village, Otakar, then returned before dark to the army post at Shemdinli, where the colonel debriefed us in his office. About that time, there was a knock on the padded door. A young officer stood at attention and reported that three village guards, of the village of Umurhi, had seen a tiger. Word about our visit had apparently spread. "When was this?" the Colonel asked.

"Five days ago."

"Ah, I don't believe this," the colonel said. "I was there three days ago. They would have told me."

"Not," I suggested, "if they were out hunting and not guarding the village."

"Just so," the colonel said. "I'll have the men come to Shemdinli."

There were three of them, the village guards from Umurhi. And yes, they were hunting goats instead of standing guard, which is why they didn't mention it to the colonel. All three men were wearing Kurdish native costume, and sometimes they spoke Kurd, which would have made it difficult for me to write a cuddly Kurd story about how the Turkish military was suppressing the dress, language, and culture of the people. We were sitting in the officers' club.

The men had been out hunting wild goats in what are called the Honeycomb Cliffs, about six kilometers north of the village. It is a labyrinthine area, very steep and rugged. They had taken the central gate into the mountains. The youngest of them, a thirty-year-old named Nuri Durmaz, moved off to the west, alone. "There was a little snow," he said, "not a lot. I was about halfway to the peak. There was an overhanging wall, like a cliff, and I saw something one hundred meters away. I couldn't see its head, but it was big. It would have taken two, maybe three men to carry it."

"What color was it?" Tommy asked.

"Like my pants," Nuri Durmaz said. He was wearing beige pants. "It had black stripes on the legs and resembled a large cat."

"Did you shoot it?" I asked.

"No. It was in a bad place. If I only wounded it, it could have torn me apart."

"What did you do?"

"I went to get my friends."

And here Nuri's friends chimed in with descriptions of the tracks: talons as long as a man's finger, the little ball of snow in the center of the track. There were other such animals up in the Honeycomb Cliffs, said a man named Bedri Geokalp. He'd seen the same tracks in about the same place almost exactly a year ago.

I brought out some pictures I'd copied for just this purpose. There was a depiction of the Anatolian panther, a kind of leopard, also thought to be extinct; a photo of a lynx, which exists in these mountains; and another photo of a Caspian tiger taken many years ago in an Iranian zoo. Nuri discarded the panther and the lynx. "This one," he said, holding up the picture of the tiger.

"What do you think," I asked Saim, of the Forestry Department.

"I'd say fifty percent credibility."

The Duck and I both thought it was a 70 percent sure thing. The colonel said, "I don't have an opinion to be expressed in a percentage, but I believe in nature. This is a wonderful thing for Turkey and the world. I will inform my lieutenant in charge of the area to monitor the situation. I will give him a camera and ask him to use his night-vision goggles whenever possible."

Nuri said, "The next time I see this animal, I will kill him for you."

"I don't think you should do that," the colonel said. This opinion was expressed as an order. But then the colonel softened his voice: "If these men publish an article, and if peace is established, you will find that people with cameras will come here, and, to your delight, they will put much money in your pocket."

"This is true?"

"This is true."

"I can almost smell that tiger," Tommy was saying. We were on our way to Iraq, in an effort to enter the Honeycomb Cliffs from the south side of the range. The colonel had been kind enough to give us a glimpse of a classified map. The Honeycomb Cliffs were a tangle of closely spaced topographic lines stretching about ten kilometers east to west, and four kilometers north to south. The highest point was 2,173 meters, and the tiger had been sighted at about 1,200 meters, call it 3,600 feet.

The colonel had told Saim that—if he were ordered to do so—he could use military resources to search for the tigers: super-night-spotting scopes, sensitive remote cameras, helicopters, and—most important—manpower. If Saim, acting as a Forestry Department official, were to write to the colonel's superiors, that order could come through in as little as three or four months.

"What is the best way to word such a request?" Saim asked.

And the colonel dictated the letter for him.

For now, however, our search was over. The Honeycomb Cliffs were ground zero in the war against the PKK, and there was no way we were getting in there. On the other hand, both Tommy and I had noticed that the cliffs stretched into northern Iraq.

So we bid good-bye to Colonel Eshrem, then rode with Saim and Mr. Security to the town of Sirnac, where we parted in an orgy of embraces and kissed cheeks. Saim refused to take any money, despite the contract we'd signed. He was a man of great honor, and high emotion, and he wouldn't take our money "for the sake of the tiger." He said: "You have done a wonderful thing."

We rented a car and driver in Sirnac, then made a run for the border. There would be no problem getting into the Kurdish-held territory: Tommy had worked with several aid agencies, helping Kurdish refugees when Saddam Hussein rolled his tanks on his own people after the Gulf War. He still had friends among the Iraqi

Kurds, and, in fact, the Kurdish cap he wore, the one I always thought of as a yarmulke, was a treasured gift from one of those folks.

At the border, however, a Turkish official refused to stamp us out of the country. We spent two days there while Tommy worked the public phones calling his friends in Ankara in an effort to, in his words, "find someone who'll squash this little prick for me."

For two days, I sat against a wall while Tommy stood at the phone, talking Tommy talk as only Tommy can talk. "Look," he was saying to some English-speaking Turkish official in the capital, "we're not actually going into the mountains." (Not unless we could get into Iraq, he failed to say.) "We're just doing what we did in Turkey. We talk to the police and to the military and to the people in the villages. We raise people's consciousness, get them thinking about what it means if this animal still exists."

Day two at the border was now slipping into day three. "All we really want to do is make people aware of this magnificent creature," Tommy was saying.

Sitting there, listening to all this, it occurred to me that maybe that was enough. For now. Maybe, as Saim said, we had actually done something wonderful. People should be made aware. Because, in my almost expert opinion, the tiger is out there.

Bug Scream

The bug scream is a distinctive human sound. It is not characterized by volume, or intensity, or duration, but by the very sound itself: a kind of high-pitched, astonished loathing that combines the "eeewww" of disgust with the "waaah" of abject terror. Eeewaah. Every human has produced a bug scream at one time or another and every human has heard someone else generate such a sound. Here is the First Rule of Vermin Shrieking: When a human being not oneself bug screams, the sound is, by instinctual definition, funny. Cahill's Corollary to the First Rule is: Bug screams screamed by individual human beings *are not funny* to the individuals screaming.

Not that I consider myself squeamish. Quite the contrary. I've actually eaten bugs. More frequently, bugs have eaten me.

Not too long ago, for instance, I was walking across the Congo Basin in company with an American scientist, a filmmaker from *National Geographic,* three Bantu villagers, and sixteen pygmies. It was hot, and the forest contained what I imagined to be the better part of all the noxious bugs that have ever existed upon the face of the earth, including bees and wasps, which I found particularly annoying, because all the creatures with stingers tended to congregate on me to the exclusion of my expeditionary colleagues.

Why me?

The scientist Michael Fay, of Wildlife Conservation International, said, in effect, "Because you're a big fat sweaty guy." He explained that all living organisms need salt, and that one of the factors limiting the abundance of life in the swampy forest was the lack of salt. The fact is, I was taller than Michael by several inches, over a foot taller than the biggest pygmy, and I outweighed everyone by fifty to one hundred pounds. Also I sweat a lot. I was, in effect, a walking salt dispenser, an ambulatory fountain of life.

There were at least half a dozen different kinds of bees in the forest, and every time I stood still for a minute or more, dozens of them took up residence on my drenched and sweaty T-shirt. Here, I thought, is an opportunity to observe nature in action. One interesting bee fact I learned is this: the little bastards generally only sting in response to dorsal pressure. If, for instance, you happen to be setting up your tent, and there are fifty or sixty bees sucking salt off your T-shirt, they will not sting unless you touch them on the back. For this reason, I found it necessary to walk with my arms held stiffly out from my sides, and to move slowly, in an angular and somewhat robotic fashion.

The problems occurred when salt-thirsty bees crawled up the sleeves of my shirt, toward the armpits, going right to the fountain of life, as it were. Then, no matter how robotically I moved my arms, there was some small dorsal pressure involved. It was worse when they crawled up the legs of my shorts.

Aside from the bees, there were tsetse flies, which can cause sleeping sickness, a disease characterized by fever, inflammation of the lymph nodes, and profound lethargy. Sleeping sickness is often fatal. And the insects that carry the disease are intensely annoying creatures.

They are long, thin, malnourished-looking flies, with skinny iridescent wings, and the ones I encountered moved so slowly I could actually bat them with a palm while they were in flight. Occasionally, I'd get a really good whack on one, and it would seem to falter in its aerodynamics, then wheel about in a lopsided loop, as if woozy and staggered. But it would stay on me. I could sometimes pop one I'd dazed three or four times using both hands—whap, bap, whap, bap—just like working out on a speed bag. The fly might back off, lose altitude, and then, as through an act of will, it would seem to straighten up and fly right, zeroing in on me again, and willing to take any amount of punishment simply to gets its filthy, disease-ridden, blood-sucking proboscis into my flesh. It was like fighting Rocky in the movies. Tsetse flies never quit.

Worse, you can't swat them on your skin, like mosquitoes. They have some kind of dorsal radar and, when threatened from above, simply fly away.

A pygmy who looked a little like a short, dark version of Jerry Lewis showed me the way to kill tsetse flies. Simple thing. Put a hand on your body some small distance from the fly and roll right over the son of a bitch from the side, like a steamroller. This process produces a nasty swatch of blood and bug guts. It is immensely satisfying.

Aside from the tsetse flies, we often encountered aggregations of fire ants, which are small and red and prone to swarming, gang stings. They frequently looked like pizza-sized hillocks of fungus on downed trees that lay across our path. Sometimes, walking along a nice, wide elephant path near such a tree, I'd see pygmies in the column ahead suddenly break into a strange hop-step sort of polka as they attempted to shake the fire ants off their bare feet and legs by stomping their feet. The convention was to yell *"Formi,"* or "ants." In fact, watching someone out ahead do the Fire Ant Polka was all the warning anyone ever needed. It's awfully funny. When someone else is dancing it.

There were also driver ants, of the type with two-inch-long pincers. It is said that various native people in Africa use driver ants to stitch up wounds. It's supposed to work like this: The ant is held in the fingers and positioned with a pincer on either side of the wound. The ant then pinches, as ants will. Driver ants will not let go. At this point, one simply twists the nasty little body off the pincers. Instant sutures.

I don't know if people actually do this or it's just one of those oft-repeated travelers' tales. I do know that a driver ant bite hurts a lot, and that once they grab onto flesh, you can't shake them off, say, a sandaled foot, no matter how hard you stomp. I had to pick driver ants off my flesh, one by one.

Among the most unbearable of the insects was a kind of sting-less bee, like a fruit fly, actually, called a melipon. Michael Fay said the word came from the Greek: *meli*, meaning honey, and *pon*, meaning, I think, incredibly annoying little sons of bitches. They arrived out of nowhere in clouds, so that, suddenly, every breath contained hundreds of melipons. They crawled into my ears and nostrils. Every time I blinked, there were several melipons ejected from my eyes, all rolled up and kicking their fragile little legs, like living tears rolling down my cheeks.

Sometimes, we crossed orderly columns of termites, thousands of them, marching along on some destructive mission or other. At night, they sometimes crawled in formation under my tent, and I could hear an unnerving clicking and clacking sound: termites, moving under my body in their thousands, all of them snapping their hideous little jaws.

None of these creatures ever caused me to produce a single dis-tressed sound beyond "oww." Halfway through my Congo walk, I believed myself almost immune to that universal human frailty, the bug scream. Vermin shrieking was something other people did, and they did it for my personal amusement.

I am, in fact, guilty of arranging certain situations designed to test and trigger the First Rule of Vermin Shrieking.

High school speech class, and here was my evil plan for the final assembly of my final year. There'd be four hundred students in the new auditorium, every seat filled, and I wanted to hear them scream.

We'd use the impressive new spotlights designed for stage plays. The best student actor I knew—and the only one I could trust to go along with me on this deal—was Dave Hanson, who would walk onstage wearing a funereal black suit. Stepping up to the podium under a single spot, Dave was to solemnly open a book, fix the au-dience with his best Vincent Price stare, and begin reading Edgar Allan Poe's merry little contemplation of corporeal decomposition entitled "The Conqueror Worm."

We knew what would happen. My fellow students, fearing Culture, would no doubt fidget for a bit. The poem postulates "an angel throng" sitting "in a theater." On the poetic stage, Poe has positioned "mimes," in the "form of God on high."

At this point, we'd begin to shrink the spot on Dave. The auditorium would become very dark as he dug down deep for his best shuddery bass voice on the verses we needed to really hammer home in order for the prank to work.

The mimes in the poem are—good Lord!—human beings. In their midst, Poe has "a crawling shape intrude." Bloodred, it writhes, it writhes. "The mimes become its food," and it—the bloodred crawling shape—is "in human gore imbued."

Dave could read that well, I knew. He'd pull the audience into the horrid realization of what this poem is all about. The last verse begins:

"Out—out are the lights—out all!"

Which is when we'd kill the spot altogether, leaving the auditorium in total darkness, while Dave gravely intoned the last lines, which are all about the poetic angel audience sobbing heavenly tears because they realize:

> "That the play is the tragedy, 'Man,'
> "And its hero is the Conqueror Worm."

Here, timing was important. We needed to hit them in the silence following Dave's recitation, but before the muttering and mumbling started. I had three confederates all set up for the non-verbal punch line. In the darkness, we'd run down the aisles of the silent auditorium, tossing out great handfuls of cooked spaghetti (still warm and a little damp). The spaghetti flingers all had a two-word line, a terror-filled scream, to be repeated as necessary: "THE WORMS . . . THE WORMS . . ."

Do it right and they'd scream. Most of my classmates would scream. Four hundred flat-out bug screams, or, more precisely, worm screams. Different creature, same sound.

One problem: along with the rest of my worm tossers, I needed a pass to be in position at the back of the auditorium. A damn fine teacher named Fred Metzner demanded to know why the four of us wanted these special passes. He wouldn't accept "It's a surprise" as an explanation. Fred Metzner had learned not to trust student surprises.

And so, my plan was foiled at the last moment. Mr. Metzner described the idea as "juvenile," though I thought it was a good deal more mature than that. It was adolescent at the very least.

One night, several weeks into the Congo walk, I was just dropping off to sleep, lying in my tent, sometime around ten in the evening, when the half-pound centipede dropped from the fabric ceiling and onto my naked, sweating chest with an audible plop. Later, under my headlamp, I was to discover that it was not one of the poisonous ones. Just a normal Congo Basin jungle centipede and only about the size of an ordinary Polish sausage. It looked naked and pink, and was curled in on itself like something the dog left on the lawn. Under my light, the bug wasn't something you'd necessarily scream about.

But, half asleep, and in the dark, I had no idea what it was. Just something wet and heavy that seemed to have been dropped from a great height. I said "eeewaah." I believe I said "eeewaah" several times in the darkness—a crescendo of half-awake terror—and when I brushed at my chest with blind, fluttering hands, I suddenly felt the heavy wormlike thing just above my wildly beating heart and swept it to the side. I said "eeewaah" several more times as I leapt to my feet, nearly stuck my head through the fabric of my tent, fell down somewhere near where "the unknown thing" had to be, then rolled over, and finally came out of my tent like a scorched cat. All the time saying "eeewaah, eeewaah, eeewaah."

The pygmies, all thirteen of them, were over in their camp, maybe fifty yards away. I could hear their battery-powered short-wave radio blasting out static-ridden music. The sound, as usual, was turned up into that range of irritating distortion in which it is impossible to tell reggae tunes from English madrigals. Pygmies, I had learned on my Congo walk, listen to the radio all night long. And they will always sacrifice fidelity to volume.

I had started out on this long jungle trek determined to get close to the pygmies, to understand their lives, their hopes, their dreams, their music. Most of all, I wanted to absorb a small measure of their knowledge of the forest. But they kept the radio on all night, never seemed to sleep, and I generally camped some distance away, just out of earshot.

So it was possible they hadn't heard me bug screaming.

But no, they were shouting and howling among themselves, and the howls were those of high-pitched and helpless laughter.

"What?" one of them called out to me in French, our only common language. I think it was Kabo, who was handsome as a homecoming king and one of the leaders. "What has happened?" he called.

I didn't know the French word for centipede. I don't know much French at all, but the word for insect isn't particularly difficult for an English speaker.

"*Insecte,*" I said.

Kabo strolled over, along with half a dozen other pygmies. I had scooped the centipede up onto a machete, using my notebook to avoid touching the thing, and was about to dump it, alive, a good distance from my tent. But the pygmies had to examine the creature that had caused me to say "eeewaah" several dozen times.

They aimed their one flashlight on the machete. The beam was very dim and yellow in color. The pygmies said some words to one another in Sangha, their native language, looked up at me, and, unnecessarily, I thought, began laughing again. They shook my hand and slapped me on the back and laughed until tears came to their eyes. It was, I thought, incredibly juvenile behavior.

Later that night, I could hear them in their camp, shouting over the static on the radio. They used the word *mundele,* "white man," which has about the same connotation that the word *gringo* has in Latin countries. The noun is sometimes merely descriptive and void of nuance. Sometimes, like *gringo, mundele* can mean greenhorn, oaf, imbecile, or doofus. The meaning depends on the context. In this case there was silence for ten or fifteen seconds, then one of the pygmies would say *mundele,* meaning me, and the rest of them would begin howling with a kind of hilarity that I believed to be entirely inappropriate to something as human and unaffected as a few dozen simple bug screams.

It was in those moments of sweaty humiliation that Cahill's Corollary to the First Rule of Vermin Shrieking was born, screaming.

The Platypus Hunter

Here is the wily Platypus Hunter, stalking the forests of the night. He steps carefully into the pulsing darkness, feeling for the trail with his foot. He breathes. Steps again. He doesn't want to use his light yet, so he is moving slowly, slowly. The great eucalyptus trees all about soar two hundred feet and more into an inky, blue-black sky, but the canopy itself is unseen above, a grand weight of leafy life vaguely delineated by the unfamiliar stars of the Australian sky. He steps again, and there is a muffled thud, which, he deduces from long experience, is the sound of his body colliding with the trunk of a tree. It doesn't even hurt. Not that much, anyway. The bark is peeling off the tree in great long strips: a stringy bark tree.

In less than four hours, the Platypus Hunter will be another year older. He feels the seasons of his life slowly flapping in front of his face like the beating of some great dark wing. You're born, he thinks; you live, you die, and to what end?

Is our journey through life a quest? For enlightenment, perhaps? For nirvana? For a Union with the One? This is why the wily Platypus Hunter is out walking into trees in the middle of the night. He's pretty much clueless in the what-does-it-all-mean department, but figures that a series of small, highly defined quests—seeing a platypus in the wild, for instance—will one day accumulate into a critical mass and then there will be a blinding light like the collision of suns. In that radiant moment, the Platypus Hunter believes, he will be able to see into the Very Core of the Universe.

I was about fifty miles north of Melbourne, on the far southern reaches of the Great Dividing Range, near the headwaters of the Yea River, where the platypus, so I imagined, frolicked. The sun had set some time ago. The moon had not yet risen, and the Hour of the Platypus was rapidly approaching.

There wasn't much that could hurt me in this forest. I suppose that wild pigs, feral for generations, might leave me bleeding from a myriad of six-inch half-moon-shaped cuts, the scimitar tusks and upper teeth gnashing together like scissors in a cacophony of snorts and grunts. Local tiger snakes are venomous and potentially deadly, as are most Australian snakes, but I'd yet to see one in two weeks of prowling the parklands above Melbourne. What they had here were koalas dozing in the trees, shy swamp wallabies—a kind of junior-sized kangaroo—as well as lyrebirds, cockatoos, and burrowing wombats, an animal that can weigh up to seventy-five pounds and that looks a bit like a cross between a tiny bear cub and a Sherman tank.

My eyes adjusted to the darkness, my confidence expanded, and I began taking two and three steps at a crack. Which was when I stepped on the tiger snake.

Everything happened very quickly. I was somewhere two or three feet above the trail, suddenly and involuntarily airborne. Gravity had no dominion over me. The tiger had twisted under my foot, and the rest of its body thrashed in the foliage to my left. Big snake, I thought urgently, five or six feet long. Lotta venom.

In the fullness of time, I found myself some distance away, dropped effortlessly into a gunfighter's crouch on the mute forest floor, right arm extended. The trigger seemed to pull itself, and the night exploded into light.

And what the beam of the spotlight I carried revealed was not, in fact, a tiger snake. It was a wide, seven-foot-long strand of stringy bark shed by one of the eucalyptus trees. Had the big rechargeable halogen spotlight been a gun, I would have fired blindly into the night. The realization was a form of enlightenment I didn't care to contemplate.

Even worse: Had anyone seen me blow away the menacing strip of tree bark?

I raked the forest with my spotlight. All the night things that crept and crawled below, that darted or soared above, were staring directly at me, in my solitary embarrassment. Their eyes, in the scalding beam of light, seemed vaguely demonic, as if the creatures in this forest were burning up from within, all their hearts on fire. Dozens of pairs of radiant eyes were focused on me, some of them red like glowing coals, others shining a pale, poisonous-looking yellow, and still others gleaming a cool and luminescent green. When I snapped off the light after about twenty seconds, the eyes in the forest faded into a darkness that was more impenetrable than before, more absolute. It would take twenty minutes or more for my own eyes to readjust. For the moment, I couldn't see my hands in front of my face. I stood alone and still and silent. Listening.

Frogs along the riverbank grunted out their lust in an irregular bass beat that croaked along in counterpoint with the high-pitched chirping of bats. Owls—there were several of them—worked the horn section, hooting out short, soft calls that seemed to arouse a kind of rage in various species of possum, which traded off in a series of angry solos: high in the trees, I heard the strange, strangled gurgling of a possum called the yellow-bellied glider, and then the piercing bark of a sugar glider.

Above and unseen, there was an air war in progress, owls and possums in combat. A "flying" possum such as the greater glider can soar the length of a football field on a wing called a patagium, a flap of skin that extends from the wrist to the ankle. Flexing at the elbows, with the forepaws tucked under its chin, the possum spreads its wings and leaps from a perch high in the trees, falling into a gradually descending glide path and sometimes swerving off at right angles to its direction of flight. Greater gliders are pursued, and sometimes even taken in midair, by what's called the powerful owl. The possum terminates its flight as a hang glider might, turning back upward into the night sky and using gravity as a brake. It lands on all fours against the trunk of a tree.

There were greater gliders in the trees above, feeding on the eucalyptus leaves. I'd seen them earlier in my light, marking them by their eyeshine, which was a brilliant whitish yellow. They were known to turn away from direct light. The brush-tailed possums stared directly into the spot, and theirs were bright red horror-film eyes.

Most animals native to Australia are nocturnal, and as it has with all nocturnal creatures, evolution has engineered their eyes to collect and concentrate available light. The retinas of night-adapted vertebrates are backed with a reflecting layer of cells called the *tapetum lucidum,* the "bright carpet." What light there is enters through the pupil and is partially absorbed by the retina, the inside back wall of the eyeball. Light that is not absorbed by the retina is reflected back into the eye by the *tapetum lucidum,* effectively giving the animal a second chance to see the image.

When a bright artificial light is directed into such an eye, it will seem to glow, as if from within. The phenomenon is called eyeshine. Various droplets of colored oil in the cells of the eyes of different species give each a distinct eyeshine. Cats' eyes seem to glow green, rabbits' are yellowish, deer's are a pale yellow, and wolves' are greenish gold. The West Indian tree boa's eyes are red-orange, and the Nile crocodile's are bright red, as are the eyes of alligators and caimans.

I once believed that the eyes of all nocturnal predators shone red. This, until very recently, was a matter of lifelong misperception. At night, in the wild, I did not want to catch the red eye, and more to the point, I did not want the red eye to catch me. In my mind, the association of predators and glowing red eyes has been reinforced by any number of flash photographs I've taken in which my friends' true and blood-ridden souls seem to flash out of bright red pinpoints in their eyes. Humans are predators, these photographs seem to say, and you can see it in our eyes.

The physics of the situation are not so damning. A flash is used in low-light situations, when the pupil is open wide so that the full force of blinding light enters the eyeball and reflects back out the still-open pupil at the same angle. What we see in those satanic red orbs staring back at us out of the latest batch of snapshots is not the predatory nature of the human soul. It is the reflection of the blood vessels in the back of the eye. Still, the camera companies have developed anti-red-eye technology in the hope, I suppose, that we will, in our photos, seem to be maturing into a kinder and gentler race.

It took nearly a century for Western scientists to conclude that an egg-laying creature could, in fact, be a mammal. Because the platypus is such a biological oddity—web-footed, fur-bearing, and duck-billed—I had assumed it was rare and endangered. In fact, the most conservative estimate is that there are tens of thousands of them inhabiting rivers and streams along the eastern seaboard of Australia, all the way from Melbourne to Queensland.

Platypuses spend their nights swimming and their days curled up in burrows dug deep into riverbanks anywhere from a foot to ten feet above the water. They dine on freshwater crayfish and worms, but the bulk of their diet consists of caddis fly larvae sunk in the mud at the bottom of the river. Diving with its eyes closed, the platypus roots around in the mud, looking for the larvae with its sensitive bill, which is soft and wet, blue-black in color, and more like a dog's muzzle than a duck's bill.

In Australia, the platypus is protected throughout its range, but it's threatened by pollution, riverbank erosion, and predation by foxes. I'd seen a few platypuses at the Healesville Sanctuary, northeast of Melbourne. It's a place where injured animals—wallabies, wombats, the whole panoply of southern Australian wildlife—are brought for rehabilitation. Platypuses, whose diet is not significantly different from that of trout, are sometimes accidentally caught on a fisherman's fly line. Some few, trapped in the stream that flows through the sanctuary, are on display in a nocturnal aquarium situation, where lights are dimmed and fragmented, like moonlight falling through foliage. There the platypuses seem to frolic, rather like otters, and they are much smaller than I would have imagined: A large adult male is about two feet long and weighs just over four pounds. The tail is broad and flat, like a beaver's, and is used as a rudder.

At Healesville, I spoke with the platypus keeper, a man who calls himself Fisk. Just Fisk. Handling a male platypus, he said, is problematic: it is the world's only venomous mammal. There are two horny spurs on the hind legs, which are connected to venom-secreting glands. Males tend to use the spurs during breeding-season altercations, which can be deadly to one or both competing platypuses. The poison is not fatal to humans, but it is painful. People stung on the hand won't be playing the guitar for several months.

In Fisk's experience, platypuses like to be stroked on the bill. They recognize individual humans and like to play. Fisk fondly recalled a platypus that would prop its little elbows on the rim of the enclosure and stare at him sitting at his desk. It's hard to get work done, he told me, when a platypus wants to party.

I had decided that, in Australia, the platypus would be my totem animal partially because of our mutual tendency to spend most of the day sleeping and most of the night frolicking about and eating. More to the point, there was something quintessentially "high school" about the creature, something endearing and adolescent and immediately accessible. Who didn't feel like a platypus in sophomore English: so strange, so different from the rest, so inherently dorky as to be unclassifiable by science. Platypus boys and platypus girls confined to Platypus High, mammals all, and some of us filled with venom.

So the platypus hunt was a personal exploration into what I'd been and what I'd become. To that end, I had scouted the Yea River during the day, looking for likely platypus habitat. The river flowed through a forest of mountain ash eucalyptus, the tallest hardwood trees in the world. Some were well over three hundred feet high, and the leaves were concentrated at the tops of the trees, so that a good deal of light fell on the forest floor, which was consequently covered with chest-high grasses and prehistoric-looking tree ferns.

The Yea was only five feet across and four feet deep where it burbled through its narrows. As it wound through the forest, it created cut banks five and six feet high, and these were places where a platypus might dig a burrow, which can be one hundred feet long.

Fallen trees, in various stages of mossy disintegration, spanned the Yea, and the river was a muddy golden color, its waters essentially a strong tea made of eucalyptus leaves. Shafts of sunlight fell on the water, and in those places the Yea looked like a golden mirror. Caddis flies were hatching out of the sun-dappled river.

These were the places I marked in my mind's map, the places I'd spotlight well after full dark.

And so, in the Hour of the Platypus, and for reasons that seemed obscure even at the time, I chose to drop to my belly and crawl through the night toward the river. No lights. At one of my intended observation sites, just off the trail that paralleled the river, a newly fallen tree formed a bridge across the Yea. I knew I was in the right spot when I found myself entangled in the exposed root system. Crawling through a big muddy root ball in the dark is an annoying and time-consuming task. It took fifteen minutes to find a position on the trunk, over the river. I took a deep breath, held it, and hit the trigger on my spot.

And, by God, there he was. The very first time I spotted the river: a platypus! Or at least something furry, swimming. A dark swirl and it was gone. The creature might have been a water rat, I suppose, but water rats don't sport beaverlike tails. At another site only two hours later, I saw another platypus.

The great dark wing has flapped once again, and here's the wily Platypus Hunter returning from the river, yet another year older and perhaps one quest wiser. Suns have not precisely collided in an explosion of white-hot light. In point of fact, the rechargeable spotlight carried by the Hunter is rapidly running out of juice. Its beam has become feeble and yellow, totally inadequate for the task at hand. Presently the damn thing simply sputters weakly and dies.

This makes walking difficult, and the tallest hardwood trees on earth assault the Hunter at every step. Stringy bark snakes litter his path.

He resolves that, in the future, he will carry two sources of light into the forest at night. And that's it, he thinks. That's the extent of the evening's epiphany, Lesson Number One out of Platypus High: Anyone who aspires to see into the Very Core of the Universe is advised to bring along two sources of light.

Fire and Ice and Everything Nice

I read the sentence a total of, oh, maybe twenty times the night before it was to be discussed in a class I was teaching on the techniques (if not the art) of travel writing.

"An initial priority for composition facilitators is to peruse, for context analysis, the local papers, and taking it seriously."

It was, and remains, the very worst lead sentence I have ever had the misfortune to read, and I remember it to this day, over fifteen years later, word for ghastly word.

Worse, I recall with a shudder the cruelty I visited upon the author, a sincere young woman who was a high school composition teacher, only a few years out of college.

This was at the University of Indiana, and the woman was taking my summer writing class because, she said, my articles on travel and adventure were popular among her students. She intended to absorb my lectures, such as they were, and convey the information to her fellow English teachers. Thus, composition instructors could inspire students to produce assignments modeled, to some degree, after the sorts of articles they preferred to read.

In an initial lecture, I'd said that travel didn't necessarily involve distance. It was a process of discovery, and could as easily be accomplished in one's hometown as in the Congo Basin. Where might a potential writer find local travel-writing ideas? Well, there were dozens of them every week in the local newspaper.

It was my first experience teaching writing of any kind, and I am afraid that clemency and compassion were not then among my small arsenal of virtues.

So there I was, standing in front of a class of twenty, all of us holding this woman's paper as if it had been used some time ago to wrap fish.

"Any comments on this before we start?" I asked. There was a silence so complete it had an odor about it. Something just vaguely sour, if not to say actually putrescent.

And then—degenerate beast that I am—I destroyed this woman, completely, and in public.

"Mr. Jones," I said. "Could you silently read the opening sentence and tell me what you think it means?" Jones was a retired history professor, and, it was obvious, a brilliant man. I stood at the front of the class, ostentatiously staring at my watch while he read.

Finally Professor Jones said, "I think it means writing teachers ought to read the newspapers."

"Me, too," I said. "But it took you forty-five seconds to come to that conclusion. You know why? Because the sentence had to be translated. It is not written in the English language."

The author sat in stunned silence. She rose slowly, eyes glazed over with what would soon be tears, and commented, quite cogently, I thought, on my teaching technique.

"You . . . asshole," she said.

This was something of a surprise since the woman was a lay teacher in a Catholic high school. Then the author of the worst lead sentence I'd ever read turned her back to me and walked toward the door. She was attempting to outrun her tears.

"Wait," I called. "Please. Let's talk about this. We want to learn how to communicate effectively with people."

The unfortunate woman stood in the open doorway, turned her now tear-stained face to me—to the class at large—and said:

"I don't want to communicate with people. I want to impact on educators."

With that she slammed the door, hard, and was gone. Exclamation point.

. . .

I was thinking about this peculiar contretemps recently. In fact, I think about it every month or so, especially when things are going well for me and I am in danger of imagining that I might be an exemplary individual. I think about it more intently when I teach travel-writing seminars, because I always use that hateful sentence as an example of a bad lead.

Now, where I live, in Montana, there is an infestation of writers. In general, those authors on the western side of the Rocky Mountains are associated in one way or another with the University of Montana and its world-class creative-writing program. These men and women generally produce highly literate and well-reviewed tomes: essays, poetry, novels. No writing down to the lowest common denominator for these folks: because they are partially funded by teaching, they have the luxury to produce literature.

Those of us who live on the arid, east side of the mountains, however, make our livings—such as they are—directly from the sales of our books or articles. When our friends from the west accuse us of pandering to the masses, as they habitually do, the usual and purposely ungrammatical reply (attributed, I believe, to Tom McGuane), goes something like this: "I done a lot of things in my life that I'm not proud of, but I never taught no goddamned creative writing." Well, I can't say that anymore. I teach one or two creative-writing courses a year, and they are all about travel and/or adventure.

I was just returning home from the Book Passage Travel Writers' Conference in Corte Madera, California. The drive took me through northern Nevada then up into southeast Oregon, and I was looking for a story. Something about travel. Or adventure. Whatever.

In Winnemucca, I glanced at the local paper, as I still advise students in search of a story to do, and found a free lecture to be given that night by "a popular short wave radio personality." I would learn "things not taught in school." The address given turned out to be in a church basement, and only about half a dozen people arrived to learn things they hadn't been taught in school. We discovered that September 9, 1999—9/9/99—was pretty much going to be doomsday. It would start with computer crashes—early computer code used four 9's to signal that the program had ended and was to be terminated. Stoplights wouldn't work. Cars would stall on the interstate, miles from anywhere. Banks would fail. People in the know—which now included the half dozen of us in the church basement—should take our money out of the bank, stock up on both food and weapons, and then begin digging out a bomb shelter. We only had three more days.

Was there a story in the end of the world as we know it? Could be, but I wasn't inspired, and drove north, into the parched cowboy country of southeastern Oregon, specifically to Harney County, a land of high-desert sage flats and sparsely timbered mountains; of fleet herds of antelope and cattle ranches. Harney extends over 10,228 square miles, which makes it the largest county in America. It is bigger than Rhode Island and Massachusetts combined. A mere seven thousand people are privileged to call Harney County home, so there is less than one person per square mile. A good place, I figured, to wait out the end of the world, now just two days hence.

I had what might be the last chocolate malt of my life at the café in Fields, Oregon, because a sign on the wall said the concoctions were "world famous," and I didn't want to die with a bad taste in my mouth. Fields is located at the southwestern edge of Steens Mountain, locally called the Steens. The mountain, a checkerboard of Bureau of Land Management, state, and private land, is a 30-mile-long fault block that rises gently from the west to a height of 9,773 feet, and then drops off precipitously, in what amounts to a sheer cliff face. From a distance, it looks like a giant wedge rising up out of the sagebrush.

This great block of land was thrust a mile above the surrounding land by pressures created in the mists of geological time when the earth's crust cooled. Millions of years later, glaciers formed near the summit of the Steens, and they slid down the western slope of the mountain, carving out verdant U-shaped valleys and deep rocky gorges so elaborately sculpted they seemed the monumental work of some mad and alien culture.

On the day the world was to end, I drove east, up the Oregon Scenic Byway, which leads to the summit of the Steens. Sage-littered antelope country gave way to juniper, and, at the higher elevations along the Blitzen River, aspen groves shivered silver and gold in a gentle aureate breeze. Toward the summit, aspen gave way to grassland matted with hearty wildflowers: asters and daisies and lacy white yarrow. September 9 is springtime at eight thousand feet on the Steens.

Presently, I found myself at a parking lot a few hundred feet below the summit proper. It was a steep, breathless climb to the top, but it took only twenty minutes or so. There was no one else there, and I sat on the summit of the Steens, staring down the abrupt and perpendicular eastern edge of the mountain's wedge.

I was looking at the Alvord Desert, which was three miles distant and almost exactly one mile below me. It was a round, flat, sandy, alkaline playa, completely uninhabited. Dust devils spun across its surface in strange and contradictory directions. It must have been well over 100 degrees down there on the sand. I, on the other hand, was cold. What had been a gentle breeze a few thousand feet below was now a gusting wind that whistled and boomed over the summit at about 50 miles an hour. The vegetation all about was of the fragile sort one finds in the high north tundra: sparse, fast-growing mosses, orange lichens on the rocks, and dwarf shrubs, inches high, hunkered down in crevasses against the wind and cold.

The sky was cornflower blue, streaked with the long, thin clouds some people call horsetails. A BLM brochure had promised that, on a clear day, I would be able to "see the corners of four states." It was a clear day and there were no conflagrations in any of the states that I could see. Late on doomsday afternoon, things were looking just peachy.

Still, I tried to contemplate the death and dissolution of civilization as we know it. Here I was, freezing in the tundra and staring down at the desert. Robert Frost had written a poem about the destruction of the world in fire, or in ice, whatever, take your pick. But, quite frankly, I wasn't inspired.

In fact, my mind was whirling with student manuscripts I had read over the years.

.   .   .

"There are no words."

Last year, one of my writers' workshop students had led off her nonfiction travel piece with that sentence, which I thought might be improved. She wanted to describe her feelings upon first landing in Antarctica. The piece as a whole was awfully good, I thought, combining, as it did, a problematic relationship with her father, who was along on the trip, and the desire to see a massive ice ridge named after her grandfather, who had been in Admiral Byrd's party. It was a real quest, filled with real emotion, and the woman had the talent to make it work.

But the lead? "There are no words."

"This," I suggested to the students at the writers' workshop, "does not fill the reader with confidence in the writer's ability to describe the interior or exterior landscape of her journey." I stifled an impulse to put my objection more bluntly. I would be risking another tearful exit if I said: "There are no words and here they aren't."

I carefully polled the other seven students in the class. "There are no words." Good lead? Or bad? And the fact is, most of them liked it.

A few nights later, my friend and colleague David Quammon came to my house for dinner. David has won awards for his essays and criticism, and for his science writing; I think he's won awards he doesn't even remember anymore, or doesn't care to talk about because he's pathologically modest. David's news was that he was building a new house, probably (I thought with that total lack of envy writers are noted for) to hold all his damn awards.

He asked me how the writers' conference was going. I said it was exhausting. I couldn't get certain manuscripts out of my mind, not because they were so bad, but because they were so close to being good.

David shook his head. He believes that no one can teach writing, that it is a solitary endeavor you do over and over again until you start getting it right.

"Tim," he said, "I think that if you just went to church and prayed real, real hard, you'd have the same effect on your students."

Gretel Ehrlich, a writer whose books I greatly admire—especially her lyrical evocation of the West in *The Solace of Open Spaces*—is of much the same opinion. Once she and I were featured speakers at a writers' conference in Montana. She gave the keynote address to the crowd of eager would-be writers, and was not at all encouraging. The speech had been written out in essay form. Gretel read it well, and with passion. Writing, she said, cannot be taught. Some teachers, she said, will tell you that there are matters of craft you can learn. This, she averred, is not so.

"Any question or comments?" she asked at the conclusion of her remarks.

The students, who'd all paid a substantial amount of money to learn to write, sat in a kind of poleaxed silence. Now, my own opinion is that elements of craft—matters of structure, organization, lead-ins, and walk-offs—can indeed be taught, and are, in fact, the only substantive principles professionals can impart to beginning writers.

So, in the silence following Gretel's request for comments, I raised my hand and said, "I thought the piece you read was very well crafted."

And now Gretel Ehrlich, in company with a certain Indiana Catholic high school lay teacher, thinks I'm a dickhead.

The sun set over Steens Mountain, and I drove down to the remote cattle town of Burns, where I lingered for days, looking for stories. As usual, my initial prioritization was to peruse, for context analysis, the local papers, and taking it seriously. It was in one of these publications that I found a short article in the foreign news section that fired my imagination.

It seemed that three Indonesian cult leaders were beaten to death by disaffected followers after their 9/9/99 doomsday prediction failed to materialize. The cult members had been told to sell their possessions and to prepare for the end of the world at 9 A.M. on September 9. But the day came and went without incident. The sun also rose on September 10 and, according to Saadi Arsam, village chief of Sukmajaya, east Java, "the members were really mad."

I wondered if the shortwave-radio personality was still in Winne-mucca, or whether he'd gone into hiding. It might be worth driving back and looking for him.

"Hey, what happened to doomsday?" would be my first question.

If the disgraced doom-monger had any sense at all, he'd decline comment. Into each life, I understood finally, there falls a time when there are no words.

The Caravan of White Gold

"Teem, wake up. There are some bandits."

An Italian—I don't recall which one—was standing over my sleeping bag and nudging my foot with his. It was about ten o'clock on a cool, clear February night in the Sahara, and I had been asleep for half an hour.

"What?"

"Some bandits have followed us up from Kidal. We have to go back to Aguelhok."

"Tuaregs?" I asked.

"Muhammad said they came from Kidal."

Muhammad, our recently hired security consultant, was a Tuareg himself. Kidal was a Tuareg town. But then again, so was Aguelhok.

I struggled out of my sleeping bag and stumbled around for a few groggy minutes in the dark. We were about three miles west of Aguelhok in the West African country of Mali and a couple hundred miles north of the Niger River, camped near the central trans-Saharan road leading north to Algeria. This was to be the last stop before a high-speed run to the historic and formerly forbidden salt mines at Taoudenni, which—we didn't know—might not even exist anymore.

Our motorized caravan was parked amid a huge jumble of rocks that had probably formed the narrows of a swift-flowing, ancient river. The rocks were black, river-rounded, the size of large trucks, and many were festooned with drawings of creatures that must have existed here in a forgotten time, when the sun-blasted sandscape had been a vast and fertile grassland. There were drawings of an elephant, an eland, an ostrich. Giraffes seemed to have been considered the most consequential of the animals depicted. There were two of them etched in ocher onto flat, black rock, set just above the sand as if in a gallery. The figures were five feet high and expertly rendered. Riding beside one of the giraffes was a man on horseback, reining his mount and preparing to throw a spear. There were already four spears in the giraffe.

I had planned to study the rock art in the morning, along with my favorite among the Italians, Luigi Boschian. Gigi, as everyone called him, was the oldest in our group, sixty-seven, but nonetheless a strong walker who wanted no help clambering over the rocks and who seemed always to know where he was when we strolled through the desert together. Our bond was this: Gigi and I were interested in the same things—history, astronomy, archaeology, geology, anthropology—the difference between us being that he had taken the trouble to do an immense amount of reading in these areas.

Our common language was Spanish, though neither of us spoke with precision, which was sometimes frustrating. I wondered, for instance, if the men on horseback depicted on the rocks could be the ancestors of the Tuareg people, who now populated the deserts of northern Mali, Niger, and southern Algeria. When I asked Gigi about it, he started at the beginning, as he tended to do. Present-day Tuaregs were the descendants of North African Berbers, who had invaded the central Sahara about 3,500 years ago. They were originally horsemen, but as the climate changed and the desert claimed the land, the horse gave way to the camel. And wasn't it interesting that while the Berbers had used chariots, the use of the wheel was eventually abandoned? Camels were the better technology.

In the course of his explanations, Gigi often got sidetracked, wandering off on some tangent or other and dithering there for half an hour at a crack. He wore desert khakis, neatly pressed, but a shirttail was always out or a pant leg stuck into a sock. His abundant white hair was properly combed in the morning, but by noon it had degenerated into a finger-in-the-light-socket situation I'd describe as a full Einstein. He was the quintessential absentminded professor, Italian style. In explanation mode, he held his hands in front of his chest, palms up and open, as if weighing a pair of melons. When our mutual incompetence in Spanish defeated us, he'd turn his palms over and drop them to his waist, as if patting two small children on the head. I thought of this as Gigi's I-can-speak-no-more futility gesture.

Now, with bandits presumably chasing us, we had to abandon the rock art.

I gathered my gear, lurched down the sand slope, and began helping with the loads. Our caravan consisted of three four-wheel-drive, one-ton vehicles modified in this manner or that for hard overland desert driving. Lanterns were glowing, and our party of just over a dozen—three West Africans from the land below the Niger River, two local Tuaregs, a cacophony of Italians, myself, and photographer Chris Rainier—was moving fast, stashing the gear any old way because it was thought the bandits were now very close.

We'd been half expecting the bastards.

No Guarantees

Aguelhok was a small, wind-scoured town of narrow, sandy streets and adobe buildings, none of which would look out of place in Taos, New Mexico. We pulled our vehicles into a large walled courtyard that seemed to be a municipal gathering place, locked ourselves behind the metal gates, and milled around in the dark, unwilling to sleep.

One of the Italians, Dario, said, "Bandits? Ha. They want us to stay here so we have to pay." Dario, I'd guess, was in his early forties, a trim, athletic man I could see snapping out orders in a corporate boardroom.

Muhammad, the Tuareg security consultant we'd hired and the

man who'd told us about the bandits, was talking to our Italian guide, Alberto Nicheli.

"I can no longer guarantee you safe passage to the salt mines," he said.

"You could this afternoon," Alberto said.

"That was before the car followed you up from Kidal."

"We can't pay you if you don't come," Alberto explained.

"This is no matter," Muhammad said.

I caught Dario's eye. We'd offered Muhammad $400 for two weeks' work; $400 is the average annual income in Mali.

"Maybe," Dario said, "this is more serious than I thought."

Gigi motioned to me. He had a map draped over the hood of the Land Rover and was displaying what can only be described, given the circumstances, as a singular lack of urgency while he traced the course of the Niger River with a finger. Could I see how it flowed east, starting in the highlands to the west, and then humped north into the Sahara like a hissing cat before turning back south and east to empty into the Atlantic at the Bight of Benin? And here, perched on top of the northern hump of the river, was Timbuktu. Geography made it the great trading city of antiquity. North African Arabs from the Mediterranean coast brought trade goods south, through the desert, while the black African kingdoms sent gold north from the forests and mountains. They met in Timbuktu.

The caravans started about the time of Christ. Around A.D. 1100, Arabs began bringing salt down from the desert to trade in Timbuktu. Salt, used to preserve and flavor food, was then a rare spice, as much in demand in certain circles as cocaine is today, and equally expensive. It was traded weight for weight with gold in the Middle Ages, and for centuries the camel train bringing salt south to Timbuktu was called the Caravan of White Gold.

And while all this was happening, Gigi explained as he weighed a pair of melons in his hands, the climate was changing, changing, changed. The giraffe-littered grassland became a desert, and the Tuareg nomads became great warriors who preyed on the caravans. They developed the mehari camel—the ultimate medieval desert-war machine—a tall, elegant beast with an elongated back that allowed riders to sit in front of the hump, down low, in sword's reach of horsemen and those fleeing on foot.

The Tuaregs, not unreasonably, sought tolls and tributes from the caravans passing through their desert. The Arab caravans—one-thousand-or-more-camel operations—were loose confederations of traders, and they did not band together for mutual defense in the manner of American wagon trains facing hostile Indians in John Wayne movies. Tuareg raiders simply rode along with caravans, located the weakest groups, cut them out of the train, and took what they wanted. These affairs were most often bloody.

Today Tuaregs are considered the finest camel breeders and riders on earth. They live the romance of their past, still herding goats, pursuing a nomadic lifestyle, and dressing as they have throughout the whole of recorded history. The men most often wear blue robes—they are sometimes called the Blue Men of the Desert—and blue or black chêches, ten-foot-long strips of cloth that are wrapped around the head and neck and can be pulled up over the nose to protect the face from blowing sand. The chêche can also be used as a mask, which is no small advantage for those engaged in the business of banditry.

An Ambush

We had started in Gao, on the Niger River, where there was a paved street or two, a market, and crowds of people clamoring for a *cadeau,* a gift. Moving slowly through the streets was a plethora of white Toyota Land Cruisers, all of them belonging to various aid agencies. My traveling companion Chris Rainier talked with a woman from the UN High Commission for Refugees, who said things in northern Mali were settling down nicely. The six-year Tuareg rebellion against the central government in Bamako was essentially over. The rebels had signed a peace treaty in Timbuktu in March 1996, during a ceremony in which three thousand weapons were burned in a great bonfire.

The droughts of the eighties and early nineties had helped fuel the rebellion, and the government had taken a unique step designed to feed hungry people: Former Tuareg rebels were allowed to enlist in the Malian army. The pay these soldiers earned fed large, extended families. In effect, the Malian government had bought off the insurrection.

Which wasn't to say that everything was hunky-dory. The Tuareg rebels were actually a loosely aligned group of several different desert factions—the Popular Movement of this town, the People's Army of that area—and not all of them were in agreement with the peace treaty. Some, it was said, were still fighting. Plus, the army hadn't been able to take every former rebel who wanted a job, so there were still some bands of hard men in the desert, former rebels who were in fact out-and-out bandits.

The woman from the UN told Chris that about a month ago, bandits had ambushed several UNHCR workers, stolen their car, stripped them naked, and driven off. It was winter, and the workers were more likely to freeze to death at night than bake to death in the day. Besides, they weren't far from town, and everyone got back all right, so there wasn't any harm done.

"What town was that?" Chris asked.

"Kidal."

The Sleeping Colonel

The Trans-Saharan Highway from Gao to Kidal was a thin red line on the map, and the line was a lie. There was no road, only a number of braided tracks in the sand, all of them running vaguely northeast and littered with the rusted and half-buried hulks of vehicles that had surrendered to the desert. In Kidal, a sprawling town of adobe houses only slightly darker than the surrounding sand, we tried to speak with the governor, the army commander, anyone who could give us information on the security situation. We wanted to go to the salt mines. Was it safe? Few answers were forthcoming.

One morning, Alberto, Chris, and I walked the red-dust streets to the largest house in town. It was said to be owned by Colonel Yat, the man thought to be the instigator of the Tuareg rebellion, a fellow, we imagined, who might have some cogent thoughts about security.

The house had a high-walled courtyard punctuated by a pair of large metal doors wide enough to admit a good-sized truck. We knocked for a long time until a gentleman inside opened one of the doors a crack. He wore threadbare black pants, a tattered red tunic, a black chêche, and rubber flip-flops. His right foot was terribly twisted. We were admitted into a large flagstone courtyard, where dozens of small trees had recently been planted. A satellite TV emblazoned with the RadioShack logo stood to one side of the house near several dozen fifty-five-gallon drums of gasoline. A white Land Cruiser—the modern equivalent of the mehari camel—was parked in front of the door. There was a bullet hole just below the backseat on the driver's side.

One tended to speculate about such vehicles. In June 1990, after soldiers massacred several Tuaregs at a famine-refugee camp just over the border in Niger, rebels ambushed a team of aid workers, stole their Land Cruiser, and used it to attack the town of Mënaka, killing fourteen Malian policemen. They escaped with guns and ammunition, and the rebellion was on. Soon there was fighting on the streets of Gao and on the blazing plain of Tanezrouft. Those are the facts. The legend is this: Colonel Yat, the man we had come to see, planned and executed the initial attacks.

The Toyota in the courtyard was white, like most aid agency cars, with a thin red stripe, and it did not carry a Malian license plate. I thought it might be a car with some history to it.

The house itself was unlike anything else in Kidal. It was a large, poured-cement building with flowing Moorish lines, painted brown and white. The man with the twisted foot knocked on an ornately carved wooden door. We stood there for some time until we were admitted by an almost preternaturally handsome Tuareg man who looked to be in his mid-thirties. He was about six feet tall, slender, wearing black slacks and gold-rimmed aviator sunglasses. His black chêche covered his mouth but not his neatly trimmed black mustache, and what we could see of his skin was that curious Tuareg color of charcoal and milk. He looked like a human sword. No names were given. No handshakes.

We said we'd like to speak with Colonel Yat, if it was possible.

Wordlessly, the man turned, motioned for us to follow, and led us across highly polished wood floors to a large dark room completely bare of furniture except for five mattresses pushed against the two far walls. Colonel Yat, we were given to understand, was the man-shaped lump under a sheet on one of the mattresses. It was late in the Muslim fasting month of Ramadan—no food or drink between sunrise and sunset—and the colonel was resting.

In whispers, we said that we could come back later, after sunset, when the colonel had refreshed himself. The man in sunglasses stared at us without expression. Colonel Yat stirred on his mattress and propped himself up on an elbow. He called out. His voice sounded sleep-clogged.

The slender Tuareg walked over, squatted by the bed, and exchanged a few words with the colonel. He walked back across the room, moving with a kind of lethal grace.

"What do you want to talk about?" he asked in heavily accented French.

"We want to talk about the current state of security in the area," Alberto said.

The man glided to the bed, whispered some words, and came back.

"Why?"

"We're journalists," I said.

When that bit of information was relayed to the colonel, he pulled the sheet up over his head and turned to the wall.

"He doesn't want to talk to any journalists," the Tuareg said.

"We're not really journalists," Alberto said.

"He won't talk to you," the man replied, and even in his bad French, it sounded like a threat.

Out of Bounds

And so we drove to Aguelhok, where we hired Muhammad, who claimed to have been an intermediary between the government and the rebels during the late war and who now said he could no longer provide security.

Alberto called us all together in the courtyard, and we stood around in the dark, shifting from foot to foot because there were decisions to be made. Alberto's clients, the Italians, were all prosperous men who'd spent dozens of vacations together traveling in the Sahara. Now they wanted to go somewhere no one else had been, someplace unique, and Alberto, a guide with a reputation for getting things done in West Africa, had suggested the salt mines. This is the nature of adventure travel at the turn of the century. Truly exotic journeys, singular and privileged, like the one the Italians had contracted for, are easily arranged. A person standing in any airport on earth is no more than forty-eight hours from Timbuktu (given the proper connections and no desire to sleep). There, in that dusty desert town, travelers congregate at the post office. Send a card to your Aunt May, postmarked Timbuktu.

These days tourists are enthusiastically welcomed to the fabled city, which was once forbidden to the world outside Africa. Those with the perverse desire to visit currently forbidden sites, people like my Italian friends, must endure various uncertainties regarding their own personal safety.

The salt mines were just such a place. "For one thousand years," Alberto had told his Italian clients, "no one from the outside could go to the salt mines. They were forbidden. You don't tell people where your gold mine is located."

In the seventies, Alberto, like many adventurous young Europeans, had made a living of sorts shipping cars from Europe across the Mediterranean to Africa and then driving them two thousand miles south through the Sahara and selling them in Mali or Nigeria or Togo or Burkina Faso. At the time, the salt mines were still operating up at Taoudenni, or so he had heard. No one he knew had ever been there. After independence from the French in 1960, the Malian government had used the mines as a political prison. Dissidents, generally from Bamako, were sent to the desert, where they were ill prepared to survive. To be condemned to work in the salt mines was tantamount to a death sentence.

Alberto became obsessed with the Taoudenni salt-mine prison

during his car-running days. As a political prison it was, of course, off limits to foreigners. Forbidden. The only outsider Alberto ever talked to who had even gotten close to the prison was an International Red Cross worker who'd driven up from Timbuktu to check on the welfare of the prisoners. A guard stopped the man at gunpoint. The relief worker, staring into the business end of the rifle, explained the concept of international law and reminded the soldier of the strict neutrality of the Red Cross, called the Red Crescent in Muslim Africa. It was his duty to see that political prisoners were treated humanely, in accordance with international law.

"Imbecile," the guard said, "there is no law here."

Alberto hatched an ill-conceived plan to dress as an Arab and try to see the mines. Good sense finally got the better of him.

In 1991, the prison was shut down. Mali, once aligned with the Soviet Union, was now moving toward a multiparty democracy. The elimination of human-rights abuses, such as forced labor in the salt mines, was a first step in securing international aid money. In 1996, a spokesman for the U.S. State Department declared Mali's human-rights record for that year "a bright spot on the African continent."

But, Alberto had heard, there were still people working in the mines, on their own, for money, and since there was a thin red line on the map but no real roads from the mines at Taoudenni to Timbuktu, Alberto figured there still had to be camel caravans, carrying salt across the flowing dunes.

Seeing this medieval anachronism—the Caravan of White Gold—well, Alberto thought and the Italians agreed, it could be the experience of a lifetime. You just didn't want it to be the *last* experience of a lifetime. And so Alberto gave us a choice: we could go back down south of the Niger River and see, oh, the Dogon cliff dwellings, a nice, culturally captivating trip with no security problems at all—a trip, in fact, that Alberto guided frequently for the company Mountain Travel-Sobek. Mali south of the Niger was safe.

Gigi and Dario wanted to wait a bit. See what happened. The two other Italians were both named Roberto. The Roberto everybody called Pepino had the heavy, ponderous dignity of a Roman emperor, and he was leaning toward retreat, as was the other Roberto, a man who reminded me of Clint Eastwood.

We decided not to decide.

Security Bandits

The next day was *eid-al-fitr,* a feast day marking the end of Ramadan. The streets of Aguelhok were thronged with people wearing resplendent new robes, all of them moving toward the mosque, where prayers were said outdoors. There were, I noticed, no cars other than our own in town.

After prayers, several families invited me into their homes, where I was invariably served tea, brewed on a charcoal brazier outside the front door. Tuareg tea is heated with an enormous amount of sugar until it boils up out of the pot and then served in a shot glass, which is always refilled twice. The first glass is said to be "strong like a man," the second "mild like a woman," and the third "sweet like love." The convention seemed to be that one shouted "hi-eee" several times during the ingestion of the tea.

So there were people shouting "hi-eee" and drinking tea, while four teenage girls, using a pair of washtubs for drums, sang a series of hauntingly melancholy songs. Two polite boys, about eight years old, had befriended me and were teaching me to say something in Arabic that they obviously considered to be just a bit naughty. Something, I imagined, in the nature of "Hello, my name is Mr. Poopy Pants."

I figured it out by the time they got to the proper name. *"Lahidahi ilalahi Muhammad . . ."*

I was laughing along with the boys and saying the naughty words—"There is no God but Allah, and Muhammad is his prophet"—when a shadow passed over. I looked up. A man in an iridescent green robe stood above me. He wore a black chêche and gold-rimmed aviator sunglasses. It was Colonel Yat's man, the human sword. He turned and walked swiftly away.

I followed at a cautious distance but lost him in the crowd. Two blocks away, parked by a curb, I found the bullet-scarred white

Toyota we'd seen at Yat's house. It was the only other car in town, and now we knew who the bandits were. And why Muhammad, the security consultant, had turned down a year's wages for two weeks of work.

Alberto, who'd independently discovered the identity of the bandits, formulated a simple plan, modeled in part on the Malian solution to the Tuareg rebellion: We'd hire the bandits themselves to provide security.

Intarka, a Tuareg desert guide we'd hired on our first trip through Aguelhok, arranged a meeting, and we squatted in the courtyard with Colonel Yat's man and his two shadowy companions. The bandits wore their chêches in mask mode. The human sword was named Mossa ag Ala (Mossa, son of Ala). His two buddies were both named Baye. (This is my brother Larry and this is my other brother Larry, I thought). And yes, for the right amount of money, they could get us to the salt mines and then safely down to Timbuktu. Negotiations began in earnest. The would-be security bandits bargained fiercely but finally agreed upon a price. We walked to an administrative center and typed out what I thought was a fairly impressive-looking contract. Mossa scrawled his name, pulled his chêche down over his mouth, and actually smiled.

And then, our security problems presumably solved, we were off to the salt mines, about five hundred miles to the north and west. Intarka navigated while Mossa, Baye, and Baye led the caravan in the white Toyota, which was essentially a rolling bomb. The bandits chain-smoked, all three of them in the front seat, while two leaky fifty-five-gallon drums full of gasoline banged around in the back of the car.

The Tuaregs decided to run overland, off the tracks in the sand that were the Trans-Saharan Highway. They wanted to avoid traffic, because traffic meant cars and cars meant bandits. Once, when we crossed some fresh tracks, the bandit car sped ahead and pulled to a stop just below a rise. Mossa jumped out and lay on his belly in the sand, glassing the plain ahead. There was a car in the distance, but no—focus, focus—it was simply a rock, glittering in the sun.

I wore a blue chêche to filter sand out of the air I was breathing.

There are many ways to wrap a chêche, but I preferred the romantic Tuareg bandit look, which left a three-foot-long tail of fabric
hanging from the left shoulder. Stand in the desert wind, and the
thing blew out behind you, Lawrence of Arabia style.

At one point, a herd of Dorcas gazelles bolted past our car. They
were sand-colored animals about the size of elongated Brittany
spaniels, sporting rabbity ears and a pair of inward-curving horns
about two feet long. The gazelles ran at speeds of over 40 miles an
hour, making comical straddle-legged leaps every few seconds.

Here's a fashion hint concerning chêches and wildlife photogra-
phy: Suppose you pull to a stop when a herd of gazelles goes leap-
ing by, jump out of the car with your camera, and slam the door
behind you. If you are wearing your chêche in the fashionable
Tuareg-bandit mode, the tail will catch in the door and abruptly
pull you to your rear as you attempt to move forward.

A chêche pratfall is a source of great amusement to Tuaregs and
Italians, to people from Togo like Daniel, the cook, and Amen, the
mechanic (the one indispensable man in our party). An event of
this nature will even draw an outright laugh from someone like
Omar, the sulky Malian driver, who generally never smiled. Slap-
stick is universal. Brotherhood through comedy.

We sped over a flat desert plain where pebbly rocks were imbed-
ded in hard sand, and our tires left tracks only half an inch deep.
The Sahara provides two environments: *reg,* which is coarse flat
sand, like the pea gravel we were driving through, and *erg,* shifting
dune sand, which we expected to hit near the mines.

Just before dusk, Intarka had us pull into a large basin behind a
low, rocky butte that would hide our campfires. The bandit car had
veered off into the distance and was running inexplicable patterns
across the sand—wide, curving turns, abrupt stops, sharp, ninety-
degree corners. The bandits rolled into camp after dark with a
gazelle they'd run to exhaustion, a method of hunting that didn't
entirely appeal to my ideas about sportsmanship. Still, they ate the
whole animal, which they grilled over a brushfire, and they gave
the rabbity, horned head to Daniel, who felt he could use it in some
fetish ceremony.

I asked Intarka, who had worked for the army during the rebellion, if he thought Mossa and his pals had really been planning to rob us. He shrugged. Would they have killed us, or merely taken the cars? Intarka said it didn't matter. "They're with us now," he said, "and their word is good."

Over by the Tuareg fire, Mossa threw down a shot glass of tea and shouted, "Hi-eee!"

The Salt Mines

Two more days of driving, while *reg* turned to *erg*. The dunes sloped gently upward where they faced the wind, then dropped off sharply on the other side. Omar couldn't seem to get the hang of driving the dunes. He'd race up the shallow slope, hit the crest of the dune, see what amounted to a cliff face dropping away below, and slam on the brakes, burying the front end of the truck two feet deep. Then it was sand-ladder time.

We dug out the wheels with shovels and hands and placed two three-foot-long tire-width metal rails in the sand underneath. Everyone pushed. Sometimes the car got going again and we ran after it, carrying the sand ladders, hoping there was some solid sand in the near distance. Often we had to dig out a second time, and a third, and a fourth. We were motoring through the Sahara three feet at a crack.

As we worked, a strong wind out of the northeast drove scouring sand before it. The seasonal *harmattan* winds carry sand from the Sahara all the way across the Atlantic and dump it on various Caribbean islands. A good blow seems to start low: it comes toward you pushing snakes of sand along the belly of the dune. Look around, and the world under your feet is alive with twisting, streaming sand snakes.

And then, half obscured by the ankle-deep sand snakes, I spied a series of tracks that looked like they had been made by three motorcycles running abreast. A closer look proved that these were camel tracks.

We saw them coming toward us: sixty camels walking single file, in three pack strings of twenty apiece. Each of the camels carried four blocks of pure white salt. The blocks were rectangular, about two inches thick, two feet high, and three feet wide. They weighed about eighty pounds apiece. Four young Tuaregs walked along with the caravan.

In exchange for *cadeaux* of tea and sugar, the Tuaregs explained the economics of the Caravan of White Gold. Salt cost about $4 a block at the mine. If you were lucky, that same block might sell for $30 in Timbuktu. This sixty-camel caravan carried about ten tons of salt and might fetch a price of $6,200.

From Timbuktu, the salt would be ferried up the Niger to the town of Mopti, where there was a paved-road system that could get it out to the whole of West Africa. Taoudenni salt was more expensive than the more plentiful sea salt, but West Africans—truly spectacular cooks who combine French technique with African ingredients and creativity—believe it is the best-tasting and are willing to pay premium prices.

Alberto and I talked about the realities of the salt trade. Camel caravans still existed, as they had in the Middle Ages, because they were the only economically feasible means of transporting salt from the mines to the Niger. "You could rent a Land Cruiser," Alberto explained. "Say your brother-in-law owns the rental company. You get it for fifty dollars a day, instead of the hundred I pay. Three days at least to drive to the mines from Timbuktu. One day to buy and load. Three days back. Seven days at a rental cost of three hundred and fifty, plus one-fifty for gas. That's five hundred dollars, not counting what you pay for a driver, food, oil, and maintenance. A Land Cruiser carries a ton. At your best price, you'd make six hundred and fifty dollars, which wouldn't even cover expenses."

"What about a ten-ton truck?" I wondered.

"Wouldn't make it through the sand."

We were now, we calculated, only miles from the mines. The next morning we rose up over a sandy hillside, crested a dune, and found ourselves staring down into a great yellow-orange basin, an enormous flatland that melted almost imperceptibly into the curve of the earth. Scattered about the sand plain at odd intervals were a number of loony, artificial-looking landmarks: a pink sand-scoured cone, a kind of lopsided pyramid, and, toward the center of the plain, a butte that looked like a many-footed sphinx. There were humans and hundreds of camels—tiny toy figures—moving about under the gaze of the sphinx. A vast area of sand and clay was cratered with small excavations, as if the place had suffered some terrible saturation-bombing raid.

A three-mile drive took us a thousand years back into history, to the periphery of the fabled Taoudenni salt mines. Men—there were no women—cautiously approached the cars. There was no electricity, no town, no road, only the desert all about and these men laboring in the sand and clay. A dozen or more of the men accompanied me as I strolled through the mines. They asked for and accepted *cadeaux* of aspirin and antibiotics, all the while pointing out the sights, such as they were.

The excavations were all of a size: rectangular holes about ten by twenty feet and perhaps fifteen feet deep. They'd been dug by hand, and the dirt was piled high around the craters.

The basin surrounding the many-footed sphinx, I imagined, had once been completely underwater: a vast inland lake, something like the Great Salt Lake in Utah. As the climate changed and the water evaporated away, minerals were deposited in the old lake bed. Centuries of blowing sand buried the salt about ten feet deep.

The good, glittering white salt was concentrated in a layer about three feet thick. It was covered over in a layer of dirty brown salt that some workers had chopped out in blocks to make small shelters. The men who dug in the pits were mostly blacks, and they used handmade axes and picks to dig out the salt, to file away the inferior brown mineral, and to smooth the edges of the blocks so they could be loaded on the camels, which knelt obediently in the sand and were loaded right at the pits. The camel drivers were Tuaregs or Arabs. Ringing the mines were sixteen different caravans of sixty to seventy camels apiece, at least a thousand animals. In the distance, I counted five more pack strings, three of which were loaded and on their way out.

At sunset, Mossa, in his capacity as security bandit, made a point of gathering everyone up and getting us all out of the mines before dark. We would camp a good distance away from the work crews, far to the northeast, on the edge of an abandoned part of the mine where old excavations were gradually filling with sand. In the morning, we'd walk through the mines one more time and leave early in the afternoon for Timbuktu, so the Italians could catch their flight. Families would be expecting them, Dario told me, and family came first.

By the next morning, the *harmattan* had kicked into high gear. The goofy landmarks—the cone and pyramid—began to shimmer and fade in the distance. Wind-driven sand snakes raced across the desert floor.

I pulled the neck portion of my chêche up over my face. Visibility was down to two hundred yards, and I wandered off into the desert to relieve myself in the privacy veil provided by blowing sand. I walked several hundred yards, then looked back. I couldn't see the camp and assumed they couldn't see me. The wind was on my left shoulder. I did my business and went back, navigating by the simple expedient of putting the wind on my right shoulder.

At camp, Amen had some bad news. Gigi was missing. Clint Eastwood–looking Roberto was sitting on the ground, beside the Land Rover, and he was literally wringing his hands in an agony of guilt. He'd been walking with Gigi. Gigi had dithered. Roberto had left him somewhere in the mines. Now he was gone.

We put together a search party and, with Dario in the lead, retraced the steps Gigi had taken. Alberto, meanwhile, had hired men on camels to ride in a widening spiral around the mines, looking for a man on foot.

Dario, athletic and decisive, ran ahead, scaling the highest of the excavations, where he'd be more likely to see Gigi, especially if he was lying injured in one of the old pits. Clint Eastwood–looking Roberto trudged through the sand in a hopeless fashion. He was known in Italy as a great hunter, but all his skills were useless to him here. The sandstorm had swept the desert floor clear of tracks. To me, the mines seemed a hopeless labyrinth. Including the abandoned sections, I estimated about five square miles of closely spaced pits, more than a thousand of them.

We straggled back into camp well after dark.

There'd been no sign of Gigi.

Strangers in the Night

After dark, Intarka stood on the roof of the Land Rover with a handheld spotlight and spun the beam through a slow 360-degree circuit. He did this tirelessly and for hours. Perhaps Gigi would see the light and follow it to the source.

Alberto drove around the mines to a small collection of salt-block houses directly opposite our camp. It was the only thing that resembled a settlement that we'd seen. Someone, we all felt, must have kidnapped Gigi. Alberto's plan was to offer money, diplomatically, for the return of our friend.

There were no police in the settlement, no soldiers, no secular authorities at all. The men of the mines, however, had submitted themselves to the moral authority of the *marabout,* a minor Muslim cleric who knew the Koran and who settled various disputes. Alberto met him in a salt-block courtyard illuminated by lanterns.

The *marabout* looked the part: an ascetic man of about fifty with an untrimmed beard going to white. He wore a brown robe and a black chêche, and he carried his authority with a degree of nobility. He told Alberto that he knew the kind of men who lived in the mines and that none of them was a killer or a robber or a kidnapper. He felt Gigi was somewhere safe, perhaps staying with people until the morning. The *marabout* offered a prayer for Gigi and said, "I think you will find your friend in one day and that he will not be injured."

Alberto arrived back in our camp and said that he'd been impressed with the *marabout.* Still, he'd organized and paid in advance for a fifty-man search party to leave at dawn. In the distance, toward the mines, we could see lights moving in our direction. They were flashlights, held by people who wanted us to know they were coming to talk and were not sneaking up on us for an ambush. There were dozens of men. We interviewed them one by one.

An Arab with a broken foot said he'd seen one of the white men walk out into the desert about noon, just when the sandstorm was at its worst.

"What did he look like?" Alberto asked.

"Blue chêche. He was the big one."

"Alberto," I said, "this guy's a moron. I'm standing right in front of him wearing a blue chêche. I'm the big one."

"Did you walk out into the desert?"

"To take a crap."

And so it went, for hours.

Clint Eastwood–looking Roberto sat in one of the cars, chain-smoking cigarettes. He blamed himself, and his eyes were red-rimmed from crying. Pepino-Roberto sat with him, assuring the grief-stricken man that Gigi's disappearance wasn't his fault. Things would work out.

At about 2 A.M. a tall Arab mounted elegantly on a sleek camel rode into camp along with four or five men on foot who seemed to be his retinue. The man wore a fine green robe and had the air of a dignitary. "Your friend," he said, "is staying with some people." He, the Arab, knew these people. He could buy Gigi back for us. It would cost 500,000 African francs, about $1,000.

Dario said, "You see, the Arab people do their business at night." It was less an expression of prejudice than one of hope. Dario had agreed with me earlier in the evening: he too thought Gigi was dead. Now, for $1,000, that sorrow could be instantly lifted from his soul.

Alberto bargained with the Arab. He would give only 50,000 francs up front, the rest to be paid when we saw Gigi alive and well. The Arab dismounted, spat on the ground, and stood too close to Alberto. "Five hundred thousand now," he said. "Then maybe you will see your friend."

Alberto turned and nodded to the white Land Cruiser behind him, where Mossa, Baye, and Baye were smoking cigarettes and monitoring the conversation. Mossa snapped on his headlights, and the tall Arab stood there blinking in the sudden glare. All three Tuaregs stepped out of the car, their black chêches worn up, in mask mode. The tall Arab, half blinded and confused, now looked as if all his internal organs had suddenly collapsed. I have seldom seen such outright fear on a man's face.

Mossa shouted three harsh words, and the tall Arab, along with his entourage, disappeared rapidly into the night.

No one slept. People kept wandering into camp with another tidbit of information. About four in the morning, a young Arab appeared and said that earlier in the evening he'd seen a white man walking toward the well at Taoudenni. This didn't seem right. The well was ten miles away and almost 180 degrees in the wrong direction. Gigi knew how to get around outdoors. Plus, Alberto had already been to the well, and none of the men there had seen Gigi.

Still, the young Arab seemed guileless. He was about eighteen and knew nothing about our offer of a reward to anyone who found Gigi alive. The Arab said he had seen an older man walking alone and a spotlight beaming in the distance.

Now, a white man walking in the desert at night was an extremely odd circumstance. So was the light. The young Arab had put the two together instantly: the light was for the white man. He had tried to tell him that, but the man just kept walking, staring at the ground and smiling vaguely. He had touched the man's arm and tried to turn him so he could see the light. But the man would not turn. He only made this strange gesture: the Arab dropped his hands to his sides.

"Wait a minute," I said, nearly shouting. "Do that again. Do it the way he did it."

The Arab turned his hands and moved them lightly up and down, as if patting two small children on the head. It was Gigi's futility gesture.

Goddamn! Gigi, still alive, was somewhere near the Taoudenni well.

Gigi in the *Tormentosa de Sable*

Alberto, Pepino-Roberto, Chris, Mossa, and I sped overland in the eerie silver light of false dawn. We skidded to a stop at the well. There was a ruined French fort, an abandoned prison, and a defunct armored personnel carrier parked nearby. The sun was just rising, an enormous sphere balanced on the horizon, and its light, in the lingering haze of the sandstorm, was the lurid red of flowing blood. When I looked back toward the prison, there was a man walking our way. He cast a shadow thirty feet long, and it rose high and red on the whitewashed walls of the prison.

"Gigi!" I screamed.

Mossa had already seen him and was running over the sand, with me sprinting behind and steadily losing ground. Mossa hit Gigi like a linebacker and nearly knocked him over with an embrace. The car sped by me. Alberto was hugging Gigi when I got there, so Mossa hugged me. His eyes were tearing over. He wasn't crying—I couldn't imagine Mossa ever crying—but he was overcome with emotion. Pepino, walking in his heavy, dignified way, was sobbing openly, drying his eyes with a clean white handkerchief.

We offered Gigi some water, and he took a small sip, as if to be polite. He'd been lost in the Sahara, without a canteen, for twenty-two hours. He drank two more sips, then patted some children on the head to indicate that, no, no, he didn't want any more.

Back at our camp, Alberto paid the Arab the promised reward. Dario and Clint Eastwood–looking Roberto were taking turns embracing Gigi. Their gestures were elegantly expressive, fully Italian. Roberto, weeping, hugged Gigi, patted him on the back, and then pushed him out to arm's length and cocked a fist as if to punch him in the mouth.

Gigi was smiling his vague smile, staring at the ground, and every time Roberto gave him a little room, he began weighing a couple of melons in explanation.

After this orgy of emotion, while everyone else was packing up for what now had to be a doubly high-speed run over the dunes to Timbuktu, Gigi and I spoke for a couple of hours. I wanted to know what happened. We spoke in Spanish, our only common language.

Gigi told me:

He'd been walking, taking pictures, dithering around as usual, when the sandstorm hit. He'd marked his position by the various oddly shaped formations on the horizon—the many-footed sphinx, the pyramid, and the cone—and felt he would be able to tell where he was at any time by using the process of triangulation. Did I understand about triangulation? Gigi began weighing some melons in his hands. *"Por exemplo,"* he said, "if I move from here to the west, the cone would change its position on the horizon. . . ."

"Sí, sí, entiendo," I said, a bit impatiently. I understood about triangulation.

Well, in a sandstorm, Gigi explained reasonably, a *tormentosa de sable,* a man cannot see the mountains on the horizon and therefore cannot use the process of triangulation in order to fix his position. He'd been concentrating on his photos, because in the sand there were bits of clay that he was interested in and . . .

"So," I said, hurrying the story along, "when you looked up from your photo . . ."

The sand, Gigi said, was blowing and he couldn't see, so he just began walking but he must have gotten turned around taking the photos, and he walked the wrong way. He was walking almost directly into the wind, to the northeast, the direction of the *harmattan,* and he should have known that was wrong, but he was thinking about other things.

I almost asked what he was thinking about but quelled the impulse. At this point we'd been working on the story for an hour.

It was actually painful, walking into the blowing sand, so Gigi sat down for an hour or two, with his back to the wind. By late that afternoon, the storm had blown itself out, but the distant mountains, his triangulation points, were still obscured in the *harmattan* haze. Gigi walked in a large circle, hoping to see the rubble and excavation of the salt mines. But it was just a level plain of sand. He sat down to think again, admired the sunset, and then got up, picked a direction at random, and began walking.

It was dark when a young man came up to him and began speaking in a language Gigi took to be Arabic. Gigi tried to project the image of an Italian gentleman out on an evening stroll, preoccupied with his own thoughts and unwilling to be bothered. The young man grabbed his arm as if he wanted him to turn and go the other way. Gigi had some preconceived notions about Arabs in the dark and so he refused to turn and see the light. In the day, Gigi said, it might have been different. He continued walking, smiling at the ground and making his it-is-useless gesture of patting children on the head. The Arab shrugged and left him. Gigi felt he'd handled the encounter well.

He walked for several more hours until he saw the lights of some campfires reflecting off a whitewashed building in the distance. As he got closer, he could see figures moving around the fires, then he could hear the shouts and laughter of people conversing in Arabic. They seemed to be camped around a well.

In the building nearest him, and farthest from the fires and the people, there were several very small rooms with bars on the windows. It was, Gigi assumed, the old prison. He chose a cell and lay down. The brick building held the heat of the day and it was all quite pleasant. The sky had now cleared, and Gigi could see the stars.

He lay on his back and formulated a plan. His friends had to get to Timbuktu to catch a flight to Bamako and then to Italy, where their families would be waiting. He expected that we would be searching for him, but he hoped we'd leave by noon, so as not to miss the flight. He didn't want to have a lot of families worried on his account.

And if we did leave, Gigi would simply walk over to the Arabs by the well, introduce himself, and ask if he could tag along on the five-hundred-mile trip back to Timbuktu. He'd be home in a couple of months.

Satisfied with his plan, Gigi fell into a sleep so profound that he didn't hear the Land Rover pull into the prison compound at eleven that night. He didn't hear Alberto and Chris and Pepino conversing with the Arabs. He'd hid himself well, and none of the men had seen him.

He woke refreshed just before dawn. As soon as the sun came

up, he walked out of the prison, on his way down to the well, to make friends with the Arabs. That's when he saw me and Mossa and Pepino. All these people sprinting over the desert in his direction, crying and shouting. It was strange.

The *Marabout's Cadeau*

We'd lost a day looking for Gigi, but there was a chance the Italians could still make their flight out of Timbuktu. However, there were thank-yous to be offered, and that would delay us. Alberto stopped at the *marabout*'s salt-block house and called off the morning's search. The men he'd hired could keep the money that had been given them. Most of them had searched for Gigi yesterday afternoon anyway, without compensation. We were very grateful.

Alberto thanked the *marabout* for his prayers and asked if there was anything he could do: Would the *marabout* accept a *cadeau*? He would not. The cleric was just happy that everything had turned out well and that our friend was safe. The *marabout*'s refusal made him all the more impressive in our eyes. We'd been bombarded by cries for *cadeaux* for weeks.

But no, after a moment's reflection, the marabout said there was something we could do. There were two Arab men who had been stranded at the mines and were unaffiliated with any caravan. Could we take them back to their homes about two hundred miles north of Timbuktu?

Yes, of course.

Both the Arabs were thin, desiccated-looking men, with strong, coppery planes in their faces and high-arched noses. They looked like Moorish versions of Don Quixote, as drawn by El Greco. The man who rode with me in the Land Rover was named Nazim, and he carried a twenty-pound bag of dates. If his good luck evaporated and he had to walk, the dates would sustain him for the three-hundred-mile trek.

Nazim had never ridden in a car before. He had to be shown how to work the door latch and the handle that rolled down the window. In thirty seconds, he had pretty much mastered the technological intricacies involved in being an automobile passenger.

The Arabs navigated. They rapidly figured out what sort of terrain was best for the vehicles and chose areas where the wind had packed sand tight to the ribs of the dunes. We flew over a roller coaster of smooth sand at 55 miles an hour. Every few hours we converged on the main camel track leading toward the mines. I counted twelve caravans heading in to the mines and eleven going out, about sixteen hundred camels in all.

It was near noon, and Nazim was getting nervous, looking around and fidgeting.

"Prayers," I shouted over the rattle of the diesel engine.

Alberto stopped the car, and Nazim, an old hand with door latches by now, jumped out and knelt in the sand, facing east. While the Tuaregs and Arabs prayed together, I scanned the line of dunes ahead, which rose and crested like so many ocean waves about to break. Bright, flashing lights seemed to be moving over the summit of the highest of the dunes, a dozen or more miles away. Although I couldn't see the camels, I guessed it had to be another caravan, fully loaded, the salt blocks glinting in the sun like a long line of signal mirrors.

We drove until well after dark and then set up camp at the base of a high dune that had the rolling sensuality of a line-drawn nude. The sand was cool and seemed luxurious. The constellations spun above, almost impossibly bright, and for a moment the Sahara seemed the most romantic spot on earth.

Many women, I knew, especially French women, travel to the desert hoping to kindle a romance with a proud desert chieftain, with someone, I imagined, exactly like Mossa. Ah, the handsome features, the noble warrior's heart, the strong, slender hands stroking underneath cotton robes with the hard stars burning overhead . . .

"I heard two American women talking about their affairs with Tuaregs," Alberto told me. "I was driving a tour. They didn't know I spoke English."

"What did they say?"

It was pretty much as I had thought. The women agreed the Tuareg men were physically beautiful, and they took these women, there in the sand, as if by right. They took them brashly and with a breath of contempt, which made it that much more exciting.

Just one thing about all that ravishing, Alberto added.

"What?"

"They said it was quick."

Alberto pronounced the word "queek."

"Queek," I repeated, secretly pleased.

"Yes, both of them agreed. Queek, queek, it is all over."

We exchanged a glance, Alberto and I. The glance said, "Maybe we are not the most desirable specimens of masculinity in this desert, but—in contrast to every offensively handsome Tuareg male alive—we would, given the opportunity, conduct this ravishment-under-the-stars business with a good deal less efficiency."

Such delusions are the salve of wounded pride.

Revenge of the Gazelles

Gradually, grudgingly, the sand began to give way to a sparsely vegetated plain that, after miles of *erg,* seemed incredibly lush. There were a few camels feeding on acacia trees, and then, as we slowed to negotiate a path through a large herd of goats, Nazim pointed to a pair of blue-and-beige open-fronted tents. He said, "Ah, ah, ah."

We stopped. A woman huddled in the nearest tent, protectively pushing a pair of youngsters behind her. Cars never came this way. Her expression seemed to say, "Nothing good can come of this." Nazim stepped out of the Land Rover and carefully closed the door behind him, as if to demonstrate new skills. The woman stared at Nazim in a kind of awed astonishment. She rose slowly to her feet, stupefied, then ran to him and hugged him tightly while the two small children pulled at the folds of his tunic.

So we delivered the *marabout's cadeau,* and thank you, Nazim, but no time for tea. It was still ten hours to Timbuktu, and sixteen hours until the Italians' flight.

We ran hard. Omar, the surly Malian driver, blew a shock absorber, there was a flat tire or two on the other vehicles, and our security bandits' gasoline drums were running low, which didn't actually stop them from chasing gazelles.

We were slaloming up and down a series of sloping dunes in the dark, about fifty miles north of Timbuktu, when the bandits finally and irrevocably ran out of gas. Mossa, Baye, and Baye got out and surrounded their vehicle. They stood with their arms crossed over their chests, staring hard at the Toyota as if it owed them some sort of an explanation.

It was a tableau I'd entitle "The Revenge of the Gazelles."

Alberto took a GPS reading while Mossa, Baye, and Baye discussed their options. It was decided that Baye and Baye would stay with the car while Mossa would come with us, continuing to provide high-class security all the way to Timbuktu, as agreed. There he'd arrange for another car and would be back to pick up Baye and Baye by and by.

The two men gave everyone a hug in the abrupt, bone-crushing manner of the desert. And then we were off again.

"Bye-bye, Baye Baye," everyone shouted from the windows. I imagine we sounded like a pack of dogs all suffering from the same strange speech impediment. "Bye-bye, Baye Baye."

"Hi-eee, hi-eee," shouted Baye and Baye.

The vehicles slipped and slid across the shifting sand. They got bogged down. They got pushed out on sand ladders. They slowed near the top of most every dune, engines roaring, slowing, slowing, stopping. We had to back down every third slope and try again. And then, at the summit of a dune that had taken us four tries to climb, I saw our destination only ten miles away. It was spread out below us in all its glittering magnificence, such as it was (I counted twenty-seven lights): the historic and formerly forbidden city of Timbuktu, where there was a reasonably comfortable hotel, cold beer for sale, a post office, and a jetport that was forty-eight hours from any major airport on earth. Some of which, I thought, were not entirely secure.

The Terrible Land

It was the greatest flood the earth has ever known: a cataclysm that literally shook the earth along a thousand-mile path. It happened this way: during the last ice age, a finger of glacier reached down into Montana and Idaho, blocking the Clark's Fork River. The river backed up, filling the deep mountain valleys of Montana and forming a lake larger than Lake Ontario. It was nearly two thousand feet deep, and when the ice dam failed, Lake Missoula drained in forty-eight hours. A wall of water moving at 65 miles an hour and carrying two-hundred-ton boulders encased in ice thundered through what is now Spokane, and blasted down the path of the Columbia River.

Starting about 15,300 years ago, there were over 40 such floods in a 2,500-year period. Human beings almost certainly occupied the Columbia River basin in that era, and stories of the flood must have passed from one generation to the next. In the manner of humans confronted by deadly forces beyond their comprehension or control, they must have regarded flood-scarred land as both terrible and sacred.

I thought about this as I stood in the path of the ancient flood and filled out form BC-3000-002 (Radiological Area Visitor Form), which I handed to an attractive young woman at the Richland, Washington, Department of Energy operations office. She gave me a radiation-measuring device called a dosimeter, a visitor's name tag to be displayed on the outer layer of my clothing, and an orientation booklet outlining security requirements and safety measures at the Hanford Site, which contains the largest repository of waste in all the hemisphere. It was my responsibility to "read and comply with all the information identified on radiological postings, signs and labels, and follow escort instructions." On page ten, there was a series of schematic drawings illustrating responses to the various emergency signals. In case of fire, for instance, a bell would ring. The bell was depicted as having eyes, a nose, a mouth, and a single, stringy arm holding a hammer. The bell was banging itself on the head with the hammer, producing a sound written as "gong, gong, gong." In another illustration, positioned above the bell, a cross-eyed siren emitted a steady blast—"HEEEEEE"—which meant "evacuation," in this case to the "staging area." The top illustration, labeled "HOWLER," was a siren with worried eyes and a mega-phone for a mouth. It's "Ah-OO-GAH" sound meant "criticality" and the required response was "RUN," though no particular desti-nation was given. Just run.

So . . . all those James Bond films were perfectly correct: when the evil scientist's lab is about to blow, the AH-OO-GAH horn really does sound. I followed my DOE escort, Eric Olds, out into the parking lot, along with the poor excuse for an evil scientist I had been corresponding with for over a year. Randy Brich was a "Tanks Focus Area" physical scientist working for the DOE, and not much into world domination. He was, in fact, an obsessed windsurfer with a minor preoccupation in mountain biking.

Randy had offered to set up a raft trip down to the Hanford Reach, inarguably the most pristine and unspoiled stretch of the Columbia River. It was, Randy said, very much as it had been when Lewis and Clark camped nearby in 1805. There were elk and sal-mon and sturgeon and egrets and herons and white pelicans and peregrine falcons and ferruginous hawks, along with pygmy rabbits and several varieties of rare wildflowers. In fact, because the area was restricted for fifty years, biologists had only recently begun an inventory of flora and fauna. In 1996, for instance, two plants previ-ously unknown to science and dozens of new species of insects, in-cluding seven new species of bees, were discovered.

Before the float trip, however, Randy thought I might want to tour the Hanford Site. The irony was that the unspoiled stretch of river and the toxic waste dump were one and the same.

We piled into a DOE van. Eric drove us to the restricted site, where we presented our credentials to armed men at a gate and rolled out onto the flat, arid landscape along the Columbia River.

The remains of a few dry orchards, untended for over fifty years, stood gnarled on the sage-littered steppe: arthritic shapes against a baleful gray sky. Apricot trees. Cherries. The people who planted the orchards back in the late 1930s and early '40s believed that the basin of the Columbia River could rival or surpass California's Central Valley in food production. Yes, the land was a steppe-shrub environment—a desert, most would say—but the Grand Coulee Dam, just upriver, had been completed in 1941. Irrigation water would be plentiful. The low-lying basin, set in the rain shadow of the Cascades, had a growing season that started two weeks earlier than California's. The future was bright.

But then, in January 1944—in the midst of the Second World War—the government claimed the cities of Hanford and White Bluffs. Over 1,300 people were given 30 days to evacuate, and the government confiscated 560 square miles of land along a 52-mile stretch of the Columbia River known as the Hanford Reach. Massive work crews—more than 150,000 men and women—hired to "do important war work" began breaking ground.

Aside from required housing, 554 mysterious buildings were constructed at Hanford in only 30 months. The soil, laid bare in the frenzy of construction, was whipped by fierce desert winds into vicious swirling dust storms that dimmed the sun, snarled traffic, and sand-blasted exposed skin. Despite the high wages paid, hundreds of workers typically left the Hanford Site after one of these "termination winds."

Only a few top scientists and engineers knew the purpose of the project. Some workers joked that it had to be President Roosevelt's summer home. But no one talked about his or her job. FBI informers were everywhere. People were fired for injudicious comments. Thefts were not prosecuted because the stolen material would become a matter of public record at a trial. The secrecy was so complete that Vice President Harry Truman was not informed about the nature of the Hanford Project until President Franklin Roosevelt died.

On July 16, the first atom bomb, code-named Trinity, was test-fired at Alamogordo Bombing Range in south-central New Mexico. It was armed with plutonium produced at the Hanford Site.

On August 6, 1945, another atom bomb exploded over Hiroshima, Japan, killing more than 64,000 people. The Hiroshima bomb was fueled with uranium produced at Oak Ridge, Tennessee. Three days later, a blast of blinding light mushroomed over Nagasaki. Seventy thousand people died. Human bodies simply evaporated at ground zero while, at the periphery of the blast, others shivered and collapsed into ashes before the nuclear termination wind.

The plutonium that fueled the Nagasaki bomb was produced at Hanford B reactor.

B Reactor was built and producing plutonium in only fifteen months. Today, it is a pile of weathered gray cement blocks several stories high, designed in the square Lego-block architecture style of the military-industrial complex. We were met at the door by a volunteer tour guide, Roger Rohrbacher, who had come to work at Hanford in the spring of 1944. "I thought I was coming to a chemical plant," he said.

We moved down a gray hallway, past water pipes stacked on water pipes, all sporting a bewildering mass of round hand cranks used to open and close valves. The Hanford Site was chosen partly because water from the Columbia could be used to cool the reactor. It required seventy thousand gallons of water a minute. Red tags hanging from some of the valves read: "Deactivated System. Deactivation Complete 2/22/68."

The reactor, Roger said, was built on a twenty-three-foot-high slab of concrete. We passed through a doorway and stared up at the front face of the reactor. It loomed three stories over us, thirty-five feet high, thirty-five feet wide, and looked like nothing so much as a giant punchboard. Except that the pins that fitted into the graphite holes were forty-five-foot-long rods. There were 2,004 of these "process tubes," which contained uranium that was converted to plutonium (and other nasty fission products) by the bombardment of neutrons.

In the dim light, the face of the atomic pile—"we called it 'the unit,' " Roger said—seemed vaguely unreal, like something designed for a Buck Rogers space opera. I glanced up into the darkness. There was a catwalk to one side of the reactor where two spectral figures in full yellow radiation suits stood looking down at us, silhouetted in the dim light from an open doorway on the third floor.

"What are they doing?" I asked Roger.

"Completing the decontamination," he said. "Desks and file cabinets and stuff up there."

We moved around the back of the pile to the control room, where there was a chair for the reactor operator. It was positioned in front of a curving green wall in which there were nine gauges. It looked a bit like the cockpit of a commercial jetliner, only much less complex. I saw something labeled "spline coiler control."

To the right of the desk where the reactor operator sat was the back of the pile, and there were the 2,004 tubes, each with its own water-flow meter. A sign said, "Caution: Bumping panel may cause SCRAM." "Scram" is the universal word for "reactor down."

During the Cold War, Roger said, eight more reactors were built at Hanford. People of Roger's generation are damn proud of the work they did at the site. In their view, it won the Second World War, and it won the Cold War. The Richland High School football team, the Bombers, wear helmets emblazoned with mushroom clouds.

All nine Hanford reactors are decommissioned now, and the DOE, after years of secrecy and downright lying, has initiated a policy of openness. Seventy-five percent of the nation's most toxic nuclear wastes, we are now told, are buried at Hanford: 54 million gallons of highly radioactive waste stored in 177 underground tanks, mostly buried in what is called Area 200. The DOE says that it will take "decades" to clean the area. The current, unofficial target date is 2035.

Officials at Hanford encourage visitors to think of the deadly toxins festering there as "legacy wastes": a legacy of the Second World War, a legacy of the Cold War, a legacy of victory.

The Columbia River rises in the Rocky Mountains of Canada. The waters flow south into the United States, abruptly turn west, and empty into the Pacific north of Portland. In between, in the state of Washington, there are ten dams along the Columbia, forming a series of lakes and reservoirs. The last of the free-flowing Columbia is the Hanford Reach, fifty-two miles of bright blue water flowing past boxlike concrete munitions plants and through a desert painted in dull, sage-stippled pastels. The land, in its undeveloped and extravagant abundance, is another legacy of Hanford, and an entirely unintended one at that.

Less than 5 percent of the 560-square-mile nuclear reservation has been developed. The river and the land, including two wildlife reserves comprising nearly ninety thousand acres, have been protected from any development for over fifty years. Now that Hanford's plutonium mission is over, the DOE plans to release the land it confiscated. The strange and fortuitous irony is that the security zone created around the nuclear munitions plants left the land undeveloped and a significant stretch of river undammed. Consequently, the Hanford Site supports populations of fish, bird, and insect life threatened with extinction elsewhere. Several species of salmon spawn in the waters below the reactors, and proponents of a Senate bill to designate the Hanford Reach a Wild and Scenic River argue that such protection is the easiest and least expensive method of the salmon-restoration programs mandated by federal courts.

Permission to camp along the reach was a matter of some bureaucratic maneuvering, requiring several weeks' effort and a slew of letters. Randy Brich, who spearheaded the effort, described it this way: a float trip courtesy of the U.S. Department of Energy, sponsored by the Desert Kayak and Canoe Club and underwritten by Battelle's Pacific Northwest national laboratory.

The river was running at about 5 miles an hour, but the waters were high, deep blue under a cobalt-blue sky, and almost glassy. Pat Wright, a Battelle safety officer, and I took turns rowing his drift boat and drinking beer, flowing gently down the stream in company with a kayak, a couple of catarafts, and a canoe. Most every floater worked at Hanford.

The gray brick buildings of the Hanford Site scrolled by on our right. Pump houses and cooling stacks and pipes running into and out of blocky gray cement buildings looked odd and out of time, rather like the shell of an old car, a Model T, for instance, rusting away in a field full of wildflowers. From a distance, the buildings were dwarfed under the overwhelming arc of sky.

As we floated by the last reactor to be decommissioned, N, there was the disconcerting sound of a cell phone ringing and Rick Raymond, a Lockheed Martin Hanford Company project manager who was paddling one of the catarafts, peeled off from our flotilla. He caught a back eddy under an unmanned, glassed-in guard tower. It was very quiet on the river. The only sounds were the whisper of the wind and the mad, birdbrained screams of mud swallows building nests on the banks of the river. In this relative silence, Rick's voice carried well and I could hear him speaking with some urgency.

Later, when he caught up with us, I accused Rick of committing business on a river trip.

"Sorry," he said. "One of our tanks is belching hydrogen." Some of the double-walled waste tanks contained a million gallons of waste: a horrifying goulash of plutonium syrup and cesium and strontium and other venomous toxins. The tanks produced hydrogen, which is a by-product of nuclear decay. Hydrogen is highly flammable. The tanks were built to vent gases, but sometimes a thick crust formed on top of the waste, and the hydrogen collected underneath in an ominous, growing bulge. In these cases, giant circulating pumps were used to vent the tank.

This was what was happening as I floated past the tank farm. An explosion in the enclosed underground tank could hurl radioactive sludge high into the atmosphere.

"Technically," he said, "it's what we in waste management call 'a bad thing.'"

Randy Brich, who was paddling a canoe nearby, recited the Hanford mantra: "A nuclear waste," he muttered, "is a terrible thing to mind."

A snowy egret rose from the banks across from the reactors and kept pace with us as we drifted along at 5 miles an hour. Ferruginous hawks worked the hillsides, river left. Ahead, along a great, ten-mile curve of river, the White Bluffs loomed six hundred feet overhead. They were crumbly sandstone deposits containing the fossilized remains of mastodons, beavers the size of bears, camels, bison: the whole ice-age menagerie.

Just across from Locke Island, a part of the bluffs had collapsed into the river, and the geologists in our group blamed irrigation on the bluffs above the cliff face, in an area known as the Wahluke Slope. Further irrigation would cause further sloughing and damage the salmon-spawning grounds. Happily, in April 1999, Secretary of Energy Bill Richardson announced the DOE's desire to preserve ninety thousand acres of the Wahluke Slope as a wildlife refuge.

We made camp at a cove set deep into the White Bluffs and then set off along a road previously used by security vehicles. The bladderpod, one of the plants new to science, grew along the tops of the bluffs. A species of mustard, the bladderpod was in early bloom and sported yellow cruciform flowers. We found several of the rare plants growing at the very tops of the White Bluffs, where they spread out and hunkered down low against the termination winds. I glanced back down the river toward the reactors, which lay along the path of the cataclysmic ice-age floods. There were forces here beyond human comprehension, and I regarded the land below as both terrible and sacred.

The House of Boots

It was no great feat of investigative journalism to find the house of Boots. The ramshackle log edifice was partially hidden behind a dozen mature trees, about a hundred yards off a gravel road a dozen miles or so outside the town of Cholila, in Chubut Province, Argentina. It was surrounded by a barbless wire fence intended to keep cows away; I had been told that no advance permission was required to examine the unmarked and abandoned complex of log buildings, so I climbed over the fence. A pasture fronting the dark structures was alive with daisies and the lazy hum of bees. The main house was pleasantly shaded by trees, and there were several outcabins strung along the banks of the slow-flowing blue waters of the Río Blanco.

The man called Boots, I had been informed, had built this homestead nearly a century ago, in 1902, after he fled to South America from the United States. In Cholila, there are those who will tell you Boots was a gunslinger and a killer. One local family believes he killed one of its forefathers during a botched and cowardly robbery. The Ap Iwans, a clan of Welsh settlers, had established a trading post to do business with the Mapuche Indians. On the night of December 28, 1909, a torch was thrown through the window of the store. The proprietor, Llwyd Ap Iwan, was inside and fired several shots to drive off the robbers, but burned his hands badly putting out the fire. The next day, they say, six outlaws, including Boots and a woman, attacked the trading post. Boots burst through the door with his pistol drawn, but Llwyd grappled with the intruder, who fell when his spurs became tangled in a rug. Despite his burned hands, Llwyd managed to get the gun away from the outlaw, but it had been modified to be cocked with the heel of the hand—to be fanned—and the trigger was missing. Llwyd was slow with the gun, and a man known in North America as the Sundance Kid stepped into the room carrying a Winchester .45 rifle and killed him.

The Welsh community was enraged. The Ap Iwans say that the outlaws were hunted down by Argentine territorial police and killed not far away, near the border with Chile. There are others in Cholila who say that the Ap Iwan family is mistaken and that Llwyd was killed by another gang of North American bandits living in the area at the time. The man who called himself Butch Cassidy ("Butch" sounds like "Boots" in a Spanish-speaking mouth) was a good neighbor and a fine rancher. According to this variation on the legend, Boots was driven from his land by political circumstances beyond his control and died either in Bolivia or back in the United States.

A breeze sighed through the tall old trees around the house of Boots, and I listened for the voices of spirits. A set of crooked steps led up to a small porch, and it was no great feat of imagination to see the place as it must have been almost one hundred years ago: graceful and rather elegant, a scaled-down version of the late-nineteenth-century cattle-baron style.

The doors were locked and the windows shut tight. I looked through panes of wavy glass into dusty, dark rooms. My own shadow slid across the floor, but I imagined dim figures, vaguely translucent, shifting through the gloom, a table set for a long Argentine lunch: one woman, two men. A linen tablecloth, fine silver, plates of beef and salad, the contented murmur of conversation.

"Step inside," a disembodied voice suggested, "for we wish to relieve you of your time and currency." Not me, I thought. But it was as if the locked door was already swinging open on ghostly, creaking hinges.

El Señor Raúl Cea, seventy-seven, is generally considered the *historiador,* the keeper of the legend. He owns a small cattle ranch set on a hillside above the Río Blanco, and I drove to visit him with an Argentine fishing buddy of mine named Eduardo, who directed me through fenced fields of fine, fat cows. Beyond the valley was the Cerro Tres Picos, an Andean wall rising stark against a cloudless sky, and the three pinnacles that gave it its name. Glaciers on the saddles between the peaks glittered in the sun.

"Raúl will talk about Boots for hours," Eduardo told me. "His wife doesn't like it. She believes he is obsessed. We should only stay for one hour, no more."

We arrived at the modest old ranch house to find Raúl Cea wrestling with a used freezer that was sitting on the tailgate of a battered Ford pickup. He was a big man, but it was my opinion that anyone who has attained seventy-seven years shouldn't be carrying around freezers single-handedly.

Eduardo and I shouldered the resolute Mr. Cea out of the way and lugged the bulky appliance into the house. We gathered around the kitchen table, and la Señora Cea graciously offered the thick green tea called mate and sat with us for a moment until it became clear that we were going to talk about the dreaded Boots. She excused herself and left the room, closing the door perhaps a bit more firmly than was absolutely necessary.

Mr. Cea told us that he was not a historian by trade, but a retired civil servant. He had been a builder, Eduardo said, and it was he who erected the stately municipal office building in Cholila. He'd also been a small-time rancher all his life—"a gaucho, a cowboy like Butch Cassidy"—and his father had known the North American outlaws well.

Butch and Sundance arrived in Cholila in the summer of 1901, Mr. Cea said. Butch called himself Santiago Ryan. Harry Longabaugh—the Sundance Kid—brought along his girlfriend, Etta Place. They claimed to be man and wife, and Sundance went by the name Enrique Place. The newcomers were granted land to develop under an Argentine law, similar to the U.S. Homestead Act, that had been enacted on October 16, 1884. (Mr. Cea, like any historian, amateur or professional, was a font of such dates.) According to the law, each head of a household was granted 2,500 hectares, or about 6,250 acres. The Ryan ranch covered 15,000 acres in all—12,500 belonging to Butch and Sundance, and 2,500 to Etta, the first woman in Argentina to be granted land under the act. This might have had something to do with the fact that Etta wore paired six-guns and was able to shoot bottles off fence posts while riding on horseback at full gallop.

In Cholila, the North Americans quickly earned the respect of the local people. They rode well, knew cattle, and Ryan and Mrs. Place spoke some Spanish. In the United States, Mr. Cea informed me, there is much controversy about Ryan. Some say he was a good man. Some say he was bad.

"When he came here," Mr. Cea said, "he was a good man."

More than ten years ago, I found myself driving through southern Argentina and stopped for a time in Río Gallegos, the last sizable outpost on the mainland before you reach the car ferry to Tierra del Fuego. It was a dreary day in late September, and the snow that lay around the small town plaza was covered with a wind-driven shroud of soot and dirt, all of it dissolving under gray, freezing rain.

My tourist map was full of interesting facts. Along this wave-battered coast of the southern Atlantic, penguins frolic on the rocks. And on February 16, 1905, the local bank was robbed by Butch Cassidy and the Sundance Kid.

A guy came from Utah to the end of the Earth to rob the bank, here? Not so very far from Antarctica? I had a hard time assimilating the idea of Wild West bank robbers in close proximity to penguins.

It took me more than a decade to get back to Argentina. I brought along a 1994 book titled *Digging Up Butch and Sundance,* by Anne Meadows. With her husband, Dan Buck, Meadows traveled to South America half a dozen times to research the life and times of Boots. "Our obsession has nearly bankrupted us," she wrote. The book is a fascinating labyrinth of conflicting stories that ends in a high mountain bowl in Bolivia where Sundance is almost certainly buried. Butch is probably there as well, but then again, there's a slight possibility that he survived and returned to the United States. The speculative historical record reads like a catalog of Elvis sightings.

By the time I turned off the paved highway and onto the gravel road to Cholila, thirty-five miles away, I was in the labyrinth myself. There were forests and rivers and lakes. The Andes looked a lot like the mountains outside my hometown in Montana, and I had a sudden apprehension of psychic danger. It was possible I too could become lost in a maze of stories; I could bankrupt myself searching for an unattainable veracity. Two days, I thought, no more—much in the way the future crack addict believes he will take a single hit on the pipe and quit.

"Ryan was born Robert Leroy Parker, in Beaver, Utah, on April 13, 1866," Mr. Cea continued. Despite my protests, he thought it was important that I revisit certain aspects of American history. The Civil War, he said, the war of brother against brother, had just ended. Some 816,000 men were dead, the most to die in any American war. In the West, banks and large cattle companies were buying up land from the widows of veterans. Justice was slow. Gangs of men, hardened fighters like Jesse James, robbed the hated banks and became folk heroes. All this, Mr. Cea said, happened in the first decade of Bob Parker's life, a time when the soul is formed. The boy saw family ranchers bilked of their land by banks, railroads, and multinational cattle companies. If Butch rustled cattle, in Mr. Cea's rendition of history, it was a form of social protest.

Butch—who worked for a time as a butcher, hence the nickname—became a ranch foreman, a natural leader who knew how to command tough men. He watched his employers, the cattle barons, stealing stock and land from poor ranchers, who had no recourse. He burned, in Mr. Cea's opinion, with a hatred of injustice, which he identified with the big and bullying corporate interests of the time.

The bad winter of 1888–1889 broke the system. Hundreds of thousands of cattle died on the range. Bosses abandoned the land and returned to their homes in Great Britain or the East. Unemployed cowboys roamed the lawless land. Butch continued robbing banks and railroads, and became famous. In 1899 he hooked up with the Sundance Kid.

Pursued by the Pinkerton Detective Agency—"actually the forerunner of your FBI," Mr. Cea said—the partners decided to flee to

South America. Modern technology, especially the telegraph, had effectively put them out of the train-robbing business.

"Why South America?" I asked.

"Europe was too socially stratified," Mr. Cea replied. "But many people in the American West knew of Patagonia." The Welsh, fleeing dead-end lives in the coal mines, had already settled in Chubut Province. Representatives of these Welsh immigrants recruited English-speaking colonists all across North America. Central Patagonia was attractive because the land looked a great deal like the American West. But there were few banks, the frontier was still open, and the cattle business was still a matter of family ranches. It was a place where a man could make an honest living raising beef.

We had been talking for an hour. Mrs. Cea came into the kitchen, passed through smiling pleasantly, and closed the door to the next room with a great deal of authority. Mr. Cea smiled after her.

The events that followed had a horrible irony, Mr. Cea continued. "When Ryan"—Butch—"arrived in Argentina, he intended to live peacefully, but instead became a catalyst for the social and political problems of the day in this country."

Behind the closed door to the living room, Mrs. Cea was rearranging furniture or perhaps using the floor as a trampoline. Raúl Cea began to speak more rapidly.

Ryan was granted land primarily because Argentina needed to develop the Cholila valley and frustrate Chilean claims on the land. After a plebiscite—"held on April 30, 1902," and presided over by Queen Victoria of England—the land was declared part of Argentina. Chileans, however, owned most of the property in the valley and apparently planned to pursue their claims by buying up all the ranches they could. The Argentine authorities gave the Ryan party homesteads—the one sizable chunk of land in the valley not yet under Chilean control—primarily because they weren't Chileans.

There are documents, Mr. Cea said, that proved they were good ranchers. As in the United States, a homesteader had to "prove up" the land, and officials were dispatched to monitor his progress.

"Remember this date," Mr. Cea said. "February fifteenth, 1905." On that day, an official named Lázaro Molinas visited Ryan's Cholila ranch under the provisions of the homestead law. He spoke with Ryan and the Places, and certified that they had nine hundred mother cows and fifty horses. Their books were in order. The report that Molinas filed, Mr. Cea said, could be found in the town records of Rawson, the provincial capital.

A Chilean-backed company called Cocham offered to buy the ranch from Ryan, but he refused. According to Mr. Cea, Chilean agents framed Ryan for the Río Gallegos robbery. "Recall the document of Señor Molinas," Mr. Cea said.

Mrs. Cea marched through the kitchen, slamming both doors.

"We should leave now," Eduardo said.

"Yes, of course," I said, making no effort to move.

Mr. Cea began speaking much faster. "Molinas talked with Ryan on February fifteenth, 1905. The bank was robbed the very next day. It is over a thousand kilometers from Cholila. Who can ride a horse one thousand kilometers in less than twenty-four hours? It is not possible!"

Sometime later, he said, a picture of Butch, Sundance, and Etta appeared on the front page of a Buenos Aires newspaper. They were identified as the persons responsible for the Río Gallegos robbery. The picture, Mr. Cea believes, was planted by Chileans. When Ryan saw the paper, he sold out to Cocham and required that they pay him in Chile. "He left on the ninth of May, 1905."

"So Butch and Sundance couldn't have killed Llwyd Ap Iwan in 1909!" I cried, as Eduardo pulled on my arm.

"No, Argentine police identified the assailants as two other North Americans, Robert Evans and William Wilson. And they were hunted down and killed near the border of Chile after the murder."

"Do you think Butch and Sundance died in Bolivia?" I asked.

"Good-bye, adios," Mrs. Cea said, as Eduardo dragged me out the door.

"I don't know," Mr. Cea said.

"Thank you for your visit," Mrs. Cea said. She was quite gracious, considering.

"Santiago Ryan," Mr. Cea said as he followed us outside, "is not a man for North America or for Argentina. He is a man for the world. He is a social enigma, a mystery of a soul haunted by injustice."

"And I saw his house."

"Oh, no," Mr. Cea said. "That was the house of Enrique and Etta. Ryan's house was in front of that. It was torn down in 1943. The logs were used for another building."

"Which one?" I asked, in the manner of the seriously obsessed.

"Good-bye, now," Mrs. Cea said, a little less graciously, and at that point we really did have to go.

This Teeming Ark

It was like trying to drink a beer on the subway at rush hour. Jostled from all sides, I stood hard against the flimsy railing of a makeshift stall trying to hold my place against various swirling currents of humanity.

Several of the drunks I'd been cultivating peeled out of the crowd to greet me.

"You are my friend," said Maurice, who, at 9 A.M., was already in the condition I aspired to achieve. "Buy me a beer."

It was his ritual greeting.

"No way in hell," I said, which was my ritual reply.

It was my tenth excruciating day aboard the *Fleuve Congo,* a conglomeration of eight mostly flatbed barges cabled to a great throbbing riverboat motoring down the Congo River. During my time on deck, I had discovered that only drunkards were intelligent enough to fully comprehend my one-hundred-word French vocabulary.

Maurice, a Congolese Bantu, like most of the other passengers, was a thin, gangly man with a goofy smile. He didn't really want a beer. He drank palm wine, which he carried with him in a greasy yellow jug that looked like it had once contained motor oil.

The temperature was rising rapidly, the beer was warm, and I was wearing shorts. My skin was a sickly pale white. I felt like a couple of dozen gallons of raw milk. Maurice pointed out all the slowly healing insect bites, the welts, the scabs on my legs.

He wanted to know what had happened to me, and I told him, for the fourth or fifth time, that I had just completed a long walk through a forest that was uninhabited.

"What were the people like?" Maurice asked.

"There weren't any people. It was uninhabited."

It was like Eden, this forest in the north of the Republic of the Congo, the former French Congo. The animals there hadn't been hunted, and they approached our party boldly: elephants and chimps and gorillas and antelope. I had been happy there. But here? On the barge? I was not happy.

"I don't like crowds, Maurice."

I told him that my entire life to date had been an exercise in avoiding crowds. I didn't know how many more days I could bear aboard this Congo River barge, along with three thousand other human beings, all of us compressed into a space about the size of a football field. For me the barge was . . . it was . . . what was the word I was looking for?

"Buy me a beer," said Maurice.

"No way in . . ." *L'enfer!* That was the word. This was my own personal hell.

I drained the beer and gave the bottle back to the man who'd sold it to me.

"Maurice," I said, "do you know God?"

"Yes."

"Have you seen him this morning?"

"No."

"Damn." I really needed to talk to God.

I was traveling with Michael Fay, a wildlife biologist, and Cynthia Moses, a filmmaker. The walk through Eden was Michael's project. His job was to inventory the flora and fauna of the forest and report back to the Congolese government with a recommendation about whether the area should be preserved as a national forest. (He thought it should.)

Cynthia documented the walk on video, and my job was to write about it. We had traveled with several Bantus and about a dozen pygmies, but it had been simple enough for me to drop back or plunge ahead of the line of march. Alone, in the forest, it was possible to imagine that I was the only human being who had ever set foot on that precise square yard of soil. Often, as I stood in such a spot, chimps gathered in the trees above, howling and screaming. They approached way too closely—well, within rifle range—because they felt it necessary to throw feces and to piss on my head, all of which suggested they regarded me as just another primate, and nothing very special, to boot. I was really quite content, alone on the forest floor and moving through the yellow, dung-studded rain.

We had stumbled out of the forest and made our way to Imfondo, on the Oubangi River, where several thousand people stood in an open courtyard while lightning ripped the sky apart and rain fell in sheets. Suddenly the rain stopped and the temperature soared. Hours passed. One elderly woman fainted in the heat. Then another fell. The paved courtyard concentrated the heat.

Michael, Cynthia, and I were the only whites, and we moved in line with the Congolese: with Habib from the Ivory Coast, with Alphonse from Gabon, with riverboat con artists and naive villagers boarding the barge for the first time. The bottleneck was the single soldier who checked everyone's papers. He wore a camouflage uniform, a brown beret, and carried an automatic pistol in a white plastic holster. His name, stitched in red on his left breast, seemed faintly mocking: "Thermometer."

A great wash of humanity carried us onto the corrugated-metal deck of the barge, and eventually, motors thrumming, we moved majestically out into the current and began floating down the Oubangi, toward the Congo and our destination, Brazzaville.

Cynthia, Michael, and I stood at the very back of the very last barge, watching Imfondo recede into the distance. On the bank to my left, there was a small village and a woman ran down the dirt path to the river, screaming at us all. She was in her late teens, I'd guess, a tall, angular young woman who flapped her arms like the blue herons that rose occasionally from the banks. Her cries couldn't be heard above the thrum and beat of our engines.

"Missed the boat," I said to Michael.

The woman dropped to her knees, turned her face to the sky,

and howled soundlessly. She beat her palms on the rain-sodden red earth, raising splashes of mud that stained her orange dress.

"Seems disappointed," Michael observed.

Cynthia thought we were like all men: cynical in the face of strong emotion. She felt sorry for the young woman.

We humped our gear through the crowds, looking for the first-class cabin we'd booked. The heart of the barge was the great river-boat called the *Fleuve Congo*. It consisted of an enormous engine room, containing two 850-horsepower engines, and a three-story wheelhouse that loomed above the eight individual barges cabled to it on the sides, on the front, on the back. Our cabin was located directly behind the engine room, in a two-story edifice that had once been a riverboat itself. The cabin was an olive-drab metal cubicle that contained a few monastic bunks along with a toilet, a sink, and an air conditioner, all of which functioned on various occasions. It felt, distressingly, like a jail cell, and the three of us escaped onto the teeming decks.

Just outside the cabin, there was a railing that gave over to the river. People dropped a bucket on a rope into the water and washed their clothes, their children, themselves. A harried mother asked me to watch one child while she bathed another. Juliet was four, and she held my index finger in her small hand while her mother washed an infant.

As I was standing there, watching Juliet, a man in clean khakis and a bushman's hat came by with a young chimpanzee that was clinging to him as if he were its mother. The chimp had a rope around its waist and the man put it on the deck. It scampered about on its feet and hands, ooffing and woofing. Juliet's mother swept her up in a single motion. People scattered in all directions. Chimps are strong and they can bite.

Cynthia, who had worked on a film about Jane Goodall and knew something about chimps, knelt in front of the animal. She held out her left palm and touched it with the bunched fingers of her right hand. A grooming gesture. The chimp took her left hand for a moment, then turned its back to her. She parted the hairs on the back of its head, grooming it, and the chimp seemed content.

The man who held the rope was named Sarafin. He was a

Congo River businessperson and had bought the orphaned chimp in a village upriver for about eight dollars. He thought he could sell it to the zoo in Brazzaville.

Michael Fay told Sarafin that, in the Republic of the Congo, any traffic in primates was forbidden. Since Michael himself consulted with the government on poaching issues, he could safely assure Sarafin that he'd be arrested at the zoo. The thing to do, he said, was to take the chimp to the primate orphanage in Brazzaville, where it would be rehabilitated, taught to hunt and forage, and eventually released into the forest.

Later, in the cabin, we talked about the encounter. Michael said he wasn't entirely sure that Sarafin would have been arrested at the zoo, though it was certainly possible. He thought the chimp and gorilla orphanage was a feel-good solution, and what was important was to stop any kind of commerce in wildlife. Sarafin was a bright young guy who had had no intention of breaking the law. He'd help pass the word.

Cynthia felt sorry for the poor chimp.

I identified with it.

There are almost no roads in the northern Congo, and people travel by river. But the *Fleuve Congo* wasn't truly about transportation. It was about commerce. Even at the smallest villages, the captain brought the engines to an idle, and people paddled out to the barges in small canoes called pirogues. They came to sell smoked fish, or oranges, or live dwarf crocodiles with their snouts wired shut, or chickens or goats. There was no refrigeration on the barges, and food was kept alive until dinner.

Sometimes, one of the flat-topped barges was uncabled at a village, and another two or three would be added. Shopkeepers, who maintained covered stalls on the various barges, sold batteries, lamps, soap, salt, shampoo, T-shirts, shorts, hard candy, and music cassettes. Bargaining was a high-volume affair. Folks shouted at one another in the way I might address someone who'd just shot my dog.

Over the space of a week, I came to see that this was the accepted manner of bargaining, and that people enjoyed it. There was always a smile hidden somewhere very close behind the seeming abuse.

Occasionally, we stopped at the larger villages, and hundreds of us—thousands—poured off the gangplanks and invaded the village, most everyone making for the forest. There were only three public toilets aboard the *Fleuve Congo*. And as folks did what they had to do, still more people from the now soiled village poured aboard the *Fleuve Congo*.

Eventually, the Oubangi emptied into the Congo proper, and in the town of Mossaka, we became deck passengers. A local politician had booked our cabin weeks before. Cynthia was concerned about the film she'd shot over the course of six hard weeks, and the captain, a fine man named Eugene Mongoli, allowed us to pile our gear in the wheelhouse.

In the early afternoon sun, the metal decks of the barges, where we lived, were hot enough to fry an egg. People sat on boards or bricks or rolls of foam padding. Sheets rigged on sticks provided some protection from the sun. At each stop, another 780,000 people boarded the barge. There was now so much sheer humanity aboard the *Fleuve Congo* that no one could take a single step without bumping into someone else.

The words most heard were "sorry," "pardon me," "excuse me." It was a world of constant apology, and my choice, as I saw it, was passive acceptance or madness: this perception despite the fact that everyone else seemed to be having a swell adventure. Cynthia obtained the captain's permission to stand on top of the wheelhouse and shoot crowd scenes along with sunrises and sunsets. Michael, already fluent in French, worked on his Lingala vocabulary, which was the local dialect. He underlined useful words in a dictionary—starting with *a*—then strolled about looking for opportunities to work "abstinence" (*ekila*) or "absurd" (*esongo na elonga*) into a conversation.

I, on the other hand, could not work. The essay that proposed itself was about heaven and hell, about the Edenic forest and the sweltering barge. Exquisitely uncomfortable and unable to write a sentence, I spent many moping hours on one of the flat-topped barges devoted to livestock: goats and pigs and chickens and me all bunched together under a tarp that provided a little bit of shade. One of the goats fell in love with a pig, to the porker's great annoyance. It was entirely *esongo na elonga*: a lesson, I thought, about all of us swirling down the drain of the behavioral sink. I was suffering a profound variety of culture shock and longed to be back in the forest, in the monkey-shit rain.

After two days on deck, I became entirely disconsolate and sought the company of drunkards. One beer, maybe two, then back to the goats: back through the general hubbub of too much humanity apologizing to itself. Excuse me, pardon me. It's too much, I thought, it's serious. *C'est trop. C'est grave.* I imagined the future of the human race as an endless ride on the Congo barge, and shuddered in the heat.

Cynthia found me hunched up and brooding among the animals. "Can I do something for you?" she asked.

"Yes," I said, "go away."

I met folks named George and Slava and Josephine and Enrique. Many of them were extremely attractive. Movie-star quality, we'd say in the United States. God, however, was easily the most handsome man I'd ever met. He stood a couple of inches over six feet: a lean, well-muscled man of about twenty-five who seemed vastly amused with life in general.

God had just graduated from college and was going to Brazzaville, where he had secured a job teaching school. Cynthia met him early on, and right away he apologized about the name. He'd grown up in a remote village where his father heard educated people talking with great respect about this person called God. It seemed a good name for a son, and young God lived half a dozen years before he realized people other than his father found the name either offensive or amusing. "But," he told Cynthia, "I'm stuck with it."

God had traveled a lot on *Fleuve Congo* and was our single best source of information. There was, for instance, no set schedule. Some nights we'd anchor in the middle of the river, some we'd run all night long. It depended a lot on Captain Mongoli's mood, and the heat of commerce conducted at various villages. God had a kind of sixth sense for the captain's humor. He'd predicted our arrival at the confluence of the Oubangi and the Congo to the hour.

Now I wanted to find out when we'd arrive in Brazzaville. My drinking buddies had varying opinions: some thought two more days, some three.

"Who knows?" Maurice asked.

God only knows, I thought, and set off to find him.

I bumped into Cynthia on the way and together we sought him out on all levels of the *Fleuve Congo* universe. He was, in fact, waiting in a long line for what was now the only functioning public toilet on the barge.

We stood with God, inching our way toward the toilet.

"Tim," Cynthia told him, "is going insane."

"How much longer?" I asked.

"Twenty-four hours," God said. "We should be in Brazzaville tomorrow morning at this time."

That, I thought, was acceptable. I could certainly bear it for one more day.

But now Cynthia had a problem. She wanted to get off the barge very quickly so she could film the disembarkation, which would be a madhouse. Everyone with something to sell, we knew, would want to get off quickly in order to get the best prices, or find the best corner to set up a makeshift stall.

"Tim and Michael can carry the gear," Cynthia said, "but could you help me get off and find a high spot to stand?"

The man said it would be no problem. Cynthia was happy: she'd get her shot, with the help of God.

I spent the remainder of the last full day drinking beer with Maurice and maundering on, mostly in English, about the difference between Eden and the end of the world as we know it. There was a reason, I informed the drunks grandly, to protect wilderness areas and it had to do with our collective future and the cost of constant apology. Maurice agreed with everything I had to say and I finally bought him the beer he didn't really want.

We pulled into the port of Brazzaville at ten the next morning, just as God had foreseen. People began pouring off the barge, but God never showed and I wasn't going to sit around waiting for him.

"Absenteeism," said Michael, trying to recall the word in Lingala.

Cynthia, who had put her faith in God, was bitterly disappointed.

"He helps those who help themselves," I muttered softly, and then grabbed my share of the gear and—apologizing all the way—got the hell off that God-forsaken barge.

Near Massacre Ranch

I was driving north, out of the flat and featureless sands of the Black Rock Desert, bouncing over a jolting gravel road that rose up into the Black Rock Mountains, a set of volcanic outcroppings with all the charm and color of a rusted anvil. Outside the air-conditioned comfort of my truck, northwest Nevada occupied itself in belching fits of ongoing and unforgiving geology. Exactly thirty-two miles out of Gerlach ("where the pavement ends and the West begins"), I acquired the second flat tire of the trip. Also my map blew away, and I made an imprudent decision that put me square in the middle of the Massacre Ranch, where, God help me, I encountered the Naked Cowboy. All that came later.

For the nonce, it was midafternoon, in late August, exactly 98 degrees in the shade—I hung a thermometer while I worked on the tire—and a blistering wind out of the north whipped itself into a series of imbecilic, whirling sand-colored funnels.

In Black Rock country, there are few road signs pointing the way (I counted four in seven days) and many, many gravel roads running in every which direction. Some of these roads are simply a pair of ruts running through the sage, and you think, "This is a cruel joke and certainly not the road indicated on the map." But it is.

A traveler in the Black Rock needs a compass and a good map from the Bureau of Land Management. Maps of Nevada, purchased in gas stations, are useless, and only include roads that skirt the desert. There are other maps, topo maps, that one might use, but the road signs have been erected by the BLM, and what the BLM calls Steven's Camp might be labeled Grassy Knob on some other map. What one map calls Table Mesa, another might call Rocky Butte. On those startling occasions when one sights a sign, it will have been erected by the BLM, which does not care what anyone else calls a certain rocky butte. To them, it's Table Mountain.

You travel into this spare, barely inhabited expanse of sage, sand flats, and bare, volcanic hills with food for two weeks, with water— fourteen gallons in my case—with extra gas, and a plethora of spare tires.

I lacked only the rubber plethora, so that when my right rear tire began to sound like a helicopter landing in the distance, I thought: Well, goodness, won't this be a jolly adventure.

Actually, I thought nothing of the sort. I thought: "I am going to find a man named B. F. Goodrich and beat him to death with a tire iron."

An adventure is never an adventure when it's happening. Challenging experiences need time to ferment, and an adventure is simply physical and emotional discomfort recollected in tranquillity. This is the definition I'd recently spouted to several hundred people who'd actually paid to hear me speak. I had attributed the basic underlying quote to Ralph Waldo Emerson. Someone pointed out that, in fact, it was the gushy Romantic poet William Wordsworth who said, "Poetry is the spontaneous overflow of powerful feelings: it takes its origin from emotion recollected in tranquillity."

So I was wrong. So what? Does that make it any less true? Adventure and poetry share a certain process.

I mean, William Wordsworth takes a walk and sees a bunch of flowers, okay? The poem doesn't spring to mind spontaneously. He goes home and thinks about it. In the fullness of time and during the doldrums of tranquillity, this little ramble in the Lake Country becomes a poem.

What was it that happened back there the other day? William Wordsworth thinks. Well, I took a walk. No, actually I wandered. I was wandering. Why? Well, because I felt quite alone in the world. Just so. I was lonely. I wandered lonely . . . as . . . as what? As a rock? Oh, heavens no. Rocks are lonely enough, one imagines, but they don't wander. So, once again: I wandered lonely as a . . . a bug. A bug? Unfortunate thought, that. Perhaps the wind? Very nearly there, but a bit too fast, actually. How about a cloud? Why, yes, a cloud. Clouds generally move quite slowly, and they do so in a properly ethereal fashion. I wandered lonely as a cloud. Jolly good!

Wordsworth went home and flopped down on the sofa with a six-pack and bag of chips. He lay there for about a week (*For oft when on my couch I lie / in vacant or in pensive mood*), and thought about how some lakeside flowers lifted his spirits one forlorn and dreary day (*They flash upon that inward eye / Which is the bliss of solitude: / And then my heart with pleasure fills, / And dances with the daffodils*).

My own peculiar situation had not yet begun to ferment into anything resembling poetry. At this point, a mere thirty-two miles from the nearest town, I lacked the necessary tranquillity and was experiencing only emotional discomfort.

There was no one on the road, and no one likely to be coming along anytime soon, which is why one needs food and water for two weeks in Black Rock country. I maneuvered the truck about in such a way that the tire in question was positioned in the late afternoon shade, then opened both of the doors to the wind in order to keep the cab cool. It worked. When the tire had been successfully changed, it wasn't much more than 110 degrees inside, quite pleasant, really, and, as I sat there sweating, it occurred to me that something was dreadfully, terribly wrong. The big BLM map, which had been spread out on the passenger's seat, was gone. Blown away. Probably wafting on the wind, winging its merry way to Reno, more than a hundred miles to the southwest. I was, at that point, experiencing a deepening and as yet unfermented adventure.

Presently, I found myself out in the sage-littered hills running around in a poetically futile series of unavailing and ever-widening circles. But, of course, the map was gone, and I was intensely annoyed, and not very tranquil, and wished that there was someone with me who might be blamed for what had happened.

"You left the doors open and the map out? In this wind? You nincompoop! We could die out here without a map."

When there is no one to blame but yourself, solitude is not bliss.

.   .   .

In the words of the immortal Steppenwolf song, I was out looking for adventure in whatever came my way. I had started the search in the Black Rock Desert proper, called the playa. It is the bed of the ancient Lake Lahontan, flat as a billiard table, seventy miles long and up to twenty miles wide. The playa occupies over one thousand square miles and is sometimes called the flattest place on earth. In 1848, emigrants on their way to the California gold-fields made camp near Double Hot Springs, at the far eastern edge of the playa, a major stop on what is called the Applegate-Lassen Trail.

A wide track enters the sand near the town of Gerlach and runs north and east, toward the black rock that gives the desert its name. In the winter, an inch of water sometimes covers the playa, and people trying to drive the desert have buried their vehicles to the axles in greasy silt then died of exposure, frozen to death out in the middle of the flattest place on earth.

In 1997, a British racing team, driving a car powered by a pair of jets, broke both the sound barrier and the world land-speed record—763.053 miles per hour—on the playa. My own drive across the sands was just a bit slower, and I dutifully kept to the established track, as per the usual BLM instructions. Dust devils danced in the distance, sometimes tracking miles across the plain to rock my half-ton truck with an audible thump, like a wrecking ball in a velvet glove. In those instances, sandstorms obscured the view briefly, then opened up to cloudless skies and terrifying monotony. Heat rose up off the scorched sand so that the flat and featureless plain ahead shimmered in rising waves, like an animated fun-house mirror.

Mirages glittered to the north. They covered the inane vacuity of the playa with mirrorlike blue waters, cool and calm as a child's dream, and they retreated before my advance, moving ever into the distance, like the rainbow's end. There were a half dozen of these lakes and they swam in the field of my parched and cracked-lipped vision like a series of especially vivid hallucinations. But mirages are not hallucinations; everyone sees them, and they are only a trick of refractive light. Emigrants, moving across the desert to the

California goldfields, wrote in their diaries that their oxen, dying of thirst, were "driven mad" by these deceptions of luminosity.

The black rock itself sits at the southern foot of the Black Rock mountain range. It is a limestone formation, several hundred feet high at a guess and much darker than the brownish-orange mountains rising above it. From the playa, the rock looks like a burned and fallen cake set on a rusted iron woodstove. Above the rock, and to the north, the entire range is ridged with terraces formed by the receding banks of the late Lake Lanhontan as it slowly sank away into sand over a period of fourteen thousand years or so.

The Double Hot Springs is set just above the sand, in a field of salt grass and sage. I camped there for three days in a solitude that was a little like bliss, only hotter. The springs are set in oblong bowls perhaps twenty feet long, ten feet wide, and about ten feet apart. The one to the east is larger, deeper, and small bubbles rise out of its emerald-black depths. Dragonflies cruise the slowly simmering pool. The one to the west is clear and cornflower blue because the underlying rocks are light in color. They form a sloping funnel that dives under an overhanging ledge and appears to plunge deep into the earth. It looked precisely like the kind of sump I had often seen while exploring caves, and every time I looked at it I had the disturbing sense of the earth turned inside out. It was always a slight embarrassment, as if I had walked in on someone naked doing something I didn't want to know about.

Ralph Waldo Emerson met William Wordsworth on a trip to England in the early 1830s. It is my entirely unfounded contention that Emerson talked about emotion recollected in tranquillity with Wordsworth, who blithely snitched the line. The proposition is self-evident. Proof is not at issue here, only exoneration.

Ralph Waldo, I also found in my research, wrote an essay containing the dictum that "Nature punishes any neglect of prudence." After changing the tire outside Gerlach, it occurred to me that if I wanted to experience a lot more adventure, or even write a poem, it would be wise, if not actually necessary, to neglect prudence. That would lead to discomfort and strong emotion, to be examined in tranquillity, provided I survived the experience.

And so, my decision made, I drove off into the desert, with no spare tire and only a schematic map—"not drawn to scale"—in an old BLM brochure I had found in the Gerlach gas station the last time I had my tire fixed there, which was yesterday. Yes, sir, I would just drive out into the desert, with no spare tire, and no map, looking for Waldo. Actually, I was looking for the emigrant trail through High Rock Canyon, driving a route I dimly recalled from the long-gone BLM map.

Every hour or so, I got out of the truck and examined my tires. The gravel road was strewn with obsidian chips, sharp as scalpels. You could perform heart surgery with some of the stones on the road to High Rock Canyon. Happily, the various tracks I chose did not go anywhere near the canyon, but dumped me out in Cedarville, California, at the far-northwest corner of Black Rock country. It was a Saturday, and the BLM office there was closed. I drove another twenty-five miles to Alturas, to buy a new tire and a topo map at the sporting goods store.

The topo included sites I didn't recall from the BLM map, including the ominous-sounding Massacre Ranch, which is on Massacre Creek, near Massacre Lake. My BLM brochure stated that local ranchers are not in the business of providing food, water, or gasoline to stranded travelers. Still, the ranch covered a lot of territory, and I tried to imagine what a Massacre Ranch buckaroo might look like while I drove over a road layered with surgical instruments. He would be a lean man, on horseback, wearing a black hat and a white hockey mask. Instead of a rifle, he would be carrying a chainsaw in his scabbard.

Not far from the Massacre Ranch, there is a place called Hanging Rock Canyon. Several families were camped nearby. I said hello and I wandered up into the mouth of the narrow canyon. The rock wall towered eighty feet overhead but looked strangely hollowed, like a domed cave room, and once again I had a sense of the earth turned inside out and naked.

In contrast, a small river ran through the valley floor, and in the well-watered shade, there were dozens of giant aspen trees growing among wild roses and waist-high stands of silver sage. The water in the stream was clear and cool and six inches deep. It was running slowly and sounded like a fountain in a backyard birdbath. A freshening breeze murmured through the trees and the sounds were like a symphony of life after the silence of the playa. It was a place I could think about, lying on the couch. Maybe write a poem.

When I got back to my truck, several people were gathered about, staring at it.

"Did you know your right rear tire is flat?" one of the men asked.

He advised me to go back to Alturas, past the Massacre Ranch, to get another tire. "I was out here last year and my car wouldn't start," he said. "We waited six days before someone came along."

"Look," I said, "I had a flat yesterday, one the day before, and now one today. What are the odds that I'll get another one?"

"One hundred percent," the fellow said.

But I went off in search of High Rock Canyon anyway, neglecting prudence once again, and driving on progressively smaller tracks through the sage for several hours. At one point, I topped a fairly steep ridge and was almost startled to see another vehicle, a battered old pickup, coming my way. In these situations, the uphill vehicle has the right of way, and I pulled off the road into the sage. The truck had Nevada plates and was pulling a horse trailer. The driver was wearing a white cowboy hat of the type called a silver belly. The name sprang to mind because the cowboy was not wearing a shirt. This was more than just a little strange. I have lived in the mountain West for over twenty years and have never seen a cowboy take off his shirt except to wash. They don't even roll up their sleeves.

As the truck passed, I could, from my position, look directly down into the cab. The driver wasn't wearing any pants either. He glanced over at me, touched a forefinger to the brim of his hat, and smiled briefly, as if to say, "Howdy, pilgrim." He did not seem to be at all disturbed by the encounter and drove off into the distance at about 10 miles an hour. Was this the stuff of poetry? Frankly, it was not something I wanted to lie on the couch and contemplate. (*And then my heart with wonder quakèd / Because the guy was bareass naked.*)

The image of the Naked Cowboy pulling a horse trailer over the naked earth troubled my mind as the sun began bleeding to death in the west. There was a lake below, shining silver in the dying light. I thought it was Summit Lake, at the head of High Rock Canyon. Unfortunately, it was not to my south, as it should have been. I turned on my dome light and studied the map. The only place where I could be looking north at a lake was two miles from the Massacre Ranch. It was, of course, Massacre Lake. Coyotes yipped and howled very near to the truck, and I spent a sleepless night camped in the cab, listening to the gentle sigh of the breeze and wondering whether it was the air escaping from my tires.

When the sun rose, I drove north and west, toward home and out of Black Rock country. I hadn't yet had the tranquillity to decide whether the experience had been a poem or an adventure. In any case, some lines from Emerson echoed in my mind:

> *Good bye, proud world! I 'm going home;*
> *Thou art not my friend, and I'm not thine.*

Or maybe that was Wordsworth.

Fubsy Hors D'oeuvres

*(with a nod to Jorge Luis Borges,
and my father, R. J. Cahill)*

In terms of bellicose behavior, the fauna of the Valdes Peninsula on the southeast coast of Argentina pretty much take the natural-history cake. Situated a little less than halfway between Buenos Aires and Cape Horn, the peninsula looks like an enormous hatchet thrust out into the Atlantic Ocean. Filmed scenes of the carnage at a place called Punta Norte, on the north end of the peninsula, live in the minds of millions of people, though the actual geography, I suspect, is a bit vague.

Here is one of those scenes: A baby sea lion is trundling along the brown pebbly beach, something of Charlie Chaplin in its endearing, awkward manner. In the surf, several large black dorsal fins, some of them six feet high, saw back and forth through the waves. Bring up the "uh-oh" music.

Close in on the baby sea lion, all bright-eyed innocence and bewilderment. It is what biologists call "fubsy." The theory has it that we, as humans, are hardwired to protect our progeny, and as a result we are also instinctively protective of creatures that possess attributes common to human infants. Clumsy animals, preferably chubby ones with large eyes, big heads, and short limbs, are said to be fubsy. This baby sea lion is so excessively fubsy that we are convinced it cannot long survive.

And so it is. On a crashing, discordant note, an immense black-and-white killer whale, an orca, makes a run for the shore, powering through the surf and skidding right up onto the sloping beach.

It's a big male weighing perhaps five tons, and it snaps up the baby sea lion like a canapé, shaking it about this way and that because orcas just hate it when their hors d'oeuvres fight back. The triumphant killer then slides back down the slope of the beach in a series of side-to-side lurches.

Several years ago, the wildlife filmmaker Paul Atkins spent six weeks at Punta Norte, shooting for the BBC series *The Trials of Life* (*with David Attenborough*). Working with the camera half in and half out of the water, he filmed the orca attacks—the killer whales charging and the sea lions fleeing. Equally compelling was his footage of the mating behavior of both elephant seals and southern sea lions, which is often brutal and bloody.

This was just one hour-long segment of *The Trials of Life*, an elegant and thoughtful twelve-part series. Sometime after the series aired, video rights were sold to Time-Life in the United States, and that company flogged a home video set in a commercial on late-night television, using the most violent clips from the series. The commercial postulated a natural world consisting entirely of fang and claw and running blood. *Hey, folks*, it seemed to shout, *how'd ya like to see animals you never even knew existed fight to the death before your very eyes?* The announcer's tag line was "Why do you think they call 'em *animals?*"

The commercial generated more than $100 million in sales, an astounding figure. Talk-show pundits took serious issue with the noisome nature of the commercial, and the BBC regretted letting go of the series for what is reported to have been a paltry sum; meanwhile, millions of people watched a thoughtful David Attenborough presentation, apparently not at all disappointed that it wasn't, in fact, some kind of natural-history snuff film.

Never mind. I was going to Punta Norte solely for the solace of violence. A project I'd recently submitted had just been seriously shredded and left bleeding on the beach.

A few miles beyond Puerto Pirámide, on the very handle of the Valdés hatchet, the pavement ended, and I drove my rental car slowly past a series of signs the Argentine government had erected to alert drivers that the gravel roads ahead were, in fact, malignant death traps. Slow down, the signs said. Don't pass. Respect the speed limit, watch out for animals crossing, slow down when approaching other vehicles, slow down altogether, señor, for the love of God and all his saints, we implore you, the dead implore you from their graves . . .

Another sign, somewhat off the subject, advised *"amigo turista"* that the entire peninsula was a reserve for the flora and fauna of the area. There was no camping, no hunting, no trekking, no rock collecting, and, along many stretches of road, no stopping to get out of the car. Period.

The land itself was littered with sagelike plants and spare grasses. To some eyes, this treeless interior plain might seem flat and featureless, though it rose and fell in a series of gentle undulations, like great sighs.

I saw a gray fox moving through the grasses and low, thorny bushes; it paused and stood like a dog on point, staring at a covey of crested tinamous, a bird I would call a partridge. In the distance, vultures drifted on thermals above what I imagined to be my recently eviscerated project. A lesser rhea, South America's version of the ostrich, trotted along ahead of me at about 15 miles an hour. Guanacos, genus *Lama,* were present in abundance. They were completely wild, and their heavy-lidded and extravagantly lashed eyes gave them an air of voluptuous indolence. Dust devils spinning over the land kicked up hundred-foot-high funnels of sandy brown soil, which approached one another and then retreated, as pretty as do-si-do.

The land did not fall off to the sea, but rose almost imperceptibly, like the lip on a dinner plate. Clay gave way to sand, and sea grasses rose all about in greenish-brown clumps. I was now moving north along the Atlantic coast, at the head of the Valdes hatchet, and decided to pull off at an empty but apparently legal parking lot.

A short path ended at a cliff face perhaps seven hundred feet high. The headlands, which rose to more than one thousand feet in some places, were ridged with the mark of retreating seas. They extended twenty miles in either direction, curving about in preposterous, looping arcs that formed windswept coves and bays.

I found a spot out of the wind, ate lunch, drank some wine for my health, and contemplated my career. It was as if the project manager had said something like "Look, Tim, this Mona Lisa thing is pretty good as far as it goes, but what's with the smile? Hell, don't get us wrong, we like enigmatic as much as the next guy, but couldn't you dial it up or down a little? Make it just a little more accessible?"

My choices were surrender or defeat. I resolved to consider the matter a little later, in the presence of inspirational bellicosity, and settled back to read a bit. Jorge Luis Borges's *The Book of Imaginary Beings* seemed appropriate: an Argentine author dealing with strange and often violent creatures born in the minds of the strangest and most violent of all animals. Somewhere just past page eighty-two (a description of the eastern dragon), I felt myself drifting off into a hazy, somnolent reminiscence.

I was, I imagine, six years old, a fubsy little guy, and my father, who was a font of zoological misinformation, had just informed me that frogs were birds, as in the terrifyingly unforgettable poem, *What a funny little bird the frog are / him ain't got no tail hardly / and when him jump / him bump his little tail / which him ain't got no hardly.*

My father also said that in certain isolated lakes set dreaming in remote Wisconsin forests, there lived a rare fish, called the goofang, that swam backward in order to keep water out of its eyes. And the gillygaloo, a bird that nested on steep slopes and laid its eggs square so they wouldn't roll down the hill.

Many of the creatures in my father's whimsical menagerie, I now realized, derived from the legends of Paul Bunyan. With the exception of the frog poem, which presented itself unbidden for my contemplation about once every two weeks, I hadn't thought about the illusory creatures that inhabited the Wisconsin of Remembrance in some time.

The Borges book brought it all back. One of the great authors of the twentieth century, Borges stumbled onto mystical Wisconsin fauna about the same time my dad was telling me about the goofang. In 1955, Borges was made director of the Argentine National Library, where he discovered "a kind of lazy pleasure in useless and out of the way erudition." *The Book of Imaginary Beings*, then, was an effort to harvest the literature of the world for "strange creatures conceived through time and space by the human imagination." Described within, one finds banshees, fairies, dragons, gnomes, elves, golems, garudas, doppelgängers, sirens, manticores, minotaurs, and nagas. More to the point, under the heading "Fauna of the United States," I found listings for the gillygaloo and the goofang.

It was, however, the entry titled "Fauna of Mirrors" that lodged itself like a burr in my imagination, where it took up permanent residence somewhere near the dreaded frog poem. In the legendary times of the Yellow Emperor, so the people of southern China say, the world of mirrors and the world of men were not separated, as they are now. "They were, besides," Borges wrote, "quite different; neither beings nor colors nor shapes were the same. Both kingdoms lived in harmony; you could come and go through mirrors." One night the mirror people invaded the earth, and there was bloody warfare, yet the "magic arts of the Yellow Emperor prevailed." The invaders were imprisoned in their mirrors and "forced to repeat, as though in a dream, all the actions of men." Spells, however, erode with the passage of time, and soon enough, the story goes, the shapes in the mirror will begin to stir. "Little by little they will differ from us," Borges wrote, "little by little they will not imitate us. They will break through the barrier of glass and metal and this time will not be defeated."

As if it wasn't hard enough to look in the mirror.

During the second apocalyptic attack, the warriors behind the glass, so it's said, will be joined by "the creatures of the water." Which, I suppose, would include sea lions, elephant seals, and orcas. Plenty of these were waiting for me thirty miles ahead, at Punta Norte. I expected it to be a sanguinary experience.

There were elephant seal calves at Punta Norte when I visited, but no adults were in evidence. The season of mating and giving birth (September) had long since passed, and adult males and females were out feeding, diving to depths of four thousand feet while the recently weaned calves basked on the beach, looking, really, like so many blubbery slugs. Very occasionally one of the weanlings moved a dozen feet or so, hunching up and down, in the manner of a caterpillar. I am pleased to report that the precise scientific term used to describe this process is "galumphing."

During the mating season, fifteen-foot-long males, weighing in excess of four tons, hold a section of beach against all comers, fighting savagely to control a harem of females. Altercations between males begin with a galumphing together, followed by a face-to-face staring contest. And these are seriously goofy faces: a male elephant seal is possessed of an inflatable proboscis that looks a bit like an upraised elephant's trunk. The combatants stand high on the tips of their front flippers, backs arched, and tower seven feet into the troubled gray sky. The animals collide, belly to belly, like sumo wrestlers, all the while butting heads like bar fighters. The butts become bites to the throat. Mouths agape, both heads rise and fall swiftly, like axes tearing into flesh. There is much blood, and it is usually all over in less than a minute, the loser galumphing away in adipose ignominy.

On this bright summer day in January, however, the southern sea lions were the show. The males are much heavier in the head and upper torso than their northern cousins and range in color from a golden brown to a deep, almost iridescent black. They have upturned noses and manes sculpted in extravagant layers, a style popular among TV evangelists. In point of fact, the male's skull carries a ridge of bone that protrudes, front to back, like a Mohawk haircut, and is designed to hold the great weight of muscle running down from the head and neck. It must have been a great strain to sit eyes forward, supporting the enormous weight, and so the males stared into the sky, heads balanced on their collars of muscle and blubber, in attitudes of magnificent disdain.

It used to be thought that female southern sea lions had no choice in mating, but recent research suggests that this is not so. Human male observers might imagine that the female calls out loudly and often in deep appreciation of the male's copulatory efforts. In fact—and it took female researchers to divine this—the female may be drawing attention to herself, saying, in effect, to the other males on the beach, "Hey, if you can get this big lug offa me, I'm yours." Thus, it's conjectured, they assure themselves that their progeny will carry the genes of the strongest male in attendance.

The pups, bleating like sheep, frolicked in the water, and there were no orcas to be seen, which was a bit of a relief, to tell the truth. The adult males, called *los machos,* roared very like lions, and their fights—there was one every two or three minutes—were brutal and brief, a matter of seven or eight tearing bites. The combatants, streaming blood, then turned away from each other and sat, back to back, heads in the air, three feet apart, like a couple of 650-pound bookends.

I felt my own chest swelling in what can only be described as a wholly fatuous case of sympathetic testosterone poisoning. It was clear that I couldn't win my own upcoming battle. So what? I'd inflict what wounds I could and leave 'em bleeding, if only a little bit. And then, by God, I'd turn away from the conflict, streaming blood, but with my head held high in an attitude of magnificent disdain.

On the beach, I saw males at war, females devoted to no one, and the pups all fubsy in the water. It was like looking into a mirror, and the mirror people were us, only we were distorted in strange ways—why do you think they call us animals?—and then, it seemed to me, thin cracks started from the center of this warped reflection, and the mirror began to bulge, ever so slightly.

Suddenly, a familiar assertion rose up, entirely unbidden, and fully illuminated the universe as I knew it.

I thought, "What a funny little bird the frog are." Not that frogs were birds, or that sea lions were humans, but it was surely possible to see them as translucent images shimmering deep within the mirror.

Gorillas in Our Schools

"I am not a gorilla scientist," I told the St. Mary's third-grade class, "but when I went to Africa, I learned something about gorilla behavior that no one knew until that day." I suspect the real scientists I was visiting in Rwanda talk about my discovery even now, almost twenty years later. And when they talk about it, I bet they laugh.

Which, I explained to the third graders, didn't make it any less of a discovery. Just because people laugh about it.

"Can you tell the class what it is you discovered?" the teacher, Miss Larson, asked. She was tall and blond and impatient with the concept of suspense.

"Well," I said, "I hurt my knee playing football in high school. Now it pops out of position every once in awhile. I fall down and scream, and I don't even know where I am, because it hurts so much. That's how I made my discovery. I contributed to the science of biology because I was such a bad football player."

The third graders weren't, I knew, particularly interested in my knee problems. I'm often invited to speak at local schools about my various travels, and I accept these invitations because I think it's a way of giving back something to the community. Also, I get to advise kids to belch at the dinner table and tell their parents that it is science.

"Do you guys want to see some pictures of gorillas?" I asked.

They did, and said so at the top of their little lungs. I asked Miss Larson to turn down the lights, and I flipped on the slide projector.

"Okay," I said, "here's the first gorilla." The on-screen image was that of a rather handsome human male wearing a photographer's vest. The children squealed with laughter.

"It's okay to laugh at this man," I said. "He's a photographer."

Nick Nichols, a *National Geographic* wildlife photographer, had given me the set of slides to show in schools.

The first real gorilla up on the screen was a frightening portrait: a head-and-shoulders shot of an adult male, mouth open in what appeared to be a scream of rage. White teeth—canines the size of small carrots—stood out against the black face.

"Scary, huh," I said. "But it's really not, because that's what it looks like when a gorilla yawns."

And I was off on Phase One of my standard grade-school gorilla lecture: They're not scary monsters at all; in fact, they're very gentle. They don't eat humans; they don't even eat meat. I showed pictures of gorillas eating bamboo and nettles. The kids, like all kids, sat there staring at Nick's photos with their mouths agape. On the grade-school slide-show circuit we like to wow 'em with charismatic megafauna.

I showed pictures of several gorillas together and explained that the animals live in family groups of two to thirty-five or more and that, most of the time, the oldest and biggest male, whose back is silver, is the boss. Silverbacks stand about five-foot-eight and weigh as much as four hundred pounds. During the day, the gorilla family will eat, rest, and move on until late afternoon. Just before it gets dark, they build a nest, almost like big bird's nest, and that's where they sleep.

I showed a picture of a blond-haired human male standing in the rain, taking notes.

"That man," I told the students, "is a scientist. His name is Conrad Aveling. He gets to study the gorillas every day, rain or shine."

To get a job like that, I said, you have to go to school for a long time and study a lot. This makes you a very precise and literal-minded person, so that if a journalist visits you and writes a story about the gorillas, you will be obligated to write him a long letter and tell him all the things he got wrong. If, for instance, the writer described a gorilla as being twice his size, the scientist would say:

"This is incorrect. The gorilla may be twice your weight, but he is not twelve feet tall."

"Field scientists," I told the third graders, "are a lot like Miss Larson, but their clothes are dirtier and they swear a lot."

After the slide show, it was time for Phase Two: I asked the shyest of the girls and the most obstreperous of the boys to assist me. The girl would sit in front of the class, in Miss Larson's chair. She would be the gorilla. The boy would be the scientist. He would try to approach the gorilla and learn about its behavior. If he did anything wrong, anything at all, the gorilla would just go away and never come back. I think this prepares boys and girls for the realities of later life. Boys more than girls, perhaps.

"It is sometimes hard to find the gorillas," I said. "You have to remember where they were the night before and start from their sleeping nests. Then you track them through the grass and bushes." Sometimes, I explained, you can smell them before you see them. The silverback has an odor like skunk and vinegar, only very faint. And then you may see them moving through the shafts of early-morning light that fall through the trees. They walk bent over, on their knuckles, and look like bears shambling through the sun. When you see them, you should fall to the ground and approach carefully.

My eight-year-old scientist began crawling up the aisle toward the gorilla in pigtails sitting in Miss Larson's chair.

Locate the silverback, I advised. Make sure he sees you. Don't get between him and any of the babies, because he will try to protect them, and then he could hurt you. Look at the silverback's face. It reads just like a human being's face. If he frowns at you, go away.

You should also know how to say some things in the mountain gorilla language.

"The gorilla hello, " I said, "sounds like this." I made my voice phlegmy and hoarse and then breathed out twice, in a kind of gentle growl. "It means, 'Hey, I don't want to fight or hurt anyone's babies.' Scientists like Mr. Aveling call that sound a double-belch vocalization." I encouraged the kids to work on their belches and to demonstrate the science they'd learned at the dinner table that evening.

As the boy scientist crawled forward, belching loudly, I advised him to keep his head down. Watch the silverback's head. Wherever it is, yours is lower. If you stand above him, he thinks you want to fight. Scientists call that an aggressive posture.

The gorilla will be watching your face, and you can smile at him, but don't show your teeth. Gorillas who show their teeth often want to fight. Look at the silverback, but keep dropping your eyes. Gorillas are like humans: they get mad at people who stare right at them for a long time.

Mr. Aveling, I said, taught me all those things about gorillas, and he was very strict. He said I should observe "proper gorilla etiquette" at all times. And it was true: If I minded my manners with the gorillas, I could sometimes sit near them and watch their behavior for hours. Sometimes I even exchanged double-belch vocalizations with silverbacks.

When the animals wanted me to go, they frowned at me and said another important gorilla word. "It's called a cough grunt," I said, "and it sounds a little like a train just starting up." I made a series of quick, soft coughs in the back of my throat. "That means 'Go away.' "

The gorilla in Miss Larson's chair did a pretty good cough grunt and the boy scientist crawled backward down the aisle. There was applause all around.

And I was into Phase Three: Only 650 mountain gorillas exist today. That's all. (Some scientists think the population in Uganda's Bwindi National Park are not mountain gorillas, but a species of the more populous lowland gorilla—or a unique subspecies. If so, there are only 320 or so mountain gorillas alive.) These numbers haven't changed much in the last couple of decades.

It is tempting, at this point, to dramatize the mountain gorillas' plight by setting up a morality play of good guys and poachers, but the real problem facing the gorillas is loss of habitat. Virunga and

Volcano national parks, where the gorillas live and are protected, are a mere 149 square miles. In the aftermath of the genocidal wars in Rwanda, over 700,000 returning refugees have flooded into the area near the base of the mountains. These people want land to farm. Families must be fed.

And yet the forests of the Virungas act as giant sponges, feeding the streams and rivers during the dry season. Destroy the forest for farms, and everyone starves during the next drought. It's a vexing problem, with no easy solutions, and what I tell the children is that the surest way to kill the gorillas is to destroy their habitat. It's true for any animal.

My friend the photographer, Nick Nichols, wanted to show the habitat problem in his pictures. One day we were standing on a very steep hillside, watching a family of about nine mountain gorillas who didn't know we were there. There were three of us—me, Nick, and Conrad Aveling. It was about noon, the hottest part of the day, and the animals had just finished feeding for the morning. The silverback was sprawled out on his back, bouncing an infant off his rather considerable belly. A female lay with her head on the male's thigh, dozing in the sun.

I felt as if I were staring down into Eden. And yet, if I lifted my gaze, I could see down past the periphery of the park, right into Rwandan farmland, which rolled bare and treeless up to the very edge of the forest. That was the picture Nick was trying to get: the gorillas at rest, the threatening farms close below.

I was just standing there, watching him work, when I shifted my weight, slipped on some moss, felt my knee pop, and heard myself saying, *"ah-ah-ah-ah-ah."* Clutching my knees to my chest had the effect of turning me into a human bowling ball, and I began rolling faster and faster down the steep and grassy slope.

I've tried to see this from the gorillas' point of view. Here you've just had breakfast, and you're ready for some quality time with the kids, followed by a nap. Then there's this hideous noise: *ah-ah-ah-ah-ah.* And when you look up, the foliage is parting in a rapid downhill vector. Whatever the horrible thing is, it's coming right at you.

The gorillas fled in all directions as I rolled directly through them and came to rest against a low shrub. My first coherent thought was that I had breached every single rule of gorilla etiquette. I sought to apologize to Conrad Aveling.

"Well, yes," he said. "On the other hand, a lot of us have wondered what would happen if a human charged a group of gorillas."

And that, I told the third graders, is how playing football very badly can lead to important scientific discoveries.

Powder Keg

It was raining fiercely along the equator the day the protestors blocked the Pan American Highway with barricades of burning tires. We had left Quito, Ecuador—where a volcano looming over the city, Pichincha, was in a state of near-constant eruption—and were driving south toward Baños, where another volcano, Tungurahua, perfectly cone shaped, was booming and roaring, spitting up great blocks of burning rock, flows of lava, and copious clouds of ash and steam. Baños, a town of some twenty thousand people situated at the foot of that bad-boy volcano, had been evacuated by the government. The townsfolk had been given a single day to get out, because the danger of a catastrophic eruption was great and imminent, or so said the geophysicists, who ought to know.

I was driving toward Baños and we'd been slaloming over the narrow two-lane highway, hydroplaning on the wet pavement, dodging axle-busting potholes as well as any number of dead dogs that littered the roadway.

"There are," I told photographer Rob Howard, "no old dogs on the Pan American Highway."

A truck passed me on the right. We took up the whole roadway, the truck and my four-wheel-drive rental vehicle, as did the pair of buses passing one another and coming the other way. Presumably, we'd all be back in a safe and sane single file several moments before the deadly collision. It was the way of the road in Ecuador, where the driving is seriously dangerous business, and people pay attention.

I slowed to allow the truck to pass, and pulled over toward the right shoulder, then had to swerve to avoid a fresh canine corpse.

"There's another one that's not going to get any older," Rob said.

"Poor son of a bitch."

And then the truck ahead of me hit its brakes hard, and when I pulled around to pass, there was no traffic coming our way. Instead, we saw black smoke rising from the roadway, and a solid wall of flames ten or fifteen feet high fiercely burning against a pewter-gray sky. Trucks and buses and cars were pulled over willy-nilly on the Pan American, and I thought we were approaching the scene of some hideous accident. Then I saw the demonstrators, most of them young and well dressed, standing four or five deep across the roadway in the rain. They were singing and shaking their fists and shouting slogans. The Pan American behind them was piled high with giant truck tires, which had been doused in kerosene and set afire.

We pulled far off the road, rolling over some green, soggy grass, parked, and walked a quarter of a mile to talk to the demonstrators. They were mostly students from the college in the nearby city of Latacunga, but there was a smattering of tough-looking older men, who represented various local labor unions. As in the United States, it is rare for these two disparate groups to join one another in a demonstration, and that fact alone suggested a unanimity of purpose and anger.

Two of the students, a handsome couple in their early twenties named Luis and Monica, said that working folks and students had come together to protest the lack of jobs and the high cost of living: inflation was running at about 60 percent, the highest rate in all of Latin America, and only a third of the working population was employed. Corruption was rampant and flaunted at the highest (and lowest) levels of government. Anger was focused on Jamil Mahuad, the president, who was said to be not only corrupt but incompetent.

Luis had no idea how long the demonstration might last, and most of the truck drivers were dozing in their cabs, waiting patiently, as if such blockades were an ordinary cost of doing business in Ecuador. The ones who weren't sleeping said they agreed with the students. The country was in bad shape. The fact that there were two live volcanoes—one threatening Quito, the capital city, and the other spitting ash all over Baños, the premier tourist destination in Ecuador—seemed to be of little matter. There was always some volcano spewing out great ash falls and burping up poison gases.

Indeed, when Alexander von Humboldt passed through Ecuador in 1802, he called the path that would become the Pan American Highway the Avenue of the Volcanoes: there was, for instance, Pinchincha, looming over the old colonial city of Quito; Cotopaxi, near Latacunga; Chimborazo, west of Ambato; and Tungurahua near Baños, not to mention a plethora of others, most of them visible to one another from the summit of one or the other trembling mountain, given a rare, clear day.

Currently, the two most obstreperous of the mountains—Pinchincha and Tungurahua—were vomiting up gas and ash and lava simultaneously. They were both on a vague schedule: Pinchincha became active every three hundred years or so, while Tungurahua erupted about once a century, so it was inevitable, in the fullness of time, that the two would become active at about the same time.

In fact, the Quechua-speaking indigenous population—various groups of Indians with remarkably varied cultures—were in agreement on one thing: when Guagua (*baby*) Pinchincha cries, Mama Tungurahua wakes up, and Daddy Cotopaxi roars. As yet, snow-capped Cotopaxi—at 19,374, it was the world's highest active volcano—was still dozing fitfully. It rose just north of us, obscured now in the rain that was falling in biblical torrents.

Luis and Monica said that if we were interested, they could show us a road around the barricades. It was the way of things in Ecuador: someone always knows a way around the obstacle. And so the people who had been blocking our way ten minutes ago got in the backseat of the car and directed us back the way we had come. We were stopped by a line of police wearing gray camouflage gear, which stood out starkly against the grassy green hillsides.

"Did you come through from the south?" a sergeant asked.

"No, we turned around."

"So the demonstration continues."

Luis said, "Yes, señor. We continue to block the Pan American."

The sergeant nodded, and all but saluted Luis.

The police, it seemed, were determined not to be provocative. They had established their lines out of sight of the demonstration, and were just waiting for it to be over, like the truck drivers, except that the police had to stand out in the rain. My impression was that the cops sympathized with the demonstrators and that Jamil Mahuad wasn't long for the office of the president.

(Indeed, several weeks after I left Ecuador, Mahuad fled the presidential palace after a chaotic but bloodless military/civilian uprising. A junta—composed of a military chief, a former Supreme Court justice, and an indigenous leader—declared they were in control of the government. Several hours later—after discussing matters of foreign aid and investment with representatives of the U.S. government—the junta declared itself dissolved, and returned power to the constitutionally elected government. Sort of. Vice President Gustavo Noboa assumed power.)

At the time, however, there along the Pan American Highway, amid the dead dogs and burning tires, I was watching the rumblings of what would very soon become a coup, and the words "powder" and "keg" kept clanging together in my mind.

Luis and Monica were pleased to help us around the barricades they themselves had erected. We were directed down a series of gravel roads that eventually led directly through the town of Latacunga. They said they did not blame the United States for the troubles in Ecuador, an attitude I've rarely encountered among South American intellectuals.

"You have good government," they said, "while ours is bad and very corrupt."

America, however, had produced something the students found dreadful and atrocious. It was called "techno music," but the U.S.

government, as far as Luis and Monica could tell, was not entirely at fault. We pulled out onto the Pan American Highway behind the burning tires, and dropped the students off to join their cohorts in protest.

We soldiered on through the rain, and turned off the Pan American Highway, east at Ambato, and drove through a small town called Pelileo, where police had barricaded the road to Baños. We convinced the officers that we were world-famous journalists, here to cover the evacuation of Baños and the eruption of Tungurahua. They let us through and we plowed down a steep grade in the general direction of the Amazon jungle. About five miles later we encountered another barricade, this one manned by the military, professional soldiers who, it seemed, didn't give a rat's ass if we were famous international journalists, movie stars, or astronauts. No one was allowed past the checkpoint.

But we had permission from the Institute of Geophysics, in Quito, to visit with scientists studying the mountain: the Americans Patty Mothes and Peter Hall.

"Ah, well," the soldiers said, "you moronic little turds," or words to that effect. In fact, we'd passed the house where the scientists were staying. It was up the hill and down a gravel road that forked many times in many directions.

In the end, we piled a pair of soldiers in the backseat and they escorted us to the house, just as the students had directed us around their own barricades. The Geophysical Observatory had been donated to the Institute of Geophysics—a teaching institution that studies earthquakes and volcanic activity in Ecuador—by a prominent local chicken farmer, and was a long white building with a red-tile roof and large picture windows. Each of the windows was taped with a big yellow X so that, in our headlights, the place looked like someone who'd been knocked seriously unconscious in a cartoon. The tape, the soldiers said, was a protection against the window-shattering sound of an eruption. Tungurahua, they said, was about ten miles away. We could actually hear it, a series of avalanches rumbling faintly in the distance.

There were soldiers camped outside the observatory in a large green canvas tent. A Sergeant Aedo escorted us into the house, where Patty Mothes was talking with a group of people who'd been evacuated from Baños. The group was well dressed—some men in coats and ties, women in dresses. Also present was a Colonel Yepes, who prefaced many of his statements about the possibility of an imminent eruption with the words "Please believe me . . ."—because, it appeared, the people didn't believe him.

The delegation from Baños wanted to return to their town, if only for a few hours. They had been evacuated for nearly two months. The people wanted to have a High Mass and a solemn parade. They wanted to do it on Sunday, five days from today. It would be a symbolic homecoming.

Patty Mothes admitted that the mountain had been quiet, seismically, of late. Sunday was a possibility. Colonel Yepes, reluctantly it appeared, okayed the five-hour return to Baños, and when the meeting was over we explained to the colonel that we were world-famous journalists and would need to accompany the people to their evacuated home. The colonel, who exuded Latin graciousness, told us there would be provisions made for the press, but the underlying message was that, frankly, he didn't give a rat's ass who we were.

No matter. We were going to Baños on Sunday and that was that.

In my quest to advance the cause of science, I was jumping up and down on solid rock at about fourteen thousand feet, just under the glaciers of Chimborazo, Ecuador's highest mountain, an inactive volcano rising 20,702 feet. Buried under my feet were a couple of geophones, sensitive devices meant to measure the movement of the rock, and convert that trembling into an electronic signal. At 210 pounds, I was the heaviest in our party, and the man most likely to advance the cause of science in this case.

Rob Howard and I had accompanied Peter Hall and his Ecuadorian associate, Viniceo "Feny" Cárceres, to the middle slopes of Chimborazo to make some adjustments to one of the more important seismic stations in the world.

The radio receiver in Peter's hand hummed with a single tone, like a mezzo-soprano holding a note.

"Okay, now jump again," Peter instructed me, and I did.

The note wavered.

"Keep jumping."

The sound coming from the receiver was now like that of a mezzo-soprano holding the note on horseback at a full gallop.

"We bring these receivers up the active volcanoes," Peter said. "When they make this wavering, waffling sound, we know the rocks below are moving. It's time to get down quick."

"Those guys who died on Pinchincha," I said, "didn't they have one of those receivers?"

"They shouldn't have been there anyway," Peter Hall said as the note continued to flutter long after my last jump. "They were told not to go."

"Weren't they students of yours?"

Peter had been the director of the Institute of Geophysics at the time.

"It was in May of ninety-three," Peter said.

"What happened?"

"We're interested," Rob said, "because we're going up there Saturday."

Peter looked to where the glaciers started, less than one thousand feet above us. The seismic station was set on a rock ledge at about fourteen thousand feet, on the northwest slope of the mountain. Below us the rock face gave way to what is called the *puna,* a steeply sloping grassland that looked rather like the moors of Scotland, minus the heather. Instead, there were blocky outcroppings of gray, lichen-encrusted rock set in a marshy valley full of tufted yellow grass. Everything was the color of a rainy autumn day.

Our cars were down there, about seven hundred feet below, parked on a muddy dirt road. It had been a stiff climb for Peter and Feny because they were both carrying thirty-pound car batteries in awkward, external-frame packs modified for the purpose. The land was boggy at first, and we stepped from tussock to tussock. Overhead, one of the last one hundred condors in Ecuador cut lazy circles through a dismal gray sky. On the ground before us, a dozen or so vicuña, slender and elegant, saw no reason to deviate from their grazing line. They called to one another in odd, high-pitched chirps and passed about fifty yards ahead of us: golden-brown animals with brilliant white bellies and long, graceful necks. Vicuña are related to llamas in the way that Fred Astaire is related to Ernest Borgnine.

Feny refused any help with the batteries, as did Peter, who had lived in Ecuador for twenty-eight years. (And people make machismo out to be a bad thing.) They struggled through the marsh to the rocks, then scrambled up another several hundred feet, gasping and bent double under the weight of the cruel batteries.

The seismic station itself consisted of a fifty-five-gallon drum buried in the ground and covered over with a solar panel. It read a signal from the geophones, buried deeper in the ground, and sent the signal to the Institute of Geophysics in Quito from an antenna set on an outcropping fifty feet above us. The station was powered by car batteries, which were charged by the solar panel. The batteries had to be replaced about once a year. Which was why we were there, standing on the ledge, waiting for Peter to tell us about the deaths on Pinchincha.

A dense fog drifted in from the north, and our world was a single shade of gray. Peter shook his head. "They were told not to go," he said again. "My wife—you met her last night, Patty?—had been in the crater the day before and she's the one who said, 'No, there's been a change of activity.' She thought there were more explosions coming on. She went back to the institute and said, 'Hey, there's something happening in Pinchincha.' One of the students, Victor, said, 'Oh, we should go up there and get some samples.' Patty said it was too dangerous. But Victor rounded up another student and they went up there early the next morning.

"Victor called down on the radio about ten that morning. Said he was up there. About eleven, the seismographs at the institute registered an explosion on Pinchincha."

"Stations like this one here," I said.

"Exactly. There are several of them up there. We were concerned about Victor. And then we couldn't reach him on the radio. They didn't come out that afternoon.

"So the next morning I went up to the summit with another fellow. We stood on the rim and then walked halfway down into the crater. That's when I saw them. With binoculars. Two bodies covered in ash at the bottom of the crater."

"What killed them," I asked, "ash? Poison gas?"

"No, they got impacted in the chest and face by rocks, big blocks . . ."

"You'd call it a cannonade?"

"I don't know if there's a good term for it, but, yeah, that captures the idea."

Rob and I thought about this for a moment. Pinchincha, for obvious reasons, was closed to casual hiking, but after much discussion and many visits to various offices, we'd obtained a variety of permissions from the institute and the military.

"Who're you going up with?" Peter asked.

"Nine-one-one," I said. This is Quito's emergency-response squad as well as its search-and-rescue organization.

"They'll be in radio contact with the institute," Peter said. "So do what they tell you."

Well, that's good thinking there, Peter, I thought, as a sudden, stiff wind ripped the fog to shreds and the condor wheeled above.

"Could you jump again?" Peter asked. "We're checking the telemetry here. How the radio signal travels all the way to the institute in Quito." There was no cellular phone link at Chimborazo, so Peter was speaking on a handheld radio to a person about thirty miles away, who simultaneously phoned each jump into the institute at Quito, where my hard-rock trampoline act was being recorded digitally. Quito called back and said, in effect, that the fat guy was coming in loud and clear.

"All right," Peter said, "they're getting the signal. Now jump again. We'll do a polarity test. What we want to know here is: When a wave comes up from below, does the rock sink first, or does it rise first? When you jump, you're pushing the rock down, so we can see how the geophone responds to it."

"How sensitive is this station?" I asked, more than a little breathless. "I mean, is it just for Chimborazo?"

"Oh no," Peter said. "On good, massive rock like this—and if an earthquake or eruption is big enough—we can pick up events from anywhere in the world. This is a vitally important station for activity in Peru, in Colombia. We report the data worldwide and it is used in calculating where the earthquake was, and how big it was. They use better stations, like the one in Pasadena, California, but this one helps, especially if the event is down in South America. Then this would be a critical station."

There were many other seismic stations along von Humboldt's Avenue of the Volcanoes in Ecuador, the most problematic being the one on Cotopaxi. The institute had sent teams of strong, young students with technical climbing experience up into the snowfields and glaciers, but they'd been stopped three times running.

"Don't you have a lot of world-class climbers coming to Ecuador?" I asked. "I bet you could get some good people to volunteer their help."

"Well, no," Peter said. "We tried that. No one wants to do it."

"Why not?"

"Because a car battery," he said sorrowfully, "is an intensely objectionable object to carry up a mountain."

Feny, meanwhile, was about to solder a resistor into the electronic guts of the station. This device would cause the geophones not to overreact to a vibration. Because all the geophones at all the seismic stations in the country had been standardized in the same way, scientists at the institute were able to calibrate the magnitude of an earthquake or an eruption.

Feny looked up from his work. "I need the oscilloscope now," he said.

Peter looked around at the gear spread out around the station, and did not like what he saw. A great sorrow clouded his face. "I thought you brought it," he said in a small sad whispery voice.

And then we looked down to the cars, seven hundred vertical feet below. They appeared to be about the size of a pair of cockroaches. Feny and Peter, who had, after all, carried the batteries, turned and regarded Rob and me.

"Hey," I said, "I've just been jumping my heart out for science."

"Rob looks to be in terrific shape," Peter said.

"He's a crackerjack," I allowed. "A regular mountain goat."

"The oscilloscope," Peter said, "is in our car, in the backseat. It's a big yellow gadget on a sling and it has an LCD window near the top. It's about the size of a long loaf of bread."

"Only a lot heavier," I said heartlessly.

Rob, the designated gofer, began trudging down the steep hillside in his own reluctant quest to advance the cause of science. When he was about ten feet below us, I said: "This is what you get for being young and strong."

"Instead of old and forgetful," Peter added cheerfully.

Twenty or thirty minutes later, Rob was splashing through the marshy land, jumping from tussock to tussock, and only about five minutes from the car.

"Geez," Peter said mildly, "I really hope I didn't lock it."

So it was a race back north, along the Avenue of Dead Dogs, the Pan American Highway, to Quito, where Pinchincha, looking mostly green and devoid of snow, loomed over the city. A reasonably fit person could walk to the lip of the crater from the city in eight or nine hours, but that would be a bad idea. Danger of eruption and serious ashfall aside, the walk winds its way up through some nasty neighborhoods where trekkers have been robbed for the contents of their backpacks, beaten up, and even raped.

Happily, Marcel Redin, the man from 911, the search-and-rescue agency, offered to drive us up past the military checkpoint, where we'd pick up our military guide, and continue on to the refuge, a kind of bunker for hikers. We also picked up Yvan, another 911 officer, and Gireya, a young woman from Lloya, a bucolic village high on the slopes of Pinchincha, a place famous for its dairy cows and cheese. She was learning about the volcano in order to inform the other villagers of its many dangers.

Marcel drove a well-maintained 911 Chevy pickup tricked out with winches and special lights. It was four in the morning and we sped through the sleeping city. There were only a few pedestrians wandering the streets. Many wore painter's masks and goggles, indicating that it was already a bad day for ashfall in the city. Pinchincha was definitely acting up.

At the military checkpoint on the road to the summit, we picked up a sergeant of the Tiger Commandos ("We are always ready"), who introduced himself as "John Baez, mountain guide." He carried radios, along with rescue gear and a full first-aid kit.

By now there were seven people in the truck, and Marcel threw the Chevy into four-wheel as we careened over the muddy path in the dark. He knew the road, which was good, because the headlights were backscattered badly due to a light ashfall. It was like driving through a combination of fog and sandstorm.

We parked just under the summit, at the refuge building, where there was running water and a toilet, along with several simple cots. A sign on the wall suggested that trekkers refrain from going down into the crater itself. "Danger," the sign read. "You could lose your life as a result of an explosive eruption due to the ejected fragments of rocks, due to poisonous gases . . ." And so on. There were a lot of ways to die in the crater.

In the spectral light of false dawn, we began trudging up the long, ash-covered talus slope to the rim of the crater, and arrived well before dawn. It was fairly clear that the mountain was active this morning, throwing up enormous amounts of ash and steam. We could see the cloud rising out of the depths of the crater, which appeared to drop below us almost a mile. A winding trail led down into the crater from our position.

There was no fire down there, only a half dozen or more places where white fumes of vaporous steam from various fumaroles rose straight up out of the lumpy, ash-covered soil. The ash cloud was billowing up out of the earth from somewhere else much farther back in the crater.

It was six-forty in the morning, and Yvan was calling down to the institute in Quito, reporting the *ceniza*, the cloud of ash and steam that now rose about a mile and a half over our heads. It was, said Sergeant John Baez, a fairly significant eruption. Happily, we were standing on the east rim of the crater, and the wind was at our backs, blowing the ash off over the virtually uninhabited areas to the west of the mountain.

The lip of the crater was 14,800 feet high, according to my altimeter, and the sky above was a pale blue interspersed with a few puffy white clouds. The ash kept rising, but the process was entirely and eerily silent. As the sun rose, the ash cloud—previously dark and malevolent—began to show its true colors. It was a subtle shade of salmon pink, a combination of steam and pulverized rock. The eruption continued for several minutes, and the cloud grew, billowing out at the edges near the top. Heavier bits of rock and cooling steam began to fall along the sides of the column, which was now mushroom shaped: well over a mile wide at our position, and four or five times that above.

I looked to the south and saw we had climbed above the clouds, which lay at about ten thousand feet, a perfectly flat layer of glittering white which took on the colors of the rising sun. The world below looked like nothing so much as a watercolor painting that might be titled "Abstract in Pastels."

And rising up out of the clouds on all sides were the volcanoes of Ecuador. I could see Cotopaxi, which had defeated the institute's climbers three times recently. It looked like the archetype of all volcanoes, perfectly shaped and snowcapped. Chimborazo lumped up just to the west, and Tungurahua—east of Chimborazo, south of Cotopaxi—was spitting out an evil column of foul black ash, easily seen against the pallid blue sky. The world consisted solely of volcanoes, some of them in eruption, and all of them rising up out of an Abstract in Pastels.

Yvan, who was still talking to the institute in Quito, said that they were getting some ominous readings from our position and that we should be prepared to evacuate.

"How do we do that?" I asked John Baez, Tiger commander and mountain guide.

"Run for your life," he advised.

"Can we go up there?" I asked, pointing to the highest point on the lip of the crater. It was about three hundred feet above us.

"If we hurry," said the sergeant.

We hustled right up there past at least three seismic stations of the type we'd seen on Chimborazo. I was tempted to jump up and down over the buried geophones. See if I could force the evacuation of Quito, a town of more than one million souls.

"But that would be wrong," Rob Howard advised me gravely.

Presently, we reached the summit, where a plaque said we were standing at 4,781 meters (15,686 feet). The eruption had subsided and I could see down into the crater, which looked like a great ashy basin studded with various gray hillocks. The volcano, we had been told, was "building domes," six of them to date, and we could see them down there, piles of whiter rock pushed up out of the earth like so many pimples.

The crater wall was not perfectly formed, but fell away sharply to the west in the way a river cuts a wide canyon out of a rock wall. We were standing on the highest spot, which was to the east. From the air, the entire crater must have looked rather like a cup tipped precipitously to the west.

Quito lies to the east, protected by the high wall of the crater, and by another mountain, Ruku, which is actually part of Pinchincha, a volcanic peak that is, for the residents of Quito, blessedly inactive. What all this meant was that if Pinchincha really blew, Quito would be largely protected. The brunt of the explosion would be directed off to the mostly uninhabited west.

(This is characteristic of eruptive volcanoes. When Mount St. Helens blew, in May 1980, nearby Portland was not much affected, but in Montana, where I live, almost seven hundred miles away, martial law was declared for a day due to heavy ashfall.)

From the summit, it was also possible to see the drainage patterns, and they all fell off to the west as well. That meant that rivers of lava would be directed away from the city. Pyroclastic flows also follow drainage patterns. These are great, heavy clouds of pulverized, incandescent rocks, vapor, and poisonous gases that can pour down drainages at over one hundred miles an hour. Some experts believe that this is probably what happened at Pompeii, under Mount Vesuvius, when it blew in A.D. 79. The people were killed by pyroclastic flows, then buried in ash.

But Quito was essentially safe. In a big eruption, a stiff wind might carry heavy ash over the city, and a number of buildings could collapse. If the ash was hot enough, there could be fires. But it wouldn't be Pompeii, or anything like it.

As I was contemplating the fate of Quito, a low, ominous rumbling rose up out of the crater, getting louder and louder. The receiver Yvan carried began making that waffling, weaving sound.

"What's going on?" I asked Sergeant Baez.

"Avalanche, I think," he said. Either the west wall of the crater was further eroding, or one of the domes was pushing up a little higher. The rumbling sounded like a jet plane taking off, and the institute called up to Yvan and suggested we evacuate the area in an orderly manner.

The roaring reverberated off the crater walls, but it stopped after a minute or so. As we scrambled down from the summit, another salmon-colored cloud billowed up out of the crater and painted the entire sky pink, the color of pulverized, incandescent rock.

When we reached the refuge, cooling gray ash fell like a light snow all around. Marcel, of 911, piled everyone into his truck, and we evacuated the area like so many bats out of hell.

Which was all just as well, since Rob and I had to drive back lickety-split down the Pan American Highway in order to be in Baños the next day for the people's five-hour visit. It would be a symbolic homecoming to a town that was well and truly menaced by an erupting volcano.

The next day's newspapers all had front-page pictures of the eruption of Pinchincha. There had been two of them. The first, at six-forty in the morning, we saw. It produced an ash cloud that rose to three kilometers and was powerful enough, so said the newspaper *Hoy,* that the mayor of Quito, Roque Sebilla, saw fit that morning to declare a combination orange and yellow alert. There were four stages of alert: white was "inform yourself and report unusual volcanic activity"; yellow was "maintain alert"; orange was "prepare to evacuate"; while red meant "run for your life." Actually, the word was "evacuate."

So the oddly silent eruption we'd seen yesterday morning had prompted the mayor to suggest that the people of Quito might begin thinking about evacuation. There had been another and much more powerful eruption later that day, just as the scientists at the Institute of Geophysics had predicted. The newspaper *El Comer-*

cio said, "The second eruption was very big and produced a column of ashes and gas higher than ten kilometers."

This gave me a great deal of confidence in the expertise of the people of the institute, but did not much settle my mind, because we were about to go into Baños, a town those same scientists thought severely threatened. They'd sent a letter to government officials to that effect in mid-October, and a day later, the people of Baños were given a single day to evacuate. Red alert. Immediately afterward, the military had formed lines around the city to prevent the possibility of looting.

But now, many of the evacuees would be going back to their town for the first time in almost two months. They were all packed inside buses, twenty-two of them, waiting for the military convoy to take them down the road to Baños, where the Amazon jungle meets the mountains.

We were waiting for the buses at the military checkpoint where we'd been stopped on our first attempt to visit Baños. Sergeant Aedo, whom we'd met at the Geophysical Observatory near Pelileo, was along to help. He'd been living in the military tent for two months, working with Patty Mothes some of the time, and had come to understand a little about volcanoes.

Yesterday, while we were on Pinchincha, he'd been about six thousand feet up on the slopes of Tungurahua, helping Patty place GPS devices used to measure the bulging of the earth. "The ground," he said, "was trembling under my feet."

"Were you scared?"

"Of course I was scared," Sergeant Aedo said sensibly.

In the weeks he'd been stationed at the observatory, the sergeant had closely monitored the four old-fashioned seismographs set up under one of the taped-over windows. When the little arm started drawing big peaks and valleys on the revolving drum, something always happened, and not much later. An explosion sounded like a mortar going off two feet away, and it wasn't a good idea to be standing near a window at that time.

We couldn't see Tungurahua from the checkpoint, but we could hear it. There was a faint rumbling, like the one at Pinchincha, and it sounded, once again, like a jet plane not so very far away. The avalanches continued for over thirty seconds. And then, in the sudden silence, there came the sound of honking horns and shouting, happy voices. The convoy of buses was moving slowly down the road. People were hanging out of the windows and sitting on the top of the buses, all of them waving little white flags and shouting, "Long live Baños."

Military vehicles led the convoy and patrolled along the sides. Sergeant Aedo talked Rob and me onto one of the buses and we were off to Baños, amid a crowd of happy, singing people. I sat next to Daniel, twenty-four, a tourist guide specializing in climbing and rafting. "Our city," he said, "waits for us."

There was a large banner hanging down behind the driver of the bus that said, "I live and shall always live in Baños." The bus's public address system was playing a cassette of songs about Baños. The songs said, "Baños is the paradise of the mountains," and "In Baños life is beautiful," and "I live and shall always live in Baños."

People sang along with the songs and waved their small white flags, most of which were emblazoned with words that echoed the songs, though some seemed to refer to this or that little bit of corruption: "Of the 10,000 American dollars, not 1,000 has arrived."

We emerged from a canyon, and I could see Baños far below, spread out on a flat bench of land just above a river. Across that river, rising abruptly, were the steep slopes of Tungurahua. It was spitting out a steady stream of black ash that combined with the clouds in the sky, and the clouds hung over the pretty city of Baños, black and heavy bellied.

Ominously, I could also see the crater, and it was tipped off in one direction, like the one on Pinchincha. Except that on Tungurahua, the crater tipped in the direction of Baños, which was basically situated at the foot of the mountain. All the drainages led directly down into the town. In a major eruption, pyroclastic flows would hit Baños in minutes. The lava would follow.

We stopped at a bridge as several soldiers uncoiled the razor wire strung across the span and continued on into the abandoned city. There was some graceful colonial architecture, and almost none of the buildings was over three stories high. Flowers grew wild everywhere, and parrots shrieked in the trees. It was a place, as the song said, where the jungle met the mountains, and one of the loveliest little towns I'd ever seen.

So it was more than strange to see such a place with no one on the streets, no one in the houses, no one anywhere. All the businesses along the empty streets—the Baños pharmacy, the travel agencies, the restaurants, the hotels—all of them were locked and shuttered. Black, ash-filled clouds hung over the ghost town of Baños.

The buses parked in front of the great Basilica of Baños, an imposing gray building entirely constructed of stones from the nearby mountains. People stood in the square in front of the church, laughing and singing and embracing one another, as lines of soldiers stood across every side street in an attempt to funnel people into the Basilica to hear the Mass.

Inside, a stern, gaunt-looking man stood at a lectern just under the altar and sang. He had an emotional, soaring voice, and his song opened up the floodgates so that most of the people standing in the pews wept openly. Behind him, a phalanx of women were placing flowers on the altar. A statue of the Virgin, holding the baby Jesus, was carried in on a pallet and placed high to the left of the altar.

All along the side walls of the Basilica, there were large oil paintings, all about ten feet wide by six high. I studied one of them, while an elderly priest chanted a prayer to the Virgin. The painting showed Tungurahua erupting, spitting fire, with clouds of smoke and ash above. The river was pink with the reflection of the fire in the sky. Below, there were two or three huts, and what appeared to be a church. Several men—farmers as well as businessmen in suits— were carrying a statue of the Virgin and the baby Jesus out of the church. In the distance, people were running for their lives along a dirt path. The runners were depicted comically, with their legs spread too far apart, their arms stretched out in front of them, and their hats flying off their heads as in a cartoon.

Underneath, there was a great deal of writing, painted by hand.

It said that the people of Baños had always protected the Virgin during eruptions of Tungurahua. It said that in the year 1797, on February 4, Tungurahua erupted violently but Baños was spared major damage, while towns farther from the mountain were all but destroyed. There were other, even more miraculous events depicted. Baños had never been utterly destroyed by an eruption of Tungurahua. Baños always protected the Virgin.

"Mary, Queen of heaven," chanted the priest.

"Queen," chanted the people.

"Mary, Queen of the earth."

"Queen."

"Mary, Queen of all the saints."

"Queen."

Presently, several men—some probably farmers, some probably businessmen—lifted up the statue of the Virgin and led the congregation out into the streets. The procession moved over the cobbled streets and through the locked and shuttered city.

People walked shoulder to shoulder, well over two thousand of them, and they filled the street from sidewalk to sidewalk for a distance of over two blocks. In some of the buildings, behind the taped-over windows, we saw starving cats. People who'd brought sandwiches tried to shove pieces of bread under the doors, or through cracks in windows broken by booming eruptions. The cats mewled piteously and some people were infuriated—with the owners of the animals or the evacuation order or both—and the mood on the street began slowly to turn sour.

I stood on a grassy hill to take a few notes, and a man who looked remarkably like the actor Charles Bronson asked me if I was a journalist. I admitted that I was, and he said I should tell the world that the politicians of Ecuador didn't care about the people. They were thieves. "If corruption was a sport," he said, "the politicians of this country would be world champions." There was no danger from Tungurahua, he said. All the stories in the paper, the evacuation of Baños: it was all just a way to shift the public spotlight off corruption.

"You don't think there is any danger?"

"None at all," the man said. In fact, he had some clothes and food in the day pack he carried and he was going to elude the police and the military. He'd stay in Baños.

"Are there others who are going to stay?"

"Many, I think," the man said.

In the distance, the procession was approaching the police line, and it appeared that the men carrying the Virgin were not going to stop. The police, not ready to use riot batons on Virgin-carrying citizens, retreated up one block, then another. As the police moved their lines, several dozen people broke out of the crowd and ran up a wooded hillside, easily outdistancing the pursuing police, who carried large plastic riot shields.

The clouds, heavy with suspended particles of ash, hung low over the city. Slender shafts of light fell on the square as the Virgin was brought back to the Basilica. It had turned cold and windy. In the empty side streets, behind the military and police lines, the wind picked up piles of black ash and sent them spinning about in shadowy whirlwinds. The ash stung my eyes, and I tasted the grit on my tongue.

Police moved down the back streets behind straining dogs. People were moving reluctantly toward the buses, pursued by the dogs in a kind of bitter slow motion. I felt a drop of rain, and then several. Finally the sky opened up and the rain fell hard, rattling the leaves of the trees lining the square.

The people of Baños, some of them crying again, began boarding their buses. They were ready to face armed soldiers and vicious attack dogs, but they didn't seem to want to get wet. Once again, I sat next to Daniel, the guide. He looked out into the rain and said: "Our city cries for us."

The Entranced Duck

I recall strolling through a Balinese temple with my younger brother, Nyoman Wirata. An important religious ceremony was about to begin, and it was likely that several of the men would fall into trances. We expected to see some socially acceptable and highly controlled violence later as priests and handlers, using blessed water, attempted to wake the men from their religious ecstasy. I had noticed that it was usually the village headman who got bloodied in the end-trance rumpus, and was working on an idea about trancing behavior.

"Older brother," Nyoman said. I was fifteen years older, and Nyoman had begun calling me "older brother," *beli*, some weeks previous. "*Beli*, look. There is your wife."

I turned to see a Western woman, improperly dressed for the ceremony. She was, in fact, wearing short shorts, revealing a sunburned pair of thighs. In contrast to the lithe and graceful Balinese women all about, the woman, an American, I feared, strode about as if stomping large, poisonous spiders with every step. The concept of respect was alien to her.

She stood in front of one of the altars and was examining the offerings: two ten-foot-high pyramids of brightly colored fruit placed on either side of a pig's head. There were a dozen sticks protruding from the head, and strung between the sticks was delicate white lace, like the finest embroidery. The lace was made of pig fat.

"Eeeyew," the woman said loudly, "gross!" Damn: an American.

"That is not my wife, little brother," I said to Nyoman. "That is your wife."

"No, big brother. I will marry Ketut in six months. You do not have a wife. Go talk to your wife. Be *Sangyang bebec* and she will love you."

"I can't do the entranced duck in a temple, Nyoman."

"In Bali, it is proper to laugh," Nyoman said, and he nudged me toward the woman, giggling.

I was staying in Nyoman's family compound, in the mountain town of Ubud, and my back window looked out on a green rice paddy. During the days, Nyoman drove me to various ceremonies in a car I had rented. Many of the remote villages we visited did not have electricity or running water.

In the Hindu-Agama religious ceremonies we sought out and witnessed, a man, self-selected, breathes the smoke of scented wood, then falls into a rapturous ecstasy, during which time he becomes, for instance, a pig. It is called "going *Sangyang.*" The supernaturally controlled pig crawls about on all fours, grunts convincingly, eats garbage, and rolls in the mud in front of the entire village. Sometimes, an entranced man will become a monkey and climb trees with startling, simian strength. *Sangyang Djarum* is the most spectacular of the trancing ceremonies, and the one most often performed for tourists. A man riding a tree branch, as a child will ride a hobby horse, runs through a rather large fire, barefoot. The fire is scattered and systematically stomped out.

In the most violent of the ceremonies, entranced men fight with sticks or swords, and yet no one is injured. At the conclusion of the event, a gang of village men, directed by a priest, or *permangku,* sprinkle blessed water on the foreheads of those who have gone *Sangyang.* As the men swim up out of the trance, they seem almost stunned, and there is a dazed, drunken expression in their eyes. They sometimes swing fists or throw elbows. Often, half a dozen men have to subdue a particularly fractious trancer. The man is tackled and held on the ground until he fully emerges from the trance. And it is almost always the headman who steps away from the pile with a bloody nose.

My theory was that trance is a socially acceptable way to channel violent and antisocial behavior in a culture that frowns on argument and aggression; a culture that values harmony and smooth interpersonal relationships.

"Why," I had asked Nyoman early on, "doesn't anyone become *bebec*, a duck, when they go *Sangyang*?" There are lots of ducks in the terraced green rice paddies of Bali.

"I think, *beli*, no one knows how to be a duck."

"Where I live, every child knows."

"Show me, older brother."

I began talking like Donald Duck and worked myself up into a fine hysterical quacking fury. Nyoman literally fell on the ground laughing. Thereafter, I found myself obliged to be *Sangyang bebec* pretty much every place we went. Every new person had to meet the entranced duck. I was quacking myself hoarse.

The amazing thing was, no matter how many times I did *Sangyang bebec*, it never stopped being funny.

My last night in Bali, during that trip, I took Nyoman and his intended bride, Ketut, to a fancy new restaurant in Ubud.

"*Beli*," Nyoman said, "you should stay here in Bali. You should marry someone here."

"Younger brother," I said, "I hardly know how to talk to Balinese women."

"It is easy. You must talk sweet. Tell them they are like flowers, like colorful little birds."

Ketut covered her mouth in the polite Balinese manner but her eyes were bright with laughter. Nyoman and I giggled like schoolboys.

And so we parted. I promised to come back. Maybe marry a Balinese woman. That was eleven years ago.

I heard news of Nyoman periodically, because I recommended his services as driver and guide to any number of Bali-bound friends. The reports were always favorable. People liked Nyoman.

A business trip to the Far East gave me an excuse to hop a short flight to Bali. People said the island had changed, and that it was now a place about tourism. The tourist dollars had bled all authenticity out of the culture, or so it was said.

My first day, I hired a car and drove from my beachfront hotel up into the mountains, where Nyoman lived, in Ubud.

Muka, my Balinese driver for the day, pointed out what was new: the double highway through Sanur, the luxury hotels, the shops where there had only been rice paddies before. Behind the shops, Muka said, there were still rice paddies. You just couldn't see them from the road.

The road to Ubud, a winding two-lane blacktop, was similarly full of shops, mostly those of family entrepreneurs who carved, say, giant kangaroos out of wood. There were silver shops, and crafts stores, and places that sold replicas of sacred and secular masks. All new.

The people in general looked healthier than I recalled.

"It is true," Muka said. Health care had improved remarkably in the past thirty years or so. Children were inoculated. Life expectancy in Indonesia as a whole has risen from 45.7 in the 1960s to 62.7. Even with the current economic problems, the country was a good deal more prosperous than it had been when I had last visited. Almost all the mountain villages now had electricity and running water, for instance.

We arrived on the outskirts of Ubud, always Bali's cultural soul. The main street was choked with shops and services, with new restaurants and upscale hotels. Traffic was constant and unrelenting. Muka and I walked up to Nyoman's family homestay, where I'd lived eleven years ago. There was a line of motorbikes parked out front, and heavy traffic was at a standstill. The sign—"Homestay Adur"—was still there, but a huge pile of rocks blocked the entrance. I climbed over, and walked up the stairs.

Balinese homes are generally walled compounds consisting of several houses. There had been three or four at Homestay Adur, but when I stepped over the threshold, I saw that all but one of the small wooden houses had been torn down. There was a huge hole in the center of what had been a graceful courtyard, and busy workmen were digging in the earth, setting the foundation for a new, central building. In the single house left standing, a dozen or more people sat at sewing machines, sweating in the heat, and making T-shirts. Nyoman, I was told, wasn't in at present. He had gone down to his T-shirt shop on the tourist beach, at Kuta. He wouldn't be back until tomorrow. I could, however, give him a call on his cell phone.

This, I reflected, was not the Nyoman who lived in memory.

Nyoman's cell phone didn't work. I liked to think that the sacred peak of Gunung Agung, an active volcano almost ten thousand feet high and locally regarded as "the navel of the world," was causing the problem.

The next day, I took a scuba-diving excursion to the island of Lembongan. The dive boat was a twenty-two-ton catamaran, with air-conditioned decks. The complicated process of outfitting dozens of divers was handled efficiently and with dispatch. The last time I dove in Bali, the equipment was ratty and the reef was so overfished that it was pretty much bereft of life. My Balinese guide, who wore a fairly expensive dive watch, said the cruise company, Bali Hai Cruises, had hired an independent marine biologist to monitor damage done to the reef by its operations. In fact, he said, the reefs were in better shape than before. Local education programs had curtailed the worst of the overfishing.

It is, I suppose, a commonplace observation, but people who are starving or fighting epidemics seldom concern themselves with environmental issues. I thought about this forty-five feet under the surface of the sea, as the current drove me along the reef at a speed of about 3 miles an hour. There were purple green tube sponges, and waving whips of golden soft corals. The reef was alive with moray eels and clown fish and all the darting, neon life of tropical seas.

Because this was a drift dive, it was hard to stop and examine any one thing very closely. I had to fight hard against the current simply to stay in one place. I wondered if what I had seen could possibly be right: Nyoman, a hotshot with a cell phone, running a sweatshop in what had been a graceful homestay? I felt I was swimming against the current of time, as expressed in measures of change. A melancholy epigram kept banging around inside my head: Life is a drift dive and then you run out of air.

Time and tide change all. Humans age, cultures evolve, and my own home continent hasn't been the same since the first American stepped onto its soil sometime deep in the ice age. This was before horses and international trade in beads and blankets; before cars and electricity and books and shopping malls; before televisions, skyscrapers, computers, and booths that sell cotton candy at county fairs. Whole waves of people changed North America: Neolithic hunters, pilgrims, and mountain men; Lewis and Clark, cowboys, and Henry Ford. African slaves. Italian and Irish and Mexican and Asian immigrants. Abner Doubleday. Abraham Lincoln. Tourists like De Tocqueville.

History is a chronicle whose function is to iterate change, and humans tolerate this current of disruption to the degree that it provides us those things we want: a decent place to live, food to eat, a quality education for our children, and some leisure time to enjoy our lives and families.

I drove up to Ubud again and finally found Nyoman at the homestay. He said the place was being torn down so that he could expand the T-shirt tailoring shop. The conditions would then be better for the employees, who were, in fact, all members of his family or very close friends. No tourists wanted to stay in the place anymore. The traffic noise was unbearable.

Nyoman had married Ketut, and they had three children.

Ketut sat with Nyoman, sometimes holding his hand as she nursed their youngest child. Nyoman said he didn't do much guiding anymore: only for friends or friends of friends. He'd traveled himself. A rich American client had bought him a ticket to the United States. He'd seen New York and Cape Cod and Miami and San Francisco. It was all very nice, especially San Francisco, but his youngest child was only four months old at the time, and he was homesick among the tall buildings.

"Remember the trancing ceremonies?" I asked.

"Yes."

"Do they still do them?"

"They are better now. The people have more money to buy better costumes. They have more time to practice, and they do them more often."

"And the headman still gets hit?"

"Always."

I liked the idea that as Bali changes, it somehow contrives to remain the same.

"I think you are married now," Nyoman said.

"It's true."

"So you are happy?"

"I think so. Most of the time."

We were silent for a moment.

"Do you remember the duck?" Nyoman asked.

"Very well."

"Please do *Sangyang bebec* again."

I quacked out the duck's furious rage. I quacked about loss and change; about the current that drives us ever forward, and entombs each moment as it passes, leaving only memories before we run out of air. I quacked so long and so fervently that I could feel moisture forming at the corners of my eyes.

It was an inspired performance. Probably the best *Sangyang bebec* I've ever done. Nyoman and Ketut collapsed in helpless laughter. The baby in Ketut's arms looked up, amused by the commotion, smiling and gurgling happily. I quacked on, a little happier now.

Time and tide change all, I thought, but the entranced duck always gets a laugh.

Castle and More Castles

All that was left of the town were its broken and weathered bones: a few ramshackle buildings with Victorian pretensions, all listing dangerously to one side or another, manifestly losing their slow-motion fight with gravity. There were some stone foundations and several piles of crumbling boards, bleached gray under a merciless blue sky. That and nothing more. Castle, Montana, dead now for over a century, is a fit subject for the most fatuous of meditations. Man is vanity, one might conclude, and yet the earth abides. Or something equally solemn and silly. If the people who populated Castle were alive today, one imagines, they'd be heavily invested in Internet stocks.

I didn't enter any of the buildings: they were prime breeding ground for hantavirus, a disease that made its appearance in 1993. It is spread by deer mice and other rodents, contained in their urine and excrement. A footstep in an abandoned building raises dust, which harbors the deadly virus. People die of respiratory complications.

So I passed near the tumble-down buildings and had a sense of unseen eyes, watching, watching. Castle now belonged to the rodents, and the virus.

There must have once been a grid of streets, but they were gone now, grown over with sage and wildflowers. My dog and I wandered through the ghost town, occasionally scaring up white-tailed deer that pogoed off into the trees, their long tails wagging over their backs like flags.

Above the town, set at the summit of the mountains, was the castle that gave the town its name: several crenellated towers that looked a bit like medieval battlements. The old town site was set on a series of rolling hills and mountain meadows alive with wild-flowers. There were purple asters and lacy yarrow, along with wild roses and Indian paintbrush and mountain bluebells. The air was alive with the hum of bees, and the wild, silvery odor of sage floated on the breeze.

The town had a six-year run of incredible prosperity, and then it died, bang, like that, in a matter of seventy-two hours. The first two hundred people had settled alongside Castle Creek in April 1887. There was silver in them thar hills, and the Cumberland mine, along with a dozen others, drew workers from all over America and Europe.

Miners made about $4 a day, which was damn good money in those days. A cowboy, by contrast, earned about a dollar a day. In Castle, early on, a house with outdoor bathroom facilities and a dry kitchen could be purchased for $100, so that an ordinary working man could buy a modest place for a little less than a month's wages. Try that today. European workers with experience in digging and blasting, notably Cornishmen, called, for some reason, "Cousin Jacks," were highly valued. There were Irishmen as well, along with a few Chinese, called "Celestials," because, at the time, China styled itself the Celestial Kingdom. The Chinese worked the tailings, piles of scrap ore Europeans and Americans could not process profitably.

A few days before my visit to Castle, I was chatting with a delegation of Chinese scientists and technicians from the Beijing Natural History Museum. They were visiting Livingston, Montana, to work with Matt Smith, of the Livingston Natural History Exhibit Hall. Matt is an artist who builds dinosaurs from bones and casts sent to his shop from all over the world. They arrive in big, battered wooden cases that look like props from an Indiana Jones movie.

Matt Smith reconstructs the dinosaurs, puts them on exhibition, then sends them off to paying customers like the Museum of Natural History in New York. He's built dozens upon dozens of creatures, including ice-age mammals, several tyrannosaurs, and a couple of quetzalcoatls, which are the largest creatures ever to fly, with a wingspan of thirty-eight feet, about as long as a school bus. More to the point, of the fifty species of dinosaurs that once existed in what is now China, Matt Smith has built or is building twenty-five of them in Livingston, Montana.

Guan Jian, the director of the Department of Paleontology at the Beijing Natural History Museum, invited Matt to a dig in southern China in December 1996, and the two men have worked closely together ever since. Matt Smith's artistry, Guan told me on one of his visits, begins at the excavation site. The biology of the creature, how it functions, is important. The geology of the region will dictate excavation techniques. Taphonomy, the study of what happens to the creature the moment it dies, is of supreme importance. How, in fact, did it die? Were the bones disarticulated by scavengers? How is it that some of the animal is preserved while other parts are missing?

Chinese workers, Guan said, were fast and efficient, but they weren't "attentive." Digging dinosaurs was a kind of hard rock mining to them.

I sort of liked the idea that—one hundred years after Chinese miners worked the discarded tailings in Castle—Matt Smith was working digs in China in a similar way.

The visiting Chinese technicians would work with Matt in Livingston. Most of them had never been to the United States. They flew into Seattle, where Matt picked them up in a rented van. Then they drove 750 miles to Montana.

In essence, all the technicians knew of the United States at the time I spoke with them was encompassed in a two-day road trip. Their impressions had to do with cars, and highways, which they found impressive and even artful. The "system of transportation" was "beautifully constructed," and it wound through a land they thought was virtually deserted. Even when they pulled into some town for lunch, the first thing they asked Matt was "Where are all the people?"

They had seen beaver and deer and eagles, which was very exciting. The United States was different from China is so many ways. For instance, if you sat down in a restaurant in America, the waiter would give you a glass of cold water, without asking. In China, you'd get a pot of hot water.

One of the technicians said, "America is only two hundred years old, and yet you are all so very interested in your history."

"What makes you think that?" I asked.

"Because every town we stopped in had one or more shops that sold old things. Everywhere you go you see the sign: 'Antiques.' " I wasn't sure this didn't say something about the acquisitive nature of Americans, but kept my own counsel on that one.

"What we especially noticed," one of the women said, "was that rich people live out of town, with a lot of land all around them. We wondered: Do they do that because they are afraid of the poor people?"

Were they? Or did it have more to do with the boom-and-bust cycle of the American West? Something to think about, anyway.

The boom:

In Castle, over one hundred years ago, shopkeepers supplied the miners, and by the time Castle's population reached several hundred, lot jumping was common. A man might find his town lot, purchased from the Castle Land Company, occupied by armed men who drove him off. A vigilance committee was formed, headed by the local postmaster. The toughs hung out in a log cabin on the slopes above town. The vigilantes rushed it one night. A man inside shouted out that the first man through the door would be shot, but the vigilantes broke down the door with a log. The lot-jumping toughs escaped through a back window, never to return.

Castle reached its peak in 1891, the year it was incorporated. It had nine stores, one bank, two barbershops, two butcher shops, two livery stables, two hotels, a photo gallery, a dance hall, a schoolhouse, fourteen saloons, one church, and seven brothels. Aside from the vigilant postmaster, there was a deputy sheriff, a justice of the peace, a chapter of the Women's Christian Temperance Union, and four newspapers. There was a permanent population of 1,500 folks. By day, the main street was jammed with outbound ore wagons pulled by teams of horses and inbound teams pulling produce, with buggies, with men on horseback, with coaches and pedestrians. People arrived daily on stagecoaches, among them prostitutes ready to work at the local "sporting houses."

The main street was now a gravel road leading up into the national forest land, high above in the Castle Mountains. All the buildings that had once lined the street were gone. To the west was the three-story skeleton of a major boardinghouse, and south of that were several weathered buildings with large bay windows looking out at the mountains above. They must have seemed graceful and luxurious in their time.

To the east, across the gravel road, was what had been the disreputable part of town. Most of the saloons and brothels had been located there, and the remains of Minnie's Sporting House lay dreaming in a high meadow.

My dog found a dead ground squirrel to roll in, and she lay on her back, paws in the air, wiggling about in what appeared to be an ecstasy of putrescence. She's a bird dog, and I believe she wants to disguise her odor. Somewhere, deep in her demented hunter's brain, she must imagine that sage hens and ruffled grouse, upon being presented with a creature streaking up on them from a distance, barking hysterically, must think: Hey, nothing to worry about here, it's just a dead squirrel.

The issue of disguise and birds was on my mind. The women who worked the brothels, such as Minnie's Sporting House, were euphemistically called "soiled doves." They arrived in the booming town carrying a trunk and, folded neatly at the bottom of each of these trunks, almost without exception, was an elaborate white wedding dress. It is true that sometimes whores married miners or shopkeepers, but more often the wedding dress was funereal garb. The soiled doves were most often buried in these gowns, and so they went into that dark night as virginal brides.

And the bust:

The year after Castle was incorporated, production of silver began to dwindle. There was a financial panic in 1893, as well, and President Grover Cleveland was convinced that the government's mandatory silver purchase program was the cause of the depression. He called a special session of Congress that summer to repeal the Sherman Silver Purchase Act. Silver prices plummeted and, in Castle, the Cumberland mine closed down immediately.

The Cumberland boardinghouse had served 135 meals the last night the mines operated. Three days later, it served 6 men, who remained to dismantle machinery. The town literally emptied out in seventy-two hours. A few families remained, but for all practical purposes, Castle was dead.

By 1936, only two people lived in the old town: the seventy-five-year-old self-appointed mayor, Joe Kidd, and the seventy-year-old constable, Joe Martino. The snows came early the winter of 1936–37, and winds drifted the snow in the coulees to forty feet or more, so that sometimes deer fell through the crusts of snow and could be found, after the thaw, starved and frozen in the tops of cottonwood trees.

There was one blizzard after another that year. Supplies were running low and Mayor Kidd hitched up a team of horses to a cutter, a light sleigh, and set out for the small ranching town of Lennep, seven miles down the canyon. He made three miles the first night, and stayed with some shepherds at their camp. At Lennep the next day, he picked up the mail, stayed the night at a local ranch, and headed back the next morning. A mile from Castle, the horses gave out and Kidd walked to Martino's house, arriving at 9 P.M. He had a cup of hot coffee and left for his own house. It was only five hundred yards away, but the mayor collapsed and died in the snow.

Martino was unable to carry the body, so he skied down to the sheep camp, and the shepherds got word to the nearest big town, White Sulphur Springs. The sheriff and coroner skied into Castle and carried Kidd's body out on a toboggan. Leaving Joe Martino as the last full-time resident of Castle. And then the rodents took over.

The big houses that so impressed the Chinese are, for the most part, trophy homes built by out-of-staters and occupied sometimes for as little as one or two weeks a year. They are springing up all throughout the West like a plague of poison mushrooms. I believe that the twenty-year bull market—what is called the wealth effect—has allowed people to build these trophies. In America, I should have told the Chinese, wealth is sometimes measured by the amount of land a person is able to post "No Trespassing" signs on.

No one knows how long the bull market will last, least of all me, but all good things come to an end. [Note: And the bull market did shortly after I wrote this.] Ask the dinosaurs. One geological moment they're standing in some fern glade of redwoods, bellowing brainlessly, masters of the earth. We were there: the mammals, or protomammals, small rat- and weasel-like creatures with sharp teeth and shining eyes. And when the dinosaurs died—when their life cycle went bust—we moved out of the shadows and took over the earth. We are the most fearsome predator the earth has ever spawned, and those creatures that know us, fear us.

Walking through the ruins of Castle, I had a sense of man as the dinosaur of this particular geological moment. There were shining eyes, watching from the shadows of ramshackle buildings. The others were there. I could hear them scurrying about when I looked in the windows where soiled doves once plied their trade.

There were others of their kind: eyes in the woodlands, under the aspens, and these eyes are watching the big trophy homes that have begun to dominate the Western landscape. There will be a bust to the boom, sooner or later, because that has always been the way. The big homes, too expensive for local folks, will fall into disrepair. The paint will peel from the walls, and the bare boards will bleach out, like bones under a desert sun. And then the watchers in the wood will move into the tumble-down buildings. The castles built by the wealth effect will lie broken and still under a merciless blue sky. And in the shadows under the shattered windows, the new inhabitants will scurry this way and that, their eyes shining, masters of all they survey.

Culinary Schadenfreude

I looked down at the quivering, white, gelatinous globules on my plate, and glanced over to the table where the Chinese were sitting. There were three of them, two men and a woman, scientists and scientific technicians: bone workers on their first full day in Livingston, Montana. They were in my hometown to help disassemble a display of Chinese dinosaurs at the Natural History Exhibit Hall here, and I had run into them at the Seattle airport the previous day. They had flown in direct from Beijing.

The only one of these distinguished visitors who spoke English asked me to call him "Brian," which, he said, sounded a bit like his actual name but was easier for Americans to pronounce. And now, after an uneventful flight, Brian and the other two Chinese folks were sitting at a long table in the basement of the local Lutheran church staring at heaping plates of lutefisk, a traditional Norwegian Christmas dinner.

Lutefisk, a fishlike substance, seems, at first glance, a revolting, jellied putrescence. Consumption is a matter of some courage. I found it necessary to sit before my plate and center myself, breathing deeply and consciously, staring at the plate as I would at a meditation mandala. Steam rose like an offering, like the soul's longing for oneness. Lutefisk, I proposed to myself, is consciousness made tangible, in the form of fish, and when I eat it, I partake of the Universal. Thus fortified, spiritually and morally—and with my courage on the ascent—I finally allowed my eyes to refocus on the plate before me and see lutefisk for what it truly was: a revolting, jellied putrescence.

Traditionally, in the ranching and farming communities of the West and Midwest, lutefisk dinners are served in Lutheran churches during the winter, just before Christmas. These are fund-raising events, and it is said that some eat lutefisk to show their devotion to Lutheran doctrine, rather in the manner of medieval saints flogging themselves bloody with whips.

The word "lutefisk" means "lyefish," which refers to the ancient Viking manufacturing process of drying fish and soaking it in lye. Lutefisk, a staple on long voyages, fueled the Viking conquest of much of Europe. This is because any person forced to eat lutefisk two nights in a row is certain to become a savage warrior.

Lutefisk won't actually kill you, though there is a rumor that, in the tiny rural town of Wilsall, about fifty miles from where I live, lye-soaked scraps were left out in back of the church—the fish is sometimes boiled in tents outside, so that the odor doesn't permeate the building for the rest of the year—and that cows from a nearby field got through the fence, ate the fish, and died.

In fact, I called the distributor of the lutefisk used there and in many other communities throughout America. The Olsen Fish Company of Minnesota sells about half a million pounds of lutefisk a year. A representative of the firm assured me that the dried fish is not "luted" in lye but in caustic soda, or sodium hydroxide, a kind of bleach used in laundry products as well as in the manufacture of explosives. Caustic soda's main virtue, in regard to dried cod, is that it breaks down fats to form soaps. Which is why lutefisk is a sort of jellied fish.

The Olsen Fish Company buys its dried cod direct from Norway, lutes it, then sends it through several rinses. When the consumer receives a shipment, it is free of toxicity, ready to boil and eat. So the rumor of the cows dying from eating lye is entirely false. They died from eating lutefisk.

I'm kidding. Lutefisk is something you kid about, anyway. I eat it and enjoy it precisely twice a year: once at the Lutheran church in

Livingston, and once at the church in Wilsall, where you have to climb over piles of dead cows to get in the door.

In Livingston, I watched the Chinese as they regarded their plates of lutefisk. We had gotten there late, which is to say, somewhere around six-thirty. Latecomers don't get large gelatinous portions of fish, but only small, quivering bites, the size of marbles, which are difficult to manipulate with a fork. It is, in the words of the late poet Richard Brautigan, like trying to load mercury with a pitchfork.

The Chinese hadn't yet tried a bite. Instead, they were speaking urgently among themselves.

I could sympathize with the Chinese, but there was another emotion tugging at me. As a travel writer, I'm usually the guest sitting at the table, staring at the food before me and wondering: Are they making fun of me here?

In northern Australia, I was served baked turtle lung, which tastes a great deal worse than it sounds. In the Peruvian Andes, I wondered what to do with the rooster's head floating in the soup, and whether I was really supposed to eat the little, stringy portions of guinea pig I'd been proudly served. My hosts in Irian Jaya treated me to a plate full of fried sago-beetle grubs, corpse-white, wormy-looking little guys about the size of my index finger from the second knuckle up. They were pretty good and tasted rather like creamy snail.

Western travelers often discuss various bizarre foods they've consumed either out of politeness or curiosity. In fact, two of my favorite recent books chronicle bizarre gustatory adventures. *Man Eating Bugs* by Peter Menzel and Faith D'Aluisio (with a foreword by Tim Cahill) concerns itself with the human consumption of insects from Uganda to Indonesia, from Australia to Cambodia. Peter had also sampled sago grubs in Irian Jaya and describes them as tasting "bacony." We get together to argue about this about once a year.

Strange Foods by Jerry Hopkins, who has eaten with local folks on six continents, features descriptions and pictures of pig ear cartilage in garlic sauce, worm-meal shakes, and five-penis wine. Jerry's thesis? "What is repulsive in one part of the world, in another is simply lunch."

Or dinner, in the case of lutefisk. Perhaps the Chinese were wondering if the mess on their plates was an elaborate joke. The tables, I thought smugly, have turned. Consider, for instance, my last dinner in Beijing.

I had arrived in Beijing carrying a pair of rifles: one .30-06, and one .22. They were for my Mongolian guides, and I had a two-day layover in Beijing before the flight to Ulan Bator. Carrying rifles out of the United States, into Canada, through Beijing, and into Mongolia was a nightmare of bureaucratic paperwork. They were expecting me at the Beijing airport, where I walked down a long corridor with armed guards in front of me and behind me. We stopped at a large room, with two couches, where a man in a Western suit asked me if I would like tea. The proper papers were signed, the guns were put into a locked safe. I was given a receipt. Then we all drank tea, with nothing much to say to one another.

I didn't want to tell them that the airline had lost one of my bags, the heavy one, containing several thousand rounds of ammunition for the rifles.

We began talking about food and the man in the suit said that, while I was in China, I absolutely had to have a traditional snake dinner. It was a man's dinner, for real men, and, as such, was manly in a vigorous, masculine manner. I gathered snake was one of those foods thought to put lead in the old pencil. Chinese men, apparently, dined on snake in large groups, all of them becoming more virile and potent with each bite. In America, the same process is associated with beer. Which, as I discovered, was not too far off the point.

I was traveling with an American named Michael Abbot and we had to make do with a two-man reptile feed. The restaurant in our hotel, as it turned out, was famous for its snake.

It was an elegant place, with ponds and bridges and fountains. When the waitress arrived at our table, I pointed to the English menu. Snake.

She said something not in my twenty-word Mandarin vocabulary, but eventually I understood that I was to get up and discuss my dinner choice with a small man standing off to one corner. The corner, I saw, was stacked floor to ceiling with glass fish tanks containing all manner of sea life. There were also chicken-wire cages, where various terrestrial animals waited to be chosen, rather like puppies in a pet shop window.

The man took me to the snake cage. There were fifteen or twenty of them in there, all twisted up together like a ball of yarn, and I understood I was to pick one out for my dinner. I have little experience in the matter of choosing a tasty snake and simply pointed at the biggest one, a creature a little over six feet long and about as big around as the business end of a baseball bat. The man opened the top of the cage, reached in, and grabbed the snake behind the head. He stood there, speaking rapidly and in an apologetic tone, while the snake hung loosely in his hand, its tail twitching and curling on the floor.

The snake, it turned out, was not venomous, and hence less effective in generating virility. The man was terribly sorry, but no restaurants in Beijing could stock poisonous snakes for a week. This was by decree of the government.

What was the reason for the rule? The snake man gestured for me to look around the restaurant. I could see the reason for myself.

The dining room was, in fact, packed with women: women obviously from Africa, Latin women, women dressed as if they lived in Saudi Arabia or Polynesia or Thailand. It was the Fourth UN World Conference on Women, being celebrated right now, in Beijing, and the government didn't want any international incidents, such as a foreign woman being killed by a venomous snake in a restaurant. Also, it might be better if the men these women encountered weren't feeling excessively, uh, manly.

So I was going to get to eat a harmless snake, which would probably only increase my potency a teensy little bit. This was well and good, since I would be dining in a room full of strange women, none of whom had expressed the slightest wish to share my company, or anything else I had to offer. What good does it do to have lead in the old pencil when there's nothing to write on?

I returned to my seat as the man dragged the snake back toward the kitchen. Almost immediately, it seemed, the waitress arrived with two small pitchers. One was perfectly clear and contained an alcoholic beverage. I didn't catch the name. *Moa tai*. Something like that. I since have been told that the generic name is *baijiu,* meaning, literally, "white alcohol." The other pitcher was filled with the snake's blood.

The waitress set two shot glasses on the table. She dropped some small, slimy nugget of snake, the gallbladder, into the blood, where it slowly sank to the bottom of the pitcher. Then she began poking at the squirmy thing with what looked like a metal chopstick. It slithered around and around on the bottom of the pitcher, but she finally punctured it, and something green—the gall?—began coloring the blood. She stirred the mixture, but the green gall didn't emulsify well, and swirled slowly around the pitcher in various viscous, amoeboid shapes, rather like a lava lamp.

That, apparently, was what it was supposed to look like, because the waitress nodded, as if at a job well done, and poured the shot glasses pretty well full with white alcohol, topped off with a dollop of lava lamp snake's blood. We should drink a toast to the coming dinner, she said, in so many gestures.

Baijiu is powerful stuff, 90 percent alcohol at a guess. It was best just to throw it down in a single gulp and get the whole thing over with. Except that the waitress filled the glasses right back up and disappeared into the kitchen. Back she came with the first course: batter-fried snakeskin. We were encouraged to drink a toast to the snakeskin. And another toast to the empty platter. A toast to the next course, which was stir-fried snake meat and vegetables. A toast to that empty platter. A toast to the courses to come, none of which I can remember, except to say that every part of the animal was served in one way or another, and it was necessary to toast every last bit of it, down to the eyeballs.

Snake, I thought, rather blearily, the dinner of alcoholics.

Michael and I paid our bill and bounced from wall to wall down the long hallway to our room. There, sitting on my bed, was the outsize duffel the airline had lost: several thousand rounds of ammunition that could, I imagined, earn me a lot of disagreeable jail time. This realization was not a comfort. I lay on the bed, worrying drunkenly about all that ammo, until the snake informed me that it wanted out, and right now.

That was my last dinner in China. Now I was watching the Chinese deal with the jellied mess on their plates, and a small, unworthy part of me thought: lutefisk is the revenge of the reptile. But they liked it. Or two of them did. Brian didn't go back for seconds, and told me later the fish wasn't "to his taste." He was polite about it, as good travelers are in foreign countries, and we laughed about the lutefisk, I perhaps more than Brian. I was pretty sure he didn't have a gun.

Swimming with Great White Sharks

The great white shark slowly cruising outside the flimsy, submerged cage in which I'd imprisoned myself was probably only twelve or thirteen feet long and weighed, at a guess, two thousand pounds. It seemed quite docile, and menacing only in its profound grace. The great white rose up to the surface, where there was a floating and iridescent smatter of chum: fish oil and sardines ladled into the water specifically to attract sharks. A disembodied seal's head floated nearby. The head was affixed to a thick yellow rope. The shark hit the seal bait with no sense of urgency whatsoever. It twisted its head slightly, in the way a human might tear at a strip of beef jerky. And while this was happening, someone above, aboard the dive boat I'd hired, was pulling on the rope attached to the seal's head so that the shark was being drawn toward the cage, where I stood breathing hard through a scuba regulator.

Presently, all I could see of the animal was its belly, white as a bedsheet. The sheer size of the fish filled my vision to its periphery, and when its leathery flesh actually touched the wire of the cage, there was an instant, thrashing jerk—all those muscles whipping and bunching inches from my face—and some part of the shark bashed into the cage, twice. It felt rather like being in a minor pile-up on the freeway: thrown helplessly forward, thrown helplessly backward, *bang,* against this side of the cage, *bang,* against that one.

The shark cut a wide circle through the sea, then disappeared into the blue-green distance.

Great whites—known to be man-eaters and sometimes called "white death"—can be found in all temperate and tropical oceans on earth. But they are most easily observed, in the wild, off South Africa, where there are an estimated two thousand of the creatures cruising between Cape Town and Port Elizabeth. The premier viewing area—probably the best spot on the planet to encounter great white sharks—is near Dyer Island, which is about seven miles off Gans Bay, a small fishing village a few hours' drive south and west of Cape Town.

Dyer Island itself is pretty much covered over in gulls and other seabirds, so that occasionally, as if on a signal, half the island seems to rise up into the air and circle about overhead, shrieking in a shrill and self-righteous manner.

Set just off Dyer Island, there is another, smaller body of land, a long, graceless pile of stones ten to forty feet high at most, and this is called Geyser Rock. It is the home of an estimated seventy thousand southern fur seals, a favorite prey of the great white shark. The seals bask in the sun on Geyser Rock, but must periodically enter the water to hunt and eat. They also become overheated in the sun, which is potentially fatal. The fur seal choice is this: stay out of the water and surely burn to death under the sun, or, what the hell, take a nice, refreshing dip in the ocean, and maybe get eaten by a huge, hungry shark.

Great white sharks circle Geyser Rock, which they seem to regard as a kind of fur seal McDonald's.

In places, less than one thousand yards separate Dyer Island from Geyser Rock. The channel between these two islands is called Shark Alley. Interested parties—tourists, photographers, scientists— can hire a "shark operator," that is, someone who owns a ski boat and a chicken-wire shark cage, and get right in the water with several great white sharks. It costs about $150 to look white death in the eye.

Gans Bay is a very small town of neat lawns and wood-frame houses, mostly painted white. It has the feel of small-town America, rural America: a place, one imagines, that values neatness and hard work; personal honesty and public decency. It sits on a coastline that could hardly be more appealing: These are the Scottish moors, with six hundred or more varieties of heather flowering in idiotic profusion because the climate is not drear and chill. It's Southern California here. Sun. Sea. Surf. A view toward Cape Town featuring purple mountains, range upon range of them, disappearing into the setting sun.

An American, standing in the midst of such soul-stirring beauty, feels, instinctively, that something is missing. Where are the trophy waterfront homes, the shopping malls and arcades and cheap amusement parks and saltwater-taffy vendors? Who left this place alone to stew in the economic stagnation of hard work and decency?

The answer is that most of the rest of the world did. In the days of apartheid and sanctions, for instance, South Africa's share of the world's tourism dollars was one quarter of one percent. These days, tourists visit local wineries, experience some of the best whale watching on earth, walk the nearly deserted white-sand beaches, and surf the perfect wave. It's heaven, as envisioned by the Beach Boys.

The emerging tourism industry, however, is not much regulated, and because South Africa is not a highly litigious country, it has, over the past few years, become one of the few places on earth where the risk-obsessed can go to put their lives on the line, with (sometimes dangerously inexperienced) outfitters offering rock-climbing or whitewater-rafting expeditions. "Sharking" is one of the new risk enterprises.

There are currently six shark operators working out of Gans Bay. Anyone with a ski boat and a welding torch can build a cage and became a shark operator. A permit or experience is not required and the money is good. The average wage in the area is about 5,000 rand (about $100) a month. Sharking pays better: a boat carrying eight paying guests at 500 to 800 rand a day ($100 to $160) is a month's wages in pocket. A year's wages in two weeks!

Consequently, competition among sharkers is fierce, and, behind the orderly and idyllic facade of the town of Gans Bay, passions and tempers run high. One sharker claims to have been shot at, probably by a competitor. Each of the operators is critical of the others, such criticisms sometimes degenerating into fistfights at the boat launch. One operator is faulted for using pig's heads as shark bait, which tourists find aesthetically unpleasing. Some operators have offended tourists by tossing cigarettes and garbage into the sea. Other sharkers are guilty of pulling great whites up to the transom of their boats so that they will thrash about in a dramatic manner, which the more aware sharkers feel is degrading to the animal, and an affront to South Africa, the first country on earth to protect great whites.

The most cogent critiques have to do with safety: Do you really want a four-thousand-pound great white shark thrashing against a boat that has no guardrails, that may be overcrowded, that is carrying tourists who range from families in matching Bermuda shorts to hot young divers from Europe and America? Shouldn't the shark cages have tops on them? Or at least extensions that rise above the sea? Shouldn't someone regulate the number of people an operator can cram onto his boat, boats that, after all, have to be able to handle ten- to sixteen-foot swells on the trip from Gans Bay to Dyer Island?

The operators and the South African Department of Transportation have been talking about regulations, a code of conduct, rules that would require a dive master and a pilot on each craft; mandate a sturdily constructed shark cage, free of rust; require operators be trained in trauma treatment and, at least, have a radio on board. Radio links to rescue helicopters have also been discussed.

But no one in Gans Bay believes new regulations will be effectively enforced. What every sharker in town knows is this: someone is going to have to die first. No one wants this to happen. Gans Bay operators are decent folks, first and foremost. And a death, or several, would be very bad for business. Still, no one doubts that the tragedy is coming, and coming soon.

The folks I chose to go with, the Great White Shark Research Institute, had the largest and safest-looking boat, a thirty-foot Dive Cat, complete with an enclosed wheelhouse, a toilet, and two clean, well-maintained 200-horsepower outboards.

The skipper, a Swede named Frederick Ostrum, brought the boat down to the dock trailered behind a battered Ford truck. The shark cage sat on the stern of the boat, and it was not the expected and reassuring rectangle of sturdy iron bars. It was, in fact, a cylinder about ten feet high and three feet in diameter, made of galvanized iron woven together in a diamond pattern. The wire was not nearly as thick as that in a Century fence, but it was somewhat stronger than chicken wire, which it closely resembled.

The cages float free, on a rope, so that they swing away from an attacking shark. The same principle makes bobbing for apples difficult. But not impossible. A spokesman for the South African Department of Fisheries has said that "if a great white wanted to destroy one of these cages, it could." Which seems reasonable on the face of it.

The Great White Shark Research Institute is sometimes criticized for being a tourist operation in the guise of a scientific institute. Whatever the fact of the matter is, on the two days I chose to dive with the GWSRI, there was an American scientist aboard, doing actual scientific work. Richard Londereraville, an assistant professor of biology at the University of Akron, had a grant to take blood samples from great whites. His mission was to find out if the ancient fish carried the hormone leptin in their blood. Leptin is created by fat cells, and controls appetite in creatures as diverse as mice and men. Sharks, however, have little or no fat. Does that mean they don't have leptin in their blood? Inquiring minds wanted to know.

Richard was handsome in a boyishly tousled way, and he showed me the implement he'd use to collect the blood. It was a simple, oversized syringe that looked like a big horse needle, with a barb halfway down its length. A piece of monofilament fishing line was connected to the plunger of the syringe, the length of it wrapped around a blue plastic plate-sized reel. The trick, Dr. Londereraville said, was to insert the needle just behind the shark's gills, where the skin is softest and the blood is fresh from the nearby heart. As the shark pulls away, you play out the line, gently pulling back on the plunger so that the syringe fills with blood. It wasn't like DNA work: you needed a lot more blood to test for the presence of a hormone.

Once the syringe was full of blood, Richard would yank the line, which would free the barb from the shark. In ten days of work, he'd collected three good samples.

"So," I said, "the syringe is fastened to some kind of long pole—"

"No. That doesn't work."

"How do you get the needle into the shark, then?"

"You have to do it by hand," the seriously insane Ph.D. said.

Low, a former commercial fisherman, piloted the GWSRI Dive Cat. After slaloming through sixteen-foot-high swells for forty-five minutes or so, we arrived at Shark Alley, and anchored about fifty yards from the fur seal colony on Geyser Rock. It was seven-thirty in the morning and no other operators had arrived yet.

The place smelled like a feed lot, which in fact was what it was if you were a great white shark. Seventy thousand blubbery mammals—males weigh in excess of six hundred pounds—produce an enormous amount of solid and liquid waste, so that the various gusts of wind that buffeted the Dive Cat seemed to have actual weight to them, and they hit like a slap to the face.

On the far side of the narrow island that is Geyser Rock, over on the other side of the great hillock of densely congregated furry blubber, the full force of the Atlantic Ocean exploded against a rock in a constant, booming meter. The sixteen-foot swells produced great geysers of spray perhaps forty feet high. This spray rose above the fur seal colony, and caught the sun in such a way that it fell back to sea and earth like the shards of tattered rainbows.

It was a noisy place, Geyser Rock, and the air itself was shattered by the continual barking and roaring of the seal colony. Females sounded like aggravated terrestrial cows, mooing in a kind of constant bawl, while juveniles baaed like goats or sheep, and the large males occasionally roared in the manner of some unfortunate soul suffering the agonies of projectile vomiting. The sound was constant and unrelenting: moo-baa-ralph, moo-baa-ralph.

The fur seals, scruffy, golden-looking creatures, were draped over the sandy-colored rocks in blubbery profusion, side by side, like an allegory about population dynamics, or Hong Kong, and whenever one seal needed to move any distance at all, it disturbed all the others that it touched or jostled, so that every annoyed seal had to moo or baa or vomit at the traveler.

Seals reaching the beach lay there for a while, heads in the air, bawling at the sea. These seals were joined by others, all of them vocalizing, as if daring each other and hurling curses to the sky. Finally, one, perhaps braver than the rest, would plunge into the sea, and it was as if the floodgates had opened and a hundred more would hit the surf, while their fellows above lay across the rocks, in attitudes of adipose unconcern, all of them melting in the sun like Salvador Dalí clocks.

The seals swam in "rafts," dozens of them, clustered together for the safety that can be found in numbers. The rafts hugged the shoreline, a single flipper raised to the sky, catching the cooling effect of wind against wet flesh and fur. They were dithering about in the surf, only ten yards from the safety of land, only fifty yards from the boat, and it was tempting to wave back to them. Hi, seals.

Washed up on Geyser Rock were several ship's timbers, boards forty feet long, the remnants of some historic shipwreck. Waters around the cape are treacherous, combining, as they do, currents from the Atlantic and Indian oceans running at odds to one another and to the prevailing winds. Huge waves, called Cape Town rollers, have been known to literally break bulk cargo ships in half. Waters here are unpredictable and deadly. The area, known to the rest of the world as the Cape of Good Hope, is locally known as the Cape of Storms, and, sometimes, the Cape of Souls.

Directly off the shipwreck, dozens of seals, basking in the ebbing water of a broken wave, lifted their flippers, as if to say, "We, who are about to die, salute you."

On the Dive Cat, Frederick began macerating sardines and fish oil in a fifty-five-gallon drum using a big wooden pestle. Every minute or so, Richard would ladle a great glop of broken fish into the water, and the iridescent mess would float away from the boat, mostly on the surface.

Low muscled the shark cage into the water. The cage was tied to a cleat on the boat with a yellow rope perhaps an inch in diameter, and the cage floated in the water at the transom of the Dive Cat, so that a prospective shark diver could just step from the boat into the cage.

Set close to the transom of the boat, and tightly secured to various cleats, was a standard-sized scuba tank fitted with what is called a double hooka rig: a pair of breathing regulators affixed to the tank with two hoses perhaps twenty feet long. Divers in the cage would breathe through the long hose from the tank on the boat.

The other paying passenger on the boat was Louise Murray, an English photographer with white spiky hair and milk-white skin. She smoked hand-rolled cigarettes and had once been a negotiator for British Petroleum, working deals that ran to millions of dollars. She fell into the job sometime after she joined the company and took a test that showed that she was "a risk taker." British Petroleum apparently felt it needed fearless negotiators.

Now Louise was traveling the world, publishing her photos in various scuba magazines, doing some writing now and again, and galloping through the last of her "oil money."

The chicken-wire cage was suspended by floats—cylindrical blue and white plastic objects like giant, two-foot-long sausages. The floats were placed deep into the cage so that about three feet of wire projected above the surface of the sea.

Louise and I repaired to the wheelhouse to don our wet suits, as Richard chummed for sharks, and Low worked a pocket-knife through the half-frozen head of a dead fur seal. He said that shark operators used to buy seals that had been killed in fishermen's nets, but new laws, designed to make killing seals economically unsatisfying, had stopped the practice. Now, Low and Frederick just picked up dead seals every once in awhile. I spotted a couple of them—defunct seals—rotting on the far shores of Geyser Rock. In fact, there was a seal-shaped thing with a big hunk missing in the middle directly below our boat, which was anchored in about fifteen feet of clear water. It might have been an oddly shaped rock.

"Is that a seal?" I asked Frederick.

"Yes," he said, then added, unnecessarily, I thought, "it's dead."

Richard ladled chum, while Low whirled the roped seal's head about in a great underhanded circle and tossed the bait about fifteen yards from the boat. To the west, a small squall, like a bruise against the sky, stood on dark and slanting pillars of rain. A freshening breeze slapped the boat with the heavy, deep brown odor of fur seal.

"The smell," Frederick said, "isn't too bad today."

"It isn't?"

"No." The temperature stood at 60 degrees. On really hot summer days, 100-degree scorchers, Frederick said, fur seal excrement literally baked on the stones of Geyser Rock, and tourists who'd come to risk their lives diving with white sharks spent most of an eight-hour day vomiting into the sea, chumming the waters with last night's dinner and unconsciously imitating the sounds of the fur seal bulls only fifty yards away.

"There's a shark out there," Low said, in the way another man might say, "Oh, look, a robin."

I stared out to sea, in the vicinity of the floating seal's head, and saw what looked to be a shadow on the surface of the sea.

Louise and I were struggling with our weight belts. I needed seventeen pounds to be neutrally buoyant in order to stand comfortably upright on the bottom of the cage.

Frederick and Low said they had seen the shark come up below the frozen seal's head and then glide slowly past it. "We call that a dummy run," Frederick said.

"Shouldn't I be getting in the cage?" said Louise, the certified risk taker. She was standing on the transom of the boat, about three feet off the surface of the sea, and out beyond her, I could now see the dorsal fin of the shark cutting through the water, leaving twin ripples drifting off to each side. Definitely a great white.

Frederick tugged on the rope that pulled the shark cage to the transom of the boat. Louise sat with her feet dangling over the water, then lifted them into the cage. She held the regulator in her hand, adjusted her mask, cradled her camera in her right arm, like an infant, and turned to me.

"Bring my second camera," she said. "Be careful with it."

So it appeared I was going to get into the water. I sat on the transom with my feet in the cage, bit down on the regulator, adjusted my mask, and, as I did so, the shark rose out of the water and hit the seal's head with a kind of indolent indifference. It was not at all like a trout hitting a fly on the surface of a stream. Instead, everything happened very slowly, very deliberately, and there was no sense of urgency in the shark, only a kind of regal indifference. The sun caught my mask at an angle, so what I saw was a blurred and brilliant glare, with a great triangular head shimmering in the center as it rose languidly from the sea, mouth agape. Rows of glittering triangular teeth ridged the palate, and the great white's eyes were a pure and ghostly white.

Great whites are possessed of a nictitating membrane, a leathery eyelid that comes up from below and protects the shark's eyes from the thrashing death throes of its prey. The membrane is pure white, so the shark rose like a particularly vivid nightmare, with gleaming rows of teeth and spectral white demon's eyes completely devoid of pupils.

Because of the membrane covering its eyes, the shark was effectively blind at the moment of the munch. Low tugged the rope and gently pulled the bait toward the boat as the great white moved blindly forward, mouth open in a behavior Frederick called "gaping."

"I'll bring him right up to the cage," Low said. "Get in."

"You get knocked out of the cage," Frederick said, "swim down."

"Down?"

"They hit things struggling on the surface."

And so, cradling Louise's second camera, and biting down hard on my regulator, I dropped into the cage, where everything turned gray-green and I was looking at the world through a mesh of chicken wire, while Louise stood at the slitted window in the cage, her camera at the ready. Say I lost the regulator: How long could I stay below the surface of the sea, with a great white shark circling above? Two minutes? How long is a great white shark's attention span?

And then I saw the shark, perhaps forty feet in the distance, a dim abstraction, like a notion of grace half formed in the mind, something brilliant but hazily apprehended. There was a curious feeling of dread without vulnerability, as in a dream.

Louise and I stayed underwater for perhaps half an hour, and the shark circled back a few times, always gliding off at meditative distances. Occasionally, chilled and shivering uncontrollably, the two of us rose to the surface, and sat, somewhat awkwardly, on the floats set about the interior of the cage, so that we were still surrounded by the wire that rose above the surface of the sea.

"How big was that guy?" I asked Frederick. I figured twenty feet.

"About eleven feet," he said. "Weighed maybe fifteen hundred pounds."

"I thought it was bigger."

"Adrenaline magnification," Frederick explained.

"Biggest one caught around in these waters," Low added, "was just over twenty feet. Biggest one I've seen here in Shark Alley was about seventeen feet. Weighed probably four thousand pounds."

We saw six sharks that day. There were two other shark operators, with boats full of paying customers, anchored no more than a stone's throw from us. While that felt a little crowded, the next day was a circus.

Here we are, four out of six operators, all of us anchored side by side in Shark Alley, in the one area just off the shipwreck where the water is relatively flat. There is, however, enough surge and surf that the boats are swinging widely on their anchor lines and banging, one against the other, so we are pushing boats off the Dive Cats with long poles, which is not something one really wants to worry about a whole hell of a lot because there are three (count 'em, three) great white sharks in the water, circling the boats, and there are three cages, containing five divers, in the water, not to mention three scuba divers, who are swimming around just under our boat. These divers are not in a cage. One of them, an American scientist named Mark Marks, habitually swims with great whites in this exposed fashion. Other operators think this is dangerous, and feel that when he's eventually killed, business will suffer.

Marks is working with a French film crew, and at the moment, he is acting as a safety diver for the cameraman, who, when looking through the lens of his camera, cannot see sharks coming at him from odd angles. Marks hovers above the Frenchman, holding a weighted, three-foot-long board carved into the shape of a killer whale. The board is painted with the orca's distinctive black-and-white markings. Killer whales are one of the few creatures in the sea that might prey on sharks. Even great whites.

Anchored next to the French party was a small, seventeen-foot boat, boasting twin 75-horsepower Yamahas. Counting the captain, there are ten people aboard. The swells had diminished to a mere twelve feet, but this is the Cape of Storms, the Cape of Souls, and the boat, rated for six passengers, was dangerously overloaded. Low told me he had quit work for a rival shark operator because he tolerated such conditions. "I think people will die here," Frederick said. "Not from the sharks, maybe. But for sure, a boat will go down. An overloaded boat, like that one."

I glanced over at the wreckage on Geyser Rock, and thought about trying to swim the fifty yards, boat to shore. The boat closest to Geyser Rock has deployed a cage whose floats are positioned on the top rim so that when the divers, two American men in the thirties, surfaced to the warmth of the sun, they sat on the floats, with their butts hanging out in the shark-infested water. Occasionally Frederick or Low would yell over helpful advice, like, "For Christ's sake, get in the cage, there're sharks coming your way."

Having seen any number of sharks rise two or three feet out of the water to take seal bait, I found this cage just a little scary. A white shark could easily rise up and put his great conical head in the cage, where the animal would be trapped, swimming around like some doofus at a party with a lampshade on his head. Except, of course, there would be divers crouching at the bottom of the cage. This scenario is not at all fanciful. It has happened. The photographer cowering at the bottom of the cage got a lot of good pictures and was not injured. But what an advertisement for the topless shark cages: Sharks can get in, but they can't get out.

Louise was down in our cage, with Frederick watching the circling great whites, and Low ready at the line that held the cage. In a bad scenario, a shark could get wrapped in the rope and toss Louise out of the cage. Low stood ready to uncleat in an instant. Meanwhile, boats were bashing up against one another, mostly because the other operators had come out alone, with no dive master or assistants, so that they felt an obligation to watch the sharks and their clients, and couldn't spare the attention necessary to reanchor or even prevent the constant and irritating collisions.

As I pushed the French vessel off the Dive Cat with a long pole, the biggest of the great whites made a dummy run at our bait, rose blind and gaping, then engulfed the entire seal's head in its mouth. Low pulled the shark to the transom of the boat—it was a fifteen-footer—and Richard, the leptin collector, leaned over the transom and tried to plunge his syringe into the powerful, thrashing beast, which was more than a little tricky. He missed twice. The French boat thudded into the Dive Cat as the shark at our transom boomed against the boat, threw up a great waterspout of spray, then caromed off the nearby cage, bouncing Louise back and forth against the chicken wire before it turned and dove slowly toward the French cameraman, whose video housing was snowy white, and very prominent against the blue-gray sea.

Then something remarkable happened. Marks, the safety diver, pulled the black-and-white painted board from under his chest and flashed it at the shark, rather in the way horror film actors hold up crosses to vampires. Did the shark apprehend the board as a killer whale in the far distance? Did it calculate its chances against a mammal that can weigh in excess of five tons, and that hunts in packs? I don't know, but the great white shark did not just turn away from the three-foot-long board. It veered off in several sharp thrusts, the fastest I'd seen a great white shark move in over twenty hours of observation.

Louise crawled out of the cage, blue-lipped and shivering, shaking uncontrollably as she tried to get a topside shot of another shark taking our bait, which it shook about for a time. Little bits and pieces of what used to be a seal floated to the surface. I pushed boats off the Dive Cat while Dyer Island seagulls swooped to the surface of the sea and picked at the floating leftovers. This seemed less than gallant, a way of profiting from death and tragedy. I told Louise that I thought of these particular seagulls as "lawyer birds."

She was thoughtful for a moment.

"We do that too," Louise said.

"What?"

"Journalists. We write about death and tragedy. For money."

And I guess we do. Right now, I thought, I am one of the journalist birds circling over Shark Alley, and we are all shrieking in our shrill and self-righteous manner about choosing the proper operator, about inexperienced sharkers and overloaded boats, about operators with no radios, no links to rescue helicopters, and no trauma training. Soon enough, we'll be swooping down to pick at the various remains of the inevitable disaster, the one no one wants and everyone expects.

With that unlovely thought in mind, and with a certain amount of confidence in my own operator, I dropped back down into the chicken wire, and played another one-sided game of bumper tag with a couple of thousand pounds of white death.

Atlatl Bob's Splendid Lack
of Simple Sanity

Atlatl Bob Perkins called me from the Rabbit Stick encampment, along the banks of the Henry's Fork River, just outside of Rexburg, Idaho. Rabbit Stick is an annual weeklong gathering of people allied with the Society of Primitive Technology.

"How are you, Bob," I said, then winced. When you say how are you to Atlatl Bob Perkins, he invariably says, "I'm at the top of the food chain."

"I'm at the top of the food chain," Bob said.

"The Society of Primitive technology"—I didn't know how to phrase this—"has, uh, telephones at Rabbit Stick?" I asked.

"I'm on a cellular," he explained.

The irony, apparently, was lost on Bob, who, in fact, has his own web site (atlatl.com).

"So," Bob said, "you coming down or what?"

The Rabbit Stick encampment is about a four-hour drive from my house.

"I'll be there."

"We still going to do Australia?"

Bob and I have been talking about going to Australia together for the past decade. Aboriginal hunters, in certain areas, still use the weapons Aztecs called atlatls. Bob Perkins is perhaps America's best-known atlatl maker and theoretician. This is not to suggest in any way that he is universally respected. Bob lacks scientific credentials in the field of archaeology, for one thing, and, for another, it is generally felt, not without reason, that my friend is nuts as a bunny.

But, hey, since when has simple sanity been the measure of a scientist or an artist? Bob does what he does because he can do no less.

Here's what happened to the poor guy. He was an engineering student at Montana State University, an institution that forced him to take some humanities courses in order to obtain a degree. Bob decided on archaeology, which he figured for a gut course. It was there he discovered the spear-throwing system called the atlatl.

The device comes in two parts: a thick stick, about two feet long, with a point generally made with the prong of a deer horn, at one end. The second part, the dart, can be six feet or longer. It is generally fletched with feathers, like an arrow. The feathered end of the dart fits into the notch of the stick, which is the atlatl proper. Holding the throwing stick in one hand, an ice-age hunter would notch the dart onto the point and, holding the dart with a thumb and forefinger, hurl the stick overhand, in the manner of a man serving a tennis ball.

The dart can easily be thrown one hundred yards, and is heavy enough to pierce armor, as the Spanish conquistadors discovered in their first encounters with the Aztecs. Ice-age hunters brought down North American imperial mammoths with atlatls. The weapon has been used almost worldwide for over fourteen thousand years. Some Australian aboriginals still hunt with the device, which they call a woomera.

So Bob Perkins, the incipient engineer, wrote a paper on the physical mechanics of the atlatl. It was, he discovered, a system of fiendish ingenuity and not, as might be supposed, a simple spear-throwing harpoon. Quite the contrary. The atlatl was a device that stored energy and released it in carefully timed phases. The throwing stick was flexible, bending backward as the hunter served the dart. Toward the top of the throwing arc, the dart itself humped up, like a hissing cat—storing energy—then bent down as the throwing stick released its own energy. Or something like that.

Bob was awed by such stone-age genius, and was certain that the Paleolithic atlatl maker understood the principles of wave mechanics and propulsive physics. Perkins graduated in engineering and immediately got into the business of atlatl manufacture and sales, an idea whose time had come, and gone, and has now come again. The business is currently thriving.

I purchased my first atlatl from Bob fifteen years ago—it's a collector's item called the Mammoth Hunter—and found that I could throw a heavy dart the length of a football field with the kind of accuracy that would generally allow me to hit the side of a barn. Just the action of throwing the gadget forced me to imagine how Paleolithic man must have hunted. It would be like this:

The various animals, in their multitudes, would probably be found at the edge of the retreating glaciers, where there would be running water and strong katabatic winds to drive off clouds of biting, stinging insects. The streams would be populated by beavers the size of cows, but you'd probably want that giant mammoth, feeding over there in a field of alpine wildflowers. More meat on a mammoth standing fourteen feet at the shoulder.

There might be as many as twenty hunters in your clan group. If I were one, I'd position a line of atlatl tossers one hundred yards or more from the great beast and loft darts at it until one or more hit. Then I'd send in the young hotshots looking to make reputations and have them finish off the wounded and enraged animal.

This process of both building and using stone-age tools is called "experiential archaeology." It forces one to contemplate prehistory in a fairly visceral manner and it is precisely what Rabbit Stick is all about.

The Rabbit Stick gathering was a conglomeration of about 350 people, instructors and students (who paid a $195 fee), all interested in learning various skills now considered useless and time-consuming: tanning buckskin, making watertight jugs from reeds, knapping flint (making stone tools), creating friction fires, turning the remains of dead animals and plants into clothes, finding and preparing edible plants, and, in general, eking out a living in the wilderness. These skills are invaluable to the person who, for whatever reason, finds himself wandering around in the woods completely naked. Rural exhibitionists, for instance.

The encampment was set along the river, which was lined with aspen and cottonwoods just turning gold in the early autumn weather. There were dozens of tepees set up and people wandered about, some of them dressed in buckskin and other homemade duds. The morning I arrived, a school bus from nearby Rexburg disgorged a phalanx of orderly preteens who strolled among the groups of people sitting in the sun weaving blankets and making soap. I followed them about. Steve Watts, president of the Society of Primitive Technology, a calm, bearded man, told the students that human beings, and their predecessors, have been on Earth for over a million years and that for 99 percent of that time, they lived as hunter-gatherers. "I don't care what race you are, or where you come from," Watts said, "you are standing here today because your ancient ancestors were successful hunter-gatherers." Today, he said, there is no reason to tan a hide in order to make a shirt. The urge to do so, he thought, comes from somewhere else, somewhere deeper inside the human soul.

I peeled off from the kids and met some of the instructors. Almost every one of them has a nickname: Dogface George, who runs dogsleds; and Abo Boy, who makes containers and atlatl darts from river cane; and Roadkill, whose specialty eluded me. I asked around for Atlatl Bob.

"You mean the big, Neanderthal-looking guy?" someone asked. "He's sitting over there." Bob's thinning hair was longer than I recalled and hung down over his shoulders. He was wearing a buckskin poncho, along with some kind of strange woven skirt. Since he was barefoot, I couldn't help but notice that every one of his toenails was painted a different garish color.

Several students were sitting around a washtub working on their atlatls. The tub contained buffalo tendons soaking in water. The buffalo had been donated from a private ranch, and the tendons, taken from above the loin, could be peeled in such a way that they formed thin strings, which were being used to tie what is called a timing stone to the back of each carefully crafted throwing stick. Like rawhide, the tendons would tighten as they dried, holding the stone tight to the stick. The stone delays flex in the throwing stick in order to store more energy in the dart.

"Hey, Bob," I said. "Where's Buddy?"

"Ahh, you missed it. We ate him last night.

"Top of the food chain, huh?"

"Sadly," Bob said, in a rare moment of introspection.

Buddy has come to Rabbit Stick for years with Bob, and he always sleeps in the same tepee, which makes some people think Bob is strange, in that Buddy is a lamb.

Every spring, Bob buys a new lamb, and the lamb is always named Buddy. Bob stakes Buddy out on a rope in his yard in Manhattan, Montana. Buddy mows and fertilizes the lawn in exchange for food and beer. Buddy drinks beer out of a nippled baby bottle. Occasionally, visiting Bob, we've all sat in the backyard—me, Bob, and Buddy—swilling beer and talking about atlatls and Australia. Bob's theory—not surprising, considering his obsession— is that human beings are differentiated from other animals not by language or laughter, but by our ability to accurately throw stuff. "We're small, we're weak, we're slow: What other advantage do we have against, say, a mammoth?"

"So a major-league pitcher is the acme of human civilization," I suggest.

"Exactly."

"Bahhh," argues Buddy, speaking for the nonhuman world.

Bob, a former marine, can't bring himself to personally slaughter the lamb. It happens this way: one day, when the leaves on the aspen have turned yellow and the grass has stopped growing, Buddy downs as many bottles of beer as he wants. After Buddy passes out, he is taken on a short drive and comes back several days later, wrapped in little white packages of freezer paper.

"You know I became a Mormon," Bob said.

"What? No more beer?"

"Not for a year and a half."

The last day Atlatl Bob drank he was driving south, down Interstate 5, on the way to the Valley of Fire State Park to participate in the world atlatl competition. His van broke down somewhere south of Mesquite, Nevada, which is still over one hundred miles from Las Vegas. It is desolate country, with sage-littered hills rolling out forever, in all directions.

Bob, of course, had Buddy with him in the disabled van. Now, the sad fact is this: no rational driver is going to pick up a big, Neanderthal-looking hippie guy leading a lamb on a leash. Hitchhiking was out of the question. But there was a dirt road into the rolling hills which must have been a ranch access. Bob figured he could walk to the ranch and call a tow truck. He began moving west, and the rising sun cast shadows before him: there on the ground was a long, pastel-pink silhouette that was Bob, and a shorter one that was Buddy. They walked for half an hour. Buddy gamboled out ahead. He leapt and ran and circled Bob and then, about a mile and a half from the road, Buddy decided he was done for the day.

So Atlatl Bob picked up his lamb and put him over his shoulders. Carried him back to the van on the interstate, walking directly into the sun, and into, what was for Bob, a new day.

He'd been considering joining the Mormon Church.

A few years previous, he'd been driving down the same road, going to the same event, and stopped at the casino hotel in Mesquite, where he gambled for a time while his girlfriend chose to sleep in the room. When he came up, she'd made it clear that she wasn't interested in anything that Bob might have in mind. Not entirely happy about this turn of events, Bob had slunk off to the bathroom and read the *Book of Mormon,* which he had found in the drawer of the bedroom table. A lot of it had made good sense to Bob Perkins.

So there he was, out in the cool of the morning desert, carrying Buddy back to the van, thinking about Mormonism and reflecting that, with Buddy over his shoulders, he must look a little bit like the depiction of Jesus he'd seen a lot. Christ carrying the lost lamb back to the fold.

In the midst of this divine perception, Bob felt a spreading warmth flowing down over his shoulders. It felt like Revelation until he realized that Buddy had pissed on him. I wonder, Bob thought, if this ever happened to Jesus?

And then another, much stranger, and more life-altering thought occurred to Atlatl Bob Perkins.

He thought: I believe I ought to stop drinking and become a Mormon.

The last full day of Rabbit Stick featured various events on the "weapons range." Bob and a dozen others tossed atlatls at a paper target on stacked hay bales from distances of fifteen and twenty meters. Bob scored the only direct bull's-eye, but lacked winning consistency. "At least I didn't embarrass myself," said the Neanderthal Mormon with painted toenails.

Later, we all stood around tossing rabbit sticks at fuzzy toy bunnies of the type carried about by toddlers around Easter. A rabbit stick looks a bit like a boomerang elongated on one end, and American Indians used them as throwing sticks in order to brain bunnies and other small game. The stick is thrown underhand, in the way you'd skip stones across water, and it spins low over the ground like a horizontal airplane prop. At twenty meters, most of us proved that we'd have made excellent Paleolithic conservationists. The toy bunnies sat before us, motionless and mocking. After several dozen attempts, one fellow actually hit the largest of the toys and literally knocked the stuffing out of it. We whooped and howled out of that portion of our souls that still resided in the stone age.

On our way back to the campsite, I asked Bob about his toenails.

"Oh, some women staked me out on the ground and painted them," he said.

"Women?"

"They were from Canada," Bob explained.

Atlatl Bob is a star at Rabbit Stick and women, inexplicably in my view, seem to find him irresistible. As we strolled through camp, Bob talked about a type of atlatl that cut through the air in such a way that the act of throwing and the flight of the dart were very nearly silent, and so would not startle grazing animals. "It's stone-age stealth technology," Bob said. He was very excited about it.

I considered the terrifying prospect of Australia. I'd have to sit next to Atlatl Bob for a fifteen-hour flight, another four-hour flight, and a six-hour drive. The payoff was that, in the end, we'd meet someone Bob had studied and admired all his adult life. It would be as if an art historian was offered an opportunity to meet Michelangelo.

I saw, in my mind's eye, that artist's image of God and Man, reaching out to touch one another, as on the ceiling of the Sistine Chapel, except in my vision, God was an Australian aboriginal and Man was a big, Neanderthal-looking hippie guy, an ex-Marine and teetotaling Mormon whose toenails were painted all sorts of different colors.

I decided that, like Atlatl Bob Perkins, I shouldn't ever let simple sanity stand in my way.

Stutter

Grant Thompson, the head honcho at Tofino Expeditions, a kayaking outfitter in Seattle, sa-sa-sa-sa . . . stutters. We were paddling together in the Queen Charlotte Islands, about fifty miles off the coast of northern Canada, and had set up our camp for the night. I went for a solitary walk in the thick, temperate-zone rain forest, and—duh—fell off a cliff about fifteen feet high. Landed on my head. Grant bandaged up the worst of my wounds and called in a medical evacuation seaplane on his emergency radio. Because the connection was scratchy and intermittent, it was necessary to state our location quickly and without delay.

He was absolutely flawless.

I thought about this. As a young man, he once told me, he'd "used" his verbal hitch when talking to young women, because it made him seem su-su-su . . . sensitive, and hence da-da-da . . . desirable. And now, as a kayak guide, driving a van full of boats into Mexico, he allowed himself to stutter so helplessly when dealing with Mexican customs officials that the officers just gave up and waved him through the border with only a minimum of hassle.

"So," I said after Grant finished the call, "you don't stutter at all in an emergency."

"Yeah," he said, "but that's ba-ba-ba-"

"Between you and me," I suggested.

"Easy for you to say," Grant said, without the hint of a stutter.

Fully Unprepared

Televised baseball. October play-offs. Someone hits the ball and there it goes out into center field, caroming off walls and various players before rocketing toward home, where two men in different-colored uniforms collide in a cloud of dust, and the ball comes whipping out of the flying debris and whirls around the infield so that it seems as if I'm watching a kind of giant human animated pinball machine.

For someone mainlining morphine, baseball proceeds at an exceedingly expeditious pace.

Immediately, and without preamble, something else indescribably complex was happening on television and it had to do with lizards and frogs and beer. A nurse, I noticed, was standing by the side of my hospital bed.

"How are we feeling this morning?" she asked.

"We're a little," I glanced up at the ceiling, looking for a suitable word, "fuzzy." I was not capable of saying: "We're intensely apprehensive less than twenty-four hours after our back surgery because our career, such as it is, will be over if, in fact, it turns out that we can't goddamn get up and walk."

"The physical therapist will be here soon," the nurse said. She promised that I'd be standing up within the hour. Standing straight and taking my first baby steps. The nurse had ginger-red hair, and was beautiful.

I always liked looking at women with red hair. Even married one once, a long time ago, when I could walk. Didn't last long, that marriage. She liked the idea of writers, if not my own peculiar manifestation of the ideal. I wasn't what you'd call a literary writer anyway; I was a travel writer, specializing, I suppose, in remote journeys and rough accommodations. Tropical forests. Bugs and butter worms. Eighty-pound backpacks. Glaciers. I was gone a lot.

She, on the other hand, had a degree in comparative literature and admired the works of sedentary French men, like Marcel Proust, who only needed the aroma of fresh-baked pastries as inspiration to scribble up mountainous reams of dense, evocative literature. Guy never went anywhere.

So: Proust. Wake up and smell the madeleines. Didn't matter if you couldn't walk. Not really. Didn't mean your career was over. Just one phase of it. One could always write *Remembrance of Things Past.*

The major problem seemed to be that there was a narrowing, a stenosis, in my lower spine, and this, so the doctors told me, is often the result of injury—a traumatic fall, for instance. Bone spurs are sometimes formed as the spine attempts to rebuild and strengthen itself. These knobby irregularities can touch and irritate the very nerves the spinal column exists to protect. Bone-strummed nerves twitch and twang in a merry galvanic polka. They trace their path through the body in a more or less constant flow of low-voltage currents that throb or sizzle or explode along their length like bolts of lightning.

In my case, the nerve that sputtered and spit fire ran down my left leg, all the way to certain toes. It was possible to relieve the pain by bending forward at the waist, while I supported myself with a walking stick. The staff I used was hand-carved and highly polished. People who hadn't seen me for a while always commented on it. "Beautiful stick," they said. That way they didn't have to say what was obvious on the face of it: that I appeared to be in substantial pain and that, even with the stick, I couldn't walk more than a few steps at a time.

"Have you injured your spine recently?" one doctor asked.

"Not recently, no."

.   .   .

Falls are almost always occasions of profound and uninvited contemplation. A slip on the ice, a quick pratfall off a child's toy, and here we go again. There's instability, disbelief, denial, a sudden sense of powers beyond human control, a short, helpless wait followed, *bang*, by impact.

One lies still, waiting for the pain. "Did I do it this time? Am I really hurt? Which parts still work?"

The bad one was in the Queen Charlotte Islands, fifty miles off the coast of northwestern Canada. Every time I look in the mirror, I see that fall. It is written across my forehead in a pair of scars three and four inches long.

The Queen Charlottes are covered in a temperate-zone rain forest that must have been connected to the mainland twenty thousand years ago or more, during the various ice ages, when great quantities of the world's water were trapped in vast, advancing glaciers. As the glaciers began to melt, and sea level rose, the Queen Charlottes were divided off from the mainland by a body of water called the Hecate Strait. Certain animals and plants survive there and nowhere else on earth. The islands are Canada's answer to the Galápagos.

My friends and I were kayaking the Queen Charlottes, and no one wanted to explore the interior with me, mainly because we were paddling past elephant seals and killer whales every day. The on-water experience should have fulfilled anyone's wildlife wow quota. But there was an endemic subspecies of black bear on the island I wanted see, and there were orchids and woodpeckers that existed nowhere else on earth.

And so I went for a walk in the dense cedar and spruce forests. I went alone, God help me, bushwhacking off trail, and I didn't see bears or even woodpeckers, though the orchids were plentiful enough and the ground was covered in several inches of soft green moss. The Queen Charlottes must be the moss capital of the earth.

At one point, a mossy cliff face blocked my path back to camp. It was an easy climb of about fifteen feet. I had to dig my hands through about ten inches of the spongy moss to find handholds in the underlying rock. Mostly, I pulled myself up with my arms, while I kicked steps into the moss as mountain climbers kick steps into steep snow slopes.

At the summit of the cliff, there was a small tree, twenty feet high, that would hold my weight if I could get a hand on it. My feet felt secure in the moss. I was standing on some kind of long, thick root set deep in the moss. It ran horizontally for over ten feet. I'd felt it with my hands on the way up, a thick, unseen thing, festooned with tendrils, and about half as big around as my wrist. Standing on it was like balancing on a thick, sagging rope.

I reached for the safety of the tree in a sweeping grab, just as the root I stood upon broke and the bottom dropped out of my world. The tips of my fingers just barely brushed against bark, and I felt myself drop away from the cliff, astonished and empty-handed. And then I was falling—somehow face first—toward the moss below, thinking all the time, "But this is totally unacceptable."

There was sense of plunging, a swan dive into the moss, and my arms were out in front of me to break the fall. My head hit something: a protruding rock. The moss muffled most of the sound, so what I heard was internal, something in my own body, and it sounded like the sharp crack of several twigs being broken at once. I pushed up off the moss, and my hands were covered in blood from the head wound.

I wanted to lie still and assess the nature of my injuries, but I needed to staunch the blood flow—tie a bandanna around my head—and I had to start moving, before my back completely seized up. There was no trail nearby, and I was wearing green and black rain gear under the heavy forest canopy. No one would ever find me here, and I had to move.

The campsite was about two miles to my south, maybe more. The South Island, Moresby, is long and narrow, shaped like a scimitar, with a spine of ridge running down its length. I was about halfway between the ridgetop and the beach. Numerous creeks poured down off the ridge to the ocean, forming deep rocky ravines the nearer they got to the ocean, and it was often necessary to stumble far up the steep, mossy slopes in order to find a narrow crossing I was able to negotiate. It was easier to move uphill bent from the waist, my hands on the moss. To crawl, in other words.

The forest was an obstacle course of downed timber. Sometimes I had to climb over great fallen cedars; sometimes I belly-crawled under them, always moving, never resting. The temptation was to lie still for a time, to rest, but I knew, with overwhelming certainty, that if I stopped, even for a minute, I would not be able to get up again. So I struggled to my feet, and each time I tried to stand erect, there was the abrupt and annoying sound of a human being screaming.

Moving overland, up and down the drainages, was impossible. I allowed the slope of the island to lead me down to the ocean, where there were sandy beaches to walk upon, for a time. The beaches all ended in rocky points, projecting far out into the ocean. I tried climbing the piles of jumbled rock that separated one beach from the other, but decided in the end that I didn't care for all the screaming involved in the effort.

Without pause, or even a great deal of conscious thought, I waded out into the ocean, still wearing my open-topped rubber boots, which immediately filled with water and weighed me down. I felt I needed the boots and didn't want to lose them in case I had to walk again.

And so I swam around the rocky points, despite the 50-degree water. It took five or ten minutes to get out beyond the breakers, which were exploding off rocky headlands. Beyond each point, there was another sandy beach. Once I built a driftwood fire and warmed up. I swam three times.

Meanwhile, my kayaking companions had initiated a search, and they found me toward dusk. I was out at the tip of one of the rocky points, dragging driftwood logs to a central location for what I hoped would be the mother of all signal fires.

Back at the camp, I lay down for a while, then found I couldn't walk, not at all, not without assistance.

My first wife was named Susan, and, toward the end of her life, she couldn't walk at all. She used to say she was five feet twelve inches tall. I think she was five-thirteen, because that is how tall I am and we saw eye to eye. We were together twelve years. Later, after the divorce, a disease she didn't deserve twisted her fingers and wrists; it dissolved the bones of her legs and left her confined to a wheelchair. She wrote poetry and published a small book. When the local paper ran an article about her that she found sentimental, she sent me a copy, with her own fanciful headline: "Crippled woman writes poetry!"

Doctors replaced her ankles, her hips, and each operation was less successful than the last. When I last saw her, she could still lift herself from the chair and even walk a few steps. I held her and her head lay on my chest. She had lost six inches to surgery. The doctors had just told her she had six months to live.

She wouldn't consider assisted suicide. As a poet, she wanted to realize the sheer astonishment of death. It was rumbling toward her, like a big, slow freight train, growing ever larger in her field of vision, and she couldn't keep her eyes off the son of a bitch. "I will be more than I once was or am now," she wrote, "fully unprepared to be dust."

After my last visit I drove back toward home through a town where the president of the United States was giving a speech. There was a massive traffic jam, stop-and-go traffic at noon, cars on either side of me. People glanced in my direction, then shifted their gaze. I was crying, in that helpless fashion in which your forehead contracts as your mouth expands. Here's a guy, I imagined people thought, with an incredibly low tolerance for heavy traffic.

The physical therapist got me up quickly enough, and though the incision hurt, as well as the places where they'd whittled on my spine, the nerve no longer sizzled and popped. I was walking upright for the first time in six months.

"Will I be able to do my work?" I asked the surgeon.

"Should be able to," he said. "If it hurts, don't do it."

The doctor was named John Lonstein, and he is a genius, or, as another surgeon explained, "the guru" of the sort of operation I needed.

"I'm supposed to fly to Chile in two weeks," I said. "It's a thirteen-hour flight."

"It should be no problem."

"There's a glacier. I want to walk up to the face of it."

"Stop if it hurts."

"When can I take off these stockings?" I was wearing a pair of tight white support-hose-type stockings given to surgical patients to prevent embolism.

"Take them off when you can walk a mile," Dr. John Lonstein said.

Three days after the operation, I went to a nearby mall, without my stick. I could walk, at least on an even surface. Hey! I could walk! But the muscles in my legs were atrophied, and I was moving at a slow, shuffling, geriatric pace. Boisterous teenagers, bouncing off one another and laughing, terrified me. I hugged the walls for safety. A mile would take an hour. Maybe two.

The surgeon said all had gone well, that I could return to my accustomed work, and that a little caution now and again would not be out of order. I took one step, one breath. One step, one breath. And now one, two, three, four, five steps in a row. I stood balanced on two legs, gasping as if I'd just run a four-minute mile.

In the past, I'd dreamed of walks like this: some nightmare bogie behind me, gaining on me, and my feet tangled in tall grass, in beds of string. Now I knew what that dream had always been about, and why I dreamed it. I put together another set of five steps, fully unprepared to be dust.

Evilfish

A recent *New York Times* story blasted dolphins right out of the water. "Evidence puts dolphins in new light, as killers," the headline read, with a zinger of a subhead: "Smiling mammals possess unexplained darker side." The story, a long front-page science-section offering, was continued seven pages later, under the subtly refined headline, "Evidence reveals dolphins in a new light, as senseless killers."

Nothing in the article was inaccurate—this was *The New York Times*, after all—and the evidence in question wasn't particularly new, though the prosecutorial zeal was certainly novel. There were three major allegations in the *Times* indictment:

The First Count: Certain bottlenose dolphins often kill their smaller cousins, harbor porpoises, seemingly for fun.

(Some definitions here: The terms "dolphin" and "porpoise" were used interchangeably by scientists and the general public until the late 1950s, probably to avoid confusion with the coldblooded dolphin fish, also called the mahimahi, a member of the mackerel family. These days, when scientists talk about "true dolphins," they are referring to toothed whales, cetaceans, of the family Delphinidae, which contains thirty-six species, ranging from the five-foot-long Hector's dolphin to the majestic, thirty-foot-long orca male. True dolphins have curved dorsal fins, conical teeth, and are often beaked. Porpoises are of the family Phocoenidae: they are mostly smaller than true dolphins, chubbier, have triangular dorsal fins, and generally lack beaks.)

Dolphins and porpoises often occupy the same territory. Off the northeast coast of Scotland, bottlenose dolphins sometimes surround a group of harbor porpoises, single out an individual, and ram it repeatedly, using their beaks to toss the unfortunate creature in the air. The porpoise dies of multiple causes, including skeletal fractures and severe internal injuries. Scientists have observed similar interactions between bottlenose dolphins and harbor porpoises off the Virginia coast. The contest is manifestly unequal. Male bottlenose dolphins can reach a length of thirteen feet and weigh in excess of 1,400 pounds, while harbor porpoises are among the smallest of the cetaceans, averaging about four feet nine inches in length and weighing 130 pounds.

Worse for the reputation of the bottlenose—our pals from the movie *Day of the Dolphin* and the television series *Flipper*—scientists don't believe the two species compete for the same food. The aggression is not territorial but apparently a form of deadly, bullying play.

The Second Count, and more damning still: Observations in both Virginia and Scotland confirm that bottlenose dolphins often kill bottlenose infants in the same way. Infanticide is a common reproductive strategy among mammals, especially in those species, such as bears, lions, and dolphins, in which females are not sexually receptive while rearing young. Female dolphins become sexually attractive to males within days after losing a calf.

The Third Count: Dolphins don't like humans that much and never have. In fact, people who have been in the water with wild dolphins have been bumped, rammed, bitten, and, in one case, even killed by dolphins. The permanent smile on the faces of some species of dolphin is purely anatomical, no more indicative of the animal's state of mind than are the tusks on an elephant. You moron.

I received half a dozen copies of the article by mail, fax, and e-mail from those friends who knew that I was working on an IMAX documentary movie about dolphins (*Dolphins*, Macgillivray-Freeman films) and a companion book (*Dolphins*, National Geographic Books). The scientists among my correspondents—and there were many, all of them consultants on either the book or the movie project—found the article "sensational," and the headlines especially inflammatory. It wasn't that we were unaware of the information in the *Times* piece, or that any such material had been excised from the book. To the contrary, it was all there, mostly in a single boxed article, written by Bernd Würsig, professor of marine mammalogy, director of the Marine Mammal Research Program, and codirector of the Institute of Marine Life Sciences at Texas A&M University. The article was titled "Reality Check."

This material was folded into a larger context, and our error, I now saw, was that we supposed our audience was composed of people who were aware that dolphins are wild animals and fierce predators. The *Times* piece supposed that its readers loved dolphins uncritically, and was designed to shock the mush-minded.

Like my scientific colleagues, I found the headlines incendiary—even irresponsible—but as a journalist, they stuck like a burr in my brain. In fact, as I reviewed my notes, I was besieged by a mind swarm of new and even more disgraceful headlines, many of which would not be suitable for *The New York Times*.

The article in question, for instance, didn't include information about gang rape among bottlenose dolphins, because, while certainly sensational and shocking, the news probably wasn't fit to print. In Monkey Mia, off Western Australia, some bottlenose dolphin herd females in estrus away from the group, where they, the females, are subjected to repeated and apparently unconsensual copulations. The males sometimes band together in what are called coalitions to fight off other bands of male dolphins, bent on the same rape themselves. ("Behind the Smile: Unspeakable Abuse.")

Additionally, dolphins do not mate for life, as is sometimes supposed. The male's contribution to rearing his progeny stops at conception. The paintings one sometimes sees of a happy dolphin family—mom and dad swimming proudly with a new infant—are not entirely accurate. The female's reproductive strategy is to mate often and apparently indiscriminately. Monogamy is seldom if ever practiced, and each of a female's offspring is likely to have been sired by a different male.

In the documentary I was working on, there is a brief and typical mating scene: it consists of a few rapid pelvic thrusts and is over in a matter of seconds. Blink, and you'll miss it. ("The Most Inconsiderate Mammal.")

Nevertheless, dolphins are extremely sexual creatures. Before the orgy, however, they tend to eat like gluttons. Dusky dolphins, off New Zealand, for instance, often herd great schools of fish to the surface, which acts as a wall. They then swirl about the bait fish, concentrating them into a compact ball. The duskies take turns swooping through the terrified fish, snapping up several in a single pass. ("Dolphins Nip Marlins.") After such a meal, the duskies in their hundreds will leap acrobatically, each one erupting out of the water sometimes dozens of times, as if in ecstatic celebration. ("Dolphins Fined for Poor Sportsmanship.") After-dinner socialization consists of flirtations, mock copulations, and repeated bouts of actual sex, often initiated by the females. ("Slutfish Bang for the Halibut.")

Okay, okay. I admit to a certain mush-brained affection for dolphins, even a slight reverence. Stories of relationships between dolphins and humans are as old as the written word, and I am a sucker for them, the more sentimental the better.

Almost 2,500 years ago, the Greek historian Herodotus wrote about a musician named Arion, a lyre player sailing home after a successful concert tour. The ship's crew, music critics all apparently, tell Arion that they are going to take his money and toss him overboard. Arion is granted his dying wish and is allowed to sing one last song. His music summons friendly dolphins, and Arion steps over the side of the boat, only to be carried ashore on the back of one of the big cetaceans. ("Dolphins Steal One from Mariners.")

In the first century A.D., the Roman naturalist Pliny the Elder wrote of a boy who rode a dolphin to school every day across the Bay of Naples. One day, tragically, the boy died. A few weeks later, the dolphin washed up on shore, dead, one is given to understand, of a broken heart. ("Boy, Dolphin in Bizarre Suicide Pact.")

Now, the truth of the matter is, as the *Times* reported, many people who have tried to swim with wild dolphins have been butted and bitten. Well, some people have been bitten by gorillas, and yet others sit in their midst unchallenged and unharmed. It is a matter of etiquette, and the protocols are different for each animal. Dolphins, for instance, find a direct approach threatening, not surprising in a creature that uses head butts to drive off sharks, discipline unruly members of the group, and sometimes kill. Rule One: Never, never, never approach a dolphin broadside and at a right angle. Let the dolphin approach you. Each encounter is taken at an oblique angle. Never chase. Don't touch.

Generally, when the dolphin has had enough of you, it will leave. There are, however, certain signals that suggest maybe you might want to get out of the water right now. Just as you wouldn't approach a dog that is growling and baring its teeth, you want to avoid a dolphin that is clapping its jaws, or that continually approaches at a right angle, or one that assumes a vertical, S-shaped posture.

I have found, in my encounters with wild dolphins, that one or two members of the group approach first, in a kind of sweeping torpedo run. Reconnaissance, probably. Others follow, and they will swirl about, in slow, oblique angles, inviting you to the dance. Now, I'm a former Big Ten swimmer—sprints and butterfly—but in the water with dolphins, I am entirely too slow, and have found that it is best for me to take the lead and let the dolphins follow. I swoop about in great loops, twenty and thirty feet in diameter, and the dolphins swim by my side, close enough to touch, and what I imagine I see in their round black eyes is a kind of gentle pity.

So why are there so many hostile encounters between wild dolphins and humans? The one reported death happened in Brazil, and the details are instructive. In March 1994, a bottlenose dolphin named Tiao began appearing on the beach near São Paulo. Tiao did not seem to be associated with any nearby dolphin group and was obviously attracted to humans. Such animals, often called ambassador dolphins, are rare. No one knows why they prefer to associate with humans rather than their own kind. But the attraction was mutual. According to the BBC "Wildlife Magazine": "At times, Tiao would be surrounded by up to 30 people, climbing on his back, tying things to his flippers, sticking things into his blow-hole, hitting him with sticks, even trying to drag him out of the water to be photographed with the family and kids on the beach." In December, after nine months of this, Tiao rammed one man to death and injured several others. It is said there was drunkenness involved, and that the man who was killed had been trying to shove a stick into the dolphin's blowhole. ("Killer Dolphin Slays High-spirited Baton Twirler.") These days, when Tiao visits the beach-front near São Paulo, people get out of the water and accord him the respect due both ambassadors and wild animals. ("Killer Dolphin Beats Murder Rap.")

In my film project, there is a sequence involving an abused ambassador dolphin in the Caribbean. Jojo, still another bottlenose dolphin, appeared one day near the beaches of the Turks and Caicos Islands. He seemed to be soliciting human companionship, but when people attempted to touch him or swim with him, Jojo became obstreperous. Some people were butted. There were injuries.

Something had to be done. While human swimmers were taught the essentials of dolphin etiquette, a dive instructor named Dean Bernal began swimming with Jojo every day in an effort to convince the dolphin that humans do have some manners. There have been no more human injuries, and Jojo the dolphin has since been named a "national treasure" of the Turks and Caicos.

Still, all is not well. Speedboats, jet skis, and other watercraft from beachfront resorts make swimming dangerous for both humans and dolphins. An eight-year-old girl was cut by a propeller, and Jojo has been hit eight times. Two of the deep propeller cuts were life-threatening. ("Human Merrymakers to Jojo: It's Payback Time, Tuna-Breath.")

The sequences of Dean and Jojo swimming together are easily the most popular among test audiences who have seen a rough cut of the IMAX documentary. They really look like two mammals at play: Dean blows an immense air bubble which expands as it rises, while Jojo follows the bubble to the surface, then scoots back to Dean as if to say, "Do it again, do it again." Or: Here are Dean and Jojo perfectly vertical in the water, with Dean pumping his arms back and forth, as if dancing, and here's Jojo mimicking Dean with his pectoral fins. It is as if each mammal is looking into some strange, shimmering mirror.

In the matter of the mirrored relationship between dolphin and man, a scientist and poet named Loren Eiseley contemplated a world in which humans lived the life of dolphins, which, in the manner of his day, he called porpoises.

> If man had sacrificed his hands for flukes, the moral might run, he would still be a philosopher, but there would have been taken from him the devastating power to wreak his thought upon the body of the world. Instead he would have lived and wandered, like the porpoise, homeless across currents and winds and oceans, intelligent, but forever the lonely and curious observer of unknown wreckage falling through the blue light of eternity.

Eisley thought that "It is worth at least a wistful thought that someday the porpoise may talk to us and we to him. It would break, perhaps, the long loneliness that has made man a frequent terror and abomination even to himself."

This long loneliness, it seems to me, is the foundation of all human science and philosophy. It is why we set up radio telescopes to scan the stars for evidence of life on other planets and why we want, so desperately, to communicate with the dolphin. We imagine that the dolphin is peaceful, loving, joyous, and wise because these virtues are the sum of our yearning. But dolphins are neither wise nor cruel. Not in the human sense. They are wild and free, and the lesson we might learn from them cannot be encompassed in any presently known language.

Given this, the desolation of our singular awareness, the most depressing headline I can conceive of might read: "Dolphins: Only Human, Fully Comprehensible."

The World's Most
Dangerous Friend

Once, years ago, a friend of mine, John C., took me to a restaurant in New York's Little Italy. When our entrées arrived, he turned to the waiter, pointed to the cannelloni on his plate, and asked, injudiciously, I thought: "What are these? Fried Hoffa fingers?" The waiter colored and said that he would consult with the chef. Presently the chef arrived at the table carrying a large cleaver in what I found to be a menacing manner. He explained that we were not being served fried Hoffa fingers. "Everything here," the chef said, gesturing vividly with the cleaver, "is *fresh* killed." John, in a kind of ecstasy of delight, said: "I think dinner ought to be fraught with danger, don't you?"

Few people, I suspect, would agree with John that veiled death threats are an aid to digestion. In fact, most people think my friend John is a jerk.

I found myself contemplating those cannelloni, jerks in general, and the pleasures of mortal peril before going off to spend several weeks this past summer in a very dangerous place with Robert Young Pelton, the author of the bestselling guidebook *The World's Most Dangerous Places*. Pelton, if I understand him correctly, believes that extreme jeopardy, encountered abroad, can be both life enhancing and numinous. The book, which Pelton insists is required reading at the CIA, is, in fact, exceptionally useful to those whose work carries them to insalubrious and sanguinary places: journalists, missionaries, mercenaries, aid workers, scientists and the like, not to mention kamikaze packbackers and other frenzied travelers. Most guidebooks focus on what is glorious; *Dangerous Places* draws a bead on what is goriest. It is a morbidly compelling compendium of horror, deeply disturbing, and often laugh-out-loud funny, which is to say, it's really good bathroom reading, and pretty good political science to boot.

The book—and Pelton's Discovery Channel TV show of the same name—consists of dispatches from the world's hot spots, along with reams of appalling statistics. There are impertinent interviews with Afghan warlords, conversations with professional assassins or with obscure rebel chieftains, not to mention such helpful advice as this on surviving a drive through a minefield: sit on your flak jacket.

Most of Pelton's readers and viewers, of course, have no intention of ever putting this counsel to use, but simply find it entertaining in a reality-based, *Survivor*-with-more-bite sort of way. Other people, particularly those such as foreign-aid workers and war correspondents who have no choice but to brave danger on a regular basis, are skeptical that Pelton is ever really in a great deal of peril. And if he is, then, said a distinguished friend of mine who has spent the better part of the last five years in war-ravaged Chechnya, "he's a voyeur of violence." So Pelton can't win: he's either a liar or a ghoul. A jerk, in other words.

Now, in my own twenty-five-year journalism career, I've traveled constantly and—always inadvertently—have found myself in a number of urban riots, negotiated with rebel factions for my safety, run from areas where various armies were shooting at one another, and been held at gunpoint more times than I care to remember. If the skeptics were wrong about Pelton's level of exposure—if he acted recklessly in seriously terrifying situations—I'd just make myself scarce and let him deal with the fallout. Jerks die.

Pelton and I conferred by phone and picked Colombia. With a suddenly booming kidnapping business; a bloody, forty-year-long civil war; two major violent leftist guerrilla factions, and even more violent rightist paramilitary groups; a military often accused of human-rights violations, not to mention the world's most active drug trade, this midsized Andean nation spans South America from the Atlantic to the Pacific. It was, hands down, the most dangerous destination we could have chosen in the Western Hemisphere. Our plan, as Pelton described it, was simple: we'd fly down to the capital city of Bogotá, and observe some scheduled military "operations" designed to show outside journalists that the army wasn't really the corrupt band of human-rights abusers everyone thought it was, then shake our hosts, and slip off into the bush to interview some seriously heinous guerrillas, the kind of "driven, resolute" people who, as Pelton describes in his newly released autobiography, *The Adventurist,* "burn fiercely, but briefly." If all went well, he told me, he should get some excellent footage for an upcoming *Dangerous Places* episode, and I'd be back fishing at my Montana summer cabin in under two weeks.

As Pelton worked out the details, I did some research of my own, boring stuff which I always find scintillating when my life is at stake. A few months earlier, I discovered, the U.S. State Department had issued an advisory that said while "U.S. citizens are warned against travel to Colombia at any time," recent events presented "additional opportunities for criminal and terrorist elements to take action against U.S. interests." The risk of being kidnapped in Colombia, the report said, was now "greater than in any other country in the world," with left-wing guerrillas accounting for most of the action and common criminals the rest, although the criminals sometimes made a quick buck wholesaling their richest hostages to the guerrillas.

I also learned that, as homicide was now the leading cause of death for Colombians above the age of ten, an antiviolence children's movement had sprung up. A ten-year-old leader of the movement had recently appeared on television pleading for an end to the violence. Several days later, three men carrying grenades and pistols dragged the fourth grader off his school bus and spirited him away, apparently as a warning to any other loudmouthed children with similar ideas. A few days later, a TV and radio satirist described as the country's most beloved humorist was brutally murdered when gunmen on motorcycles machine-gunned his Jeep Cherokee.

Robert Pelton fired off a number of e-mails to me describing many of these same events. The one he headed "Bring your bank statement" concerned the leftist Colombian Revolutionary Armed Forces, or FARC, the largest leftist insurgency in the Americas. One of their field marshals, a man whose nom de guerre is Mono Jojoy (pronounced *moan-oh ho-hoy*), had announced that FARC would begin kidnapping millionaires, a necessary step, he said, to counter government aggression fueled by its taxes on multinational organizations and "Yankee imperialism."

Research suggested that it was the worst possible time to go to Colombia, and Pelton was greatly encouraged. "Our timing," he e-mailed me, "is impeccable." You never knew what was going to happen, he continued, but there was every indication that our visit to Colombia would be exceedingly eventful. There would be five of us traveling together. "Freak-outs," he warned—facetiously, I think—"will be sold to the highest bidder."

On a flight to Los Angeles, where I would meet Pelton for the first time, I finished thumbing through *The Adventurist*. Pelton has stated that he considers himself "only a passable writer," and some reviewers have savaged him, though other readers, and I am one, have found the book perversely fascinating, despite the occasional purple extravagance in what is otherwise a pretty straightforward work.

There are gloomy descriptions of his bleak childhood on the plains of Alberta. After his parents' divorce, at the age of ten, he was sent to St. John's Cathedral Boys' School in southern Manitoba, the youngest kid in what was then known as "the toughest boys' school in North America." It was a place where kids ran fifty-mile snowshoe marathons, and paddled huge freight canoes on one-thousand-mile journeys that followed the historic routes of French fur trappers. (Twelve boys and one teacher drowned on one such escapade when their canoe capsized in the frigid waters of Lake Timmisskiming.)

Later, when his mother and her new husband decided it was time for Pelton to leave the nest, he bought a $175 Nash Rambler and lived out of the car, picking fruit to survive. He was sixteen. There are also testimonies to the lessons Pelton picked up while clawing his way to the top of the dog-eat-dog world of setting up audiovisual presentations for corporate conferences. At the pivotal moment when he decides, while standing at his father's snow-swept grave, that he's destined for something more than the AV business, he writes, in one of the most unfortunate passages in the book, that "It was time to live like the wind and die like thunder."

Still, the most dramatic parts of *The Adventurist* are those in which he details his success with his current enterprise, passages made all the more compelling by the fact that they're wholly con-firmable by other sources. In the years since the minor AV tycoon cashed out of slide shows and used the proceeds to buy the old Fielding Guides out of bankruptcy, Pelton has transformed a mori-bund guidebook company into an entire travel and danger-themed conglomerate, selling books, producing the Discovery Channel's highest-rated program, and hawking *World's Most Dangerous Places* hats, T-shirts, coffee mugs, and stickers, all of which are festooned with the logo of a laughing skull—"Mr. DP"—that Pelton designed himself.

I first met Pelton at the Los Angeles airport, about a thirty-minute drive from his house high on the headlands over the Pacific Ocean, where he lived with Linda, his wife of twenty-five years, who told me it was a waste of time worrying about Robert on his trips: he always comes back. Pelton's stunning sixteen-year-old twin daughters were both athletes: one an accomplished horsewoman, the other an avid surfer. He doted on them. He was a big man, six-foot-four, with large hands and feet, and a prominent beak of a nose, all of which, combined with a pair of piercing gray eyes, gave him the look of a slightly goofy eagle. He could, if he wanted, be intimidating, which is how I imagine lines such as "die like thun-der" got by any number of editors. ("I'm not going to tell him. *You* tell him.")

He doesn't always escape unscathed in all situations, however. I had just seen Pelton admonished by a CNN anchor in an appearance on that station an hour previous. UN personnel had recently been kidnapped in Sierra Leone and the anchor asked: "Is Sierra Leone a dangerous country?"

"Yes," Pelton said, "especially if you're a member of the UN."

"It's not funny," the anchor replied, and indeed it wasn't, though the question itself was moronically laughable, and Pelton, as I was to discover, doesn't suffer fools gladly.

His house had been built in the fifties, a kind of tract home that Pelton and Linda had transformed into a showcase on the sea. Pelton, like me, loved to cook—Italian food was a specialty—and had designed the kitchen himself.

We were going to Colombia tomorrow, which, if you believed the State Department, and I did, was the most dangerous country in the Western Hemisphere. The last time I'd been there, doing work for a multinational corporation, I'd been provided the services of a twenty-four-hour, Uzi-toting bodyguard.

Pelton and I spent our last evening in the States arguing recipes.

Soon enough, we were in Colombia.

Of course, Pelton realized that if we had any hope of experiencing genuine, bloodcurdling terror, we were going to need to break free of the regimented itinerary the army and national police had prepared for us, and to do that, we were going to need to get our hosts to trust us. For the week before we arrived, Pelton's contact in Colombia—Steve Salisbury, a freelance correspondent for *Semana,* the Colombian weekly magazine, as well as several newspapers in the United States—had been getting the ball rolling in this direction. And so on just our first full day in the country, the three of us, plus photographer Rob Howard, and Pelton's cameraman, an ex–special forces operative, Rob Krott, found ourselves inside the wood-paneled office of General Fernando Tapias, who is something like the Colin Powell of Colombia. The general was an articulate, avuncular man who said that the parallels which had been noted between the current situation in Colombia and the one in

Vietnam circa 1962 were all wrong. "People assume U.S. soldiers are involved in these operations," said the general, as Krott filmed the scene with one of Pelton's video cameras. "There are just two hundred U.S. military advisors here, and none engage in operations. Still, whenever the guerrillas lose a battle, they always claim 'it was against American troops.'"

In sum, the general said, the army was fighting a leftist insurgency. The strongest group was FARC, with as many as seventeen thousand fighters. There were two other major leftist groups. At the other extreme were the "illegal self-defense groups," rightist paramilitaries, opponents of the leftists, the strongest of which was called the AUC and headed by a man named Carlos Castaño. The general did not say that the army was often accused of turning a blind eye to massacres (of suspected leftists) committed by the paramilitaries. He did say that since both the Medellín and Cali cartels had been smashed, "narco-guerrillas" had begun taking a large piece of the cocaine and heroin trade, both from peasants who grew the stuff and the dealers who sold it abroad.

The hard reality, the general said, "is that narcotics trafficking supports these outlaw groups. It is no longer about ideology. In the 1980s, when we captured [FARC rebels] they carried books about Marx or Lenin. Now they have account books and spreadsheets."

The general was proud of the fact that numerous opinion polls gave the army a 69 percent approval rate. Only 6 percent supported FARC. As we left, we were given a brochure entitled "Guerrillas and Illegal Self-Defense Groups Guilty of Genocide." It said both rebels and paramilitaries "are systematically assassinating thousands of Colombians, not as a result of their race, religion or political beliefs, but in order to control the regions where illegal drugs are being harvested . . . to control a business that has represented over 3.6 billion dollars over the past eight years."

The brochure listed the names of 910 civilians killed by guerrillas in 1999, with 40.2 percent of the deaths attributed to FARC. Paramilitary groups had killed 743. The lists were horrifying, as were ghastly, full-color photos of members of the army who had been tortured and killed. FARC guerrillas, for instance, had captured and decapitated two soldiers, brothers as it turned out. Their heads were boxed up and sent to their mother. The severed heads were pictured right there on page three, followed by photos of dead men with their eyes gouged out or their skulls crushed.

One soldier—this photo has disturbed my sleep ever since—had had his face sliced off. "These are the guys," Pelton said, referring to the face-slicers, "we really ought to be talking to."

But first we had to let the national police fly us up to the northern town of Cúcuta and watch them blow the shit out of some coca leaves.

Since the guerrillas and paramilitaries supported themselves with "taxing" the drug trade, the government had been devoting more and more resources to obliterating coca bushes, drug labs, and harvesting sheds. Cúcuta was at the center of one of the main areas for these efforts. Just weeks before, fifty-one people had been massacred in the two towns directly to the north and west, apparently by paramilitaries and/or rebels trying to eliminate competition for their own growers and distributors, and Cúcuta itself had been the site of frequent bombings.

Our escort, Captain Fernando Buitrago of the police, had secured us rooms in a hotel chosen primarily for its proximity to the local police station. "Do not open your door to anyone," he instructed as we checked in. "Call me if someone knocks. I can tell, my friends, you are not safe here." I glanced over and saw Pelton was filling out Rob Howard's registration card.

Name: Howard the Duck
Occupation: Rich American
Reason for visit: Drug Bust

The next day we were dropped by helicopter, along with thirty other journalists, on a hillside about thirty minutes away. Down below, waist-high coca bushes stretched to the horizon. There was also a little three-walled shack with a thatched roof, some plastic bags, a bin full of silver-white coca leaves, and a few barrels of gasoline. Presently, a plane flew over, there was a loud explosion, and the drug lab exploded in picturesque billows of black flame.

Pelton was filming all this with a digital camera about the size of a box of Cracker Jacks.

"Good stuff?" I asked.

"Dog-and-pony show," he muttered.

The next day the army flew us down to Putumayo, the largest coca-growing area on earth. We were ushered into a prefabricated, tentlike building surrounded by razor wire and sandbags (Pelton began referring to it as "the circus tent"), where a Major Muriel laid out the situation for us in an interminable Power Point presentation, complete with charts, maps, graphs, and many, many words on the army's commitment to human rights. Muriel made a big point of telling us that the country's rivers had become "ribbons of commerce in drugs and arms," at which time we were led to a large pavilion overlooking one of the rivers. A young soldier stood at a lectern, reading from a script. "A narcotics lab is located across the river," he announced, and a helicopter swept out of the sky, strafing some trees on the far bank, while, on the pavilion's sound system, Kool and the Gang implored listeners to "move your feet to the rhythm of the beat." Two open boats containing a dozen soldiers each came roaring out of the fog and blasted the same broken trees with 50-caliber shells. The boats landed, soldiers poured into the forest, there were the sounds of light-arms fire, and then silence, except for the disco.

"The drug lab is neutralized," the young soldier announced, and then the army flew us back to Bogotá.

I knew, of course, that the whole thing had been one giant publicity stunt. But, to be honest, I was also feeling relieved that I'd survived another day with my face still attached to my skull. We'd been in Colombia for almost a week and all we'd done was interview some generals and attend "media events." Crap you see on television every day.

Pelton apologized for the timid nature of our research so far. In the coming days, he promised, we'd find danger if it killed us.

. . .

The next day, there was another one of those hideous crimes that happen with such appalling frequency in Colombia. In the rural town of Chiquinquira, Mrs. Elvia Cortés, a fifty-three-year-old dairy farmer whose son was a banker, had been fitted with an explosive necklace made from PVC pipe. Eyewitnesses heard Mrs. Cortés yelling, "We've paid and paid and paid." A male voice replied: "You won't pay? We'll see about that." Mrs. Cortés was seen coming out of her house wearing the bomb. Police were called and, along with an army explosives expert, worked for five hours trying to defuse it. The media were there, filming the whole thing: the woman's terror-stricken face, the policeman's caution, his attempts to calm her. No luck. The bomb exploded, killing the woman and the cop. FARC was immediately fingered for the atrocity (though the authorities would later admit that they couldn't be sure about that). At any rate, occurring as it did on the day after Mother's Day, the media began calling it the "mother bomb."

We were among the first people in the country to hear about the mother bomb, because we were at police headquarters in Bogotá listening in on 911 when it happened. The police, finally having tired of Pelton's demands for more "authenticity," were letting us spend the night with them and ride along on the call of our choice. At about ten that night, we rode with detectives who took down a car theft ring. One officer had trouble with a cranky stick shift on his car and I found myself driving it back to the station. The car jackers had been armed, but the cops were fast and efficient and no shots were fired. Pelton asked if I thought the experience was an "adventure."

"Absolutely," I said. "I usually ride in the back of police cars."

Later that night, about 3 A.M., we accompanied police raiding a house where urban militiamen, thought to be affiliated with FARC, were holed up in an apartment in northwestern Bogotá. In no time, we were speeding down unpaved roads into the heart of the barrio and scurrying through a muddy alleyway to a narrow street of two-story poured-concrete houses. One policeman—I couldn't believe this—knocked politely on the door of the suspected stronghold.

Pelton, in one of those little bits of advice to be found scattered throughout *The World's Most Dangerous Places,* had suggested I take a position behind the front wheel of any car parked on the street, where I'd be protected from bullets by the engine block. There were, of course, no cars parked on the street.

But I had a couple police in front of me, a couple behind, and they were going to have to serve as engine blocks. All of us were standing up against the wall, under the balcony of the house, to minimize the chances of anyone getting a clean shot at us. All of us, that is, except for Pelton, who was standing out in a muddy field just across the street, filming the whole thing with his tiny Cracker Jack–box camera.

Suddenly, the door swung open, the police swarmed in and came face-to-face with . . . one rather stout woman, two small children, and a fit-looking young man in his underwear. After some rummaging, the police also unearthed a bunch of unfired .38-caliber bullets and a few military-style backpacks and ski masks, but there was no denying: Pelton and I had been foiled again.

Such was the twisted state of our little waiting-for-guerrillas routine that we now started arguing about who'd been acting more irresponsibly back there. I told Pelton that I thought a field thirty yards from the front window of the house wasn't exactly the best place to stand when you're expecting a firefight. He countered that urban militiamen weren't likely to have rifles—"too conspicuous"—and he was out of pistol range, while the insurgents could have easily dropped a grenade on our heads.

We were still arguing about this two days later, out in the middle of Colombia, on the Magdalena River, the country's longest ribbon of illegal commerce. The army—along with the navy and marines—had finally caved in to Pelton's badgering, so now we were in a gunboat of the sort we'd seen in Putumayo, with Pelton and me outfitted in helmets and heavy flack jackets.

A small ferry carrying dozens of passengers hailed us urgently from a distance. The passengers shouted that a column of guerrillas was stationed on the east side of the river—they were only minutes away. All the passengers pointed in the same direction: *That way, guerrillas . . .*

Shells were jacked into the .50-caliber guns, and we coasted slowly—agonizingly slowly, in my opinion—along the east bank of the river, where grasses grew higher than a man's head.

"They're there," an officer assured me. "They see us. They won't shoot because they know they're outgunned. We're trying to draw their fire."

Great. So now Pelton had the army in on our perverse little game too. Back and forth we puttered in front of the shore. The soldiers were practically jumping up and down on the deck, yelling, "Shoot us! Shoot us!" And—nothing. Not so much as a hurled coconut.

That night over a drink in the hotel bar, as a large-screen TV replayed the terrible saga of the mother bomb for about the seven hundredth time, I finally had a chance to ask Pelton what he got out of continually putting himself in these situations.

"Look," he said, between sips of aguardiente, the licoriceish-flavored drink he favored in South America. "I know some people think a travel guide to war zones is pathetic. Big-time journalists, for instance, assume that 'little people' should not be attempting their great feats. It pisses them off, because the democratization of information and experience just might contradict the drivel they write from the hotel bar. Journalists," he said, referring to me and my colleagues, "are mostly pompous pussies."

How did this guy get to be such a jerk?

He had, I knew, essentially been abandoned by his mother at "the toughest boys' school in North America." She hadn't left a forwarding address when she dropped him off.

"My mother," Pelton said, "had her own problems." He didn't believe in whining about the past.

The school, which had been closed after the mass drowning on Lake Timmisskiming, was another story. "I don't know anyone I went to school with who does what I do. That kind of experience affects different people in different ways. I think that will be my next book. I'll go around and talk with my old classmates, see what happened to them. I want to call it *The Breaking*."

"Sounds like a project that requires some sensitivity," I said.

"Hey," Pelton said, "I got sensitivity up the wazoo."

And indeed he did. "I can go out and do what I do because of my family," Pelton said. "I'm proud that I've been married for twenty-five years and I'm especially proud of my daughters. That's where I'm grounded."

We ordered another round and discussed *The World's Most Dangerous Places.* "Look," he said, "I try to do an intelligent book for intelligent readers. You've got a guidebook on Colombia with you, right? Now you're here. Does it say anything about murder, kidnapping, war?"

"It's a little irresponsible in that way," I said.

"Exactly." Pelton sipped his drink. "My book isn't about seeking danger. It's about finding safety in dangerous situations."

We ordered another round and talked about writing. "The publishers didn't want the last book I suggested," he said. "It was going to answer all the big questions. You know, like: 'Why is there poverty?'"

"You know?" I asked.

"That's what the publishers said."

"I'm guessing they found the whole idea just a bit, oh, arrogant."

"Yeah. The imbecilic little shit suckers."

He paused to drain his glass. Up on the TV, the announcer had turned to the question of who was really responsible for the mother bomb. Was it the FARC guerrillas, as the government prosecutors still suspected, or some other party just intent on sabotaging the peace process and making FARC look bad? Despite the rebels' adamant protestations to the contrary, opinion seemed to be swinging back toward the former. "What do you say," asked Pelton, "why don't we go down to FARC-land? We can ask Mono Jojoy and the boys if they really are mama bombers."

Which, I thought, is what any really good journalist would do.

Photographer Rob "the Duck" Howard had left for an assignment in Egypt, and Rob Krott had flown to Cuba for his own wedding. So that left just me, Steve Salisbury, and Robert Pelton as the only gringos on the commercial flight to FARC-land.

San Vicente de Caguán is the capital of the region, about the size of Switzerland, which had recently been awarded to the rebels by the government as a peace gesture. It turned out to be a cattle-raising town where the inhabitants rode around on horses and wore cowboy hats. As we stepped off the plane, we met Lelo, a forty-two-year-old cabdriver who said he'd known the rebels for thirty-five years. Lelo found us a hotel that looked a lot like the cell block at the Bogotá police station, then led us over to the FARC office on the main square. Young, camouflage-wearing rebels, some of them in their midteens, sat on metal folding chairs out front drinking Cokes. All had assault rifles, machetes, and the odd grenade or two.

One of the FARC youngsters took us inside and knocked on a door plastered with a poster that depicted an American flag being flushed down a toilet. The woman who answered, a rather sour information officer named Nora, explained that interviews with Mono Jojoy or any other rebel leaders were out of the question without official "permission." We thanked her for her trouble and headed back out to the square to regroup. After a fair bit of Pelton prodding, Lelo said he could drive us to the rebel headquarters on our own.

Twenty miles down a gravel road, we pulled up to a neat complex of newly constructed buildings. "This is the rebel camp?" Pelton asked. Lelo explained that the Village of New Colombia, also called Los Posos, had been built for FARC by the government in another extravagant peace gesture. Peace talks were held in the buildings set down the hill. In the main complex, we saw FARC members sitting at banks of computers, answering e-mails.

The next day, after a quiet night at Cell Block Hotel, we were back at the rebel camp attending a public forum where concerned citizens—businesspeople, academics, students—could voice their concerns to the guerrillas' "Thematic Committee." A young man from the private-tourism sector was proposing a "tourist-friendly zone" where no one would be kidnapped and massacres would be frowned upon. The Thematic Committee took notes on the idea. Presently, a new blue Toyota Land Cruiser pulled up. Mono Jojoy swaggered into the forum and was immediately mobbed for autographs. But the stout, light-skinned revolutionary zeroed in on Pelton, who was wearing his usual vaguely military outfit of jungle pants, boots, and light green T-shirt. "You are CIA," Mono said. "You have a gun in those packs around your waist."

"I have cameras and batteries," Pelton answered. "Are you going to kidnap us?"

Mono referred us to his provision that only millionaires would be kidnapped, and then he was swallowed up by the mob like a rock star at a concert.

A FARC public relations woman named Sandra asked if we wanted to meet some FARC women. She said she knew the media always liked to take pictures of FARC women, armed and in uniform. Many of the prettiest ones were in an outdoor camp, and were said to be bodyguards for leaders like Mono Jojoy. Some of the women we met there were as young as fifteen, poor farm girls whose main attraction to the rebel effort, Sandra admitted, was the promise of regular meals. "Yes, I have killed in war," said a twenty-six-year-old insurgent named Lucero. "I take no pleasure in it. The army is filled with poor people. They are just like us."

"Do you marry?" Pelton asked.

"It is not permitted."

Lucero was, in fact, quite beautiful, especially to anyone who might have a fetish for women in uniform.

In fact, it seemed Robert was one of those people. So much for being grounded by his family. We had gathered several young women about us in the bodyguards' camp, and Robert kept probing relentlessly about sex. We learned: it was not permitted to have a family—women were given a contraceptive shot once a month; and while it was not permitted to marry, a woman could have a companion, a *socio,* if she obtained the proper permission. When your *socio* was on the front, fighting, it was okay to have sex with someone else, given permission. Jealousy was not tolerated.

Two young FARC girls in full battle gear said they'd like to sing a revolutionary song for us but first they had to get permission.

"Permission?" Robert asked, amazed. "Permission? To sing a revolutionary song?" He paused until the women were gone, then said: "These are not my favorite rebels." They had to get permission to burn fiercely but briefly. Or even get laid.

Later that night, back in San Vicente, we were at a café drinking coffee. Lucero was at the next table, sitting with a young civilian family, and she squatted down to play jacks with their little girl, the assault rifle slung expertly over her back. We watched the guerrilla and child play for some time, and a great weight of sadness descended on me. I didn't know why. Pelton expressed the idea that had been clattering around unformed in my mind.

"There," he said, "is a woman who wants a baby." And it occurred to me that Pelton's questions about the sex life of FARC women hadn't been salacious but intensely personal. The way he looked at and talked about Lucero now was the same way he'd looked and sounded when he'd talked about his own daughters.

"These girls get passed around," he leaned over and whispered. "They're sex slaves." I could almost see the sex-slaves segment on Pelton's next show, but, for some reason, it no longer seemed so cheap and exploitative. FARC-ettes were part of every story ever written on the guerrillas—the leftist version of staged helicopter strikes on nonexistent drug labs. So how come no one had ever asked them what their lives were like, these media-icon armed cuties? Pelton, who thought journalists were pompous pussies, was better than a passable reporter. I admired him his outrage. The guy grows on you.

The next night, we were invited to a rebel party at a nearby farm kept by the rebel leaders as a kind of country retreat. For the occasion, Mono Jojoy, our host, wore a black beret with a gold star "to honor Che Guevara," he said. Pelton told me he thought the beret made Mono look like a pissed-off Frenchman.

"Should we be afraid?" Pelton asked.

"Afraid?" Mono threw down another shot of Absolut, which was being passed around in small plastic glasses. "Ha, ha, ha," he said.

"Ha, ha, ha," we agreed.

"But you don't like gringos," Pelton persisted.

"I like gringos who want to help the people," Mono said. "Gringos who don't help the people . . ." He drifted off into an ominous silence.

We were all sitting on new plastic lawn chairs in front of the old farmhouse about five miles down a dirt road from San Vicente de Caguán. It was getting dark and a rebel named Cristián was sitting across from us, filling the plastic cups. There were, at a guess, a dozen heavily armed guerrillas in our party.

"The gringo human-rights workers FARC killed," Steve Salisbury said, "they wanted to help the people, no?" Three nonpolitical Indian activists—protesting oil drilling on indigenous land—had been killed in March 1999. After an international outcry, FARC admitted that it was responsible. It was thought, we were told by guerrilla sources, that the activists were spies.

A thin, intense man with a neatly trimmed beard named Ivan Ramírez made the case that the gringos had been slaughtered "in error. It was like when your planes bombed the Chinese embassy in Yugoslavia," he said. "It was an error."

Ramírez began speaking about tenets of Marxism: how the workers of the world should unite, because the only thing they had to lose was their chains; how religion was the opiate of the people; how an entrenched capitalist oligarchy exploited the poor . . .

"These are old, tired ideas," Pelton said. "They didn't work in Russia. Why do you think they would work here?"

"It will be different here. It will be Colombian Marxism." Ramírez glared at Pelton, and the mood soured as total darkness fell.

"Come on," Pelton said. "Don't pump sunshine up my ass. In what way will it be different?"

Steve Salisbury didn't like the turn things were taking and translated the question as: "You are very eloquent. Where did you study these ideas?"

"At the University of FARC," Ramírez said. He glanced around fiercely, lest anyone challenge these credentials. "The University of FARC," Ramírez said, "makes Harvard look like nursery school."

Mono turned to Pelton. "Don't take any more notes," he said. "This is a party." The vodka was doing its work, and Mono had begun slurring his Spanish. "Tell me," he said. "You are really CIA, no?"

"I am making a film for the Discovery Channel," Pelton said.

"What do you really want?" Mono asked.

"I want to film a real guerrilla camp," Pelton said. "I want to eat guerrilla food. Go on patrol."

"What is the name of your program?" one of the guerrillas asked.

"The World's Most Dangerous Places," Salisbury said, a bit apprehensively, I noticed.

"You think this is a dangerous place?" Ivan asked.

"If you're in the CIA," Pelton said.

"HA!" Mono Jojoy said. "Ha, ha, ha."

And so said we all: "Ha, ha, ha, ha."

Pelton dug into one of his bags and brought out a half dozen large Mr. DP stickers.

"It's an American military symbol," one of the rebels said, handing off the jolly skull to another guerrilla. "American military," the second man agreed.

If there is one thing FARC members hate worse than American imperialists, it's American imperialist military advisors.

"What does this mean?" Mono Jojoy asked in a menacing whisper.

Pelton said Mr. DP was actually a thoughtful kind of fellow and was meaningful to those people who really wanted to know what was happening in places that were being ripped apart by war or rebellion, places where reporting was spotty or inaccurate or colored by political agendas of one sort or another.

The guerrillas behind us were talking loudly about kidnapping and the sum of one million dollars. They knew we all spoke Spanish and they didn't care if we could hear them. They wanted us to hear them.

Pelton, ignoring what seemed to me to be a seriously deteriorating situation, described Mr. DP's philosophical connotations. Mr. DP wasn't political. Mr. DP didn't take sides. Mr. DP wanted to see for himself, talk to the people involved, directly, and if there was danger in that, why, Mr. DP laughed in the face of that danger. Mr. DP was a symbol for all courageous, intelligent, fair-minded people.

Pelton, I thought, was veering off into some serious bullshit, a perception apparently shared by Mono Jojoy, who said: *"En realidad, ustedes son los monos."* ("You guys are the real monkeys.") This was a foreboding statement. *Mono,* in Spanish, means "monkey," but in Colombia, it also refers to a light-skinned person, such as our host. I hoped he meant that our skin was lighter than his. I feared he meant that we—as obvious CIA military-advisor imperialist lackey types—were dumber than monkeys for coming here, to the heart of FARC-land.

In an attempt to defuse the situation, Salisbury began trying to joke with Mono, and at a furious and not entirely intelligible pace.

"Jojoy," Salisbury shouted, and reached out to shake Mono's hand. Pronounced "Ho-hoy," the word was a common greeting in Mono's home province of Santander. "Ho-hoy, ho-hoy," Salisbury said frantically. "In English we have a similar word, 'ahoy.' We say 'ships, ahoy.' Ha, ha, ha! Mono Jojoy, ships ahoy!"

"Shit?" Mono, who apparently knew the English word, now thought Salisbury was likening him to feces.

"No, no!" Salisbury shouted desperately. *"Ships, barcos,* boats, ah-hoy, ah-hoy there, ha, ha, ha." Steve was purposely acting like a drunken doofus. Better to have the rebels laugh in your face than slice it off.

I picked up on the strategy and turned to Cristián, who was pouring the vodka. "No more for Mr. Steve," I said. "Mr. Steve is very drunk. Ha, ha, ha. Look, Mr. Steve doesn't make any sense at all. Ha, ha." Actually, Steve had had one drink.

Mono, ignoring Salisbury, turned to Pelton and said, "We can show you a real guerrilla camp right now. You can eat real guerrilla food."

Someone else added, "You can cook guerrilla food."

"Stay as long as you like," Mono whispered.

"Maybe longer than you like," another voice added.

"We can leave right now," Mono said, a comment that had the weight of a question, like: "Would you care for a blindfold?"

Pelton, Salisbury, and I asked for a moment to confer among ourselves. We walked over to Lelo, who was waiting with the cab.

He suggested we get the hell out of there fast. Salisbury and I agreed. Pelton said, "Yeah, well . . ." and seemed to consider the proposition for a moment. Finally, he said, "Right, I think we ought to go." This was about as sensible a statement as Pelton had made in two weeks, and it was impossible not to like him for it.

For a guy who doesn't consider himself a journalist, Pelton did pretty well. We interviewed the heads of the army and national police; we met or interviewed every major FARC leader. Still, when I talk about my time with him, there are those folks of fine sensibility who remain convinced that he is a jerk. Some find his logo, Mr. DP, especially repellent. Massacres and slaughter and human suffering almost beyond imagination are not funny. Of course, neither is nuclear war and the end of civilization as we know it, but that doesn't mean *Dr. Strangelove* is a bad movie.

Sometimes, in defending Pelton, I point out that he thinks volunteer work is one of the best ways to begin to understand a dangerous place. Organizations that do good work are listed in his book. One could assist refugees searching for their relatives in Rwanda, or clean toilets in the Congo, or help clear land mines in just about half the countries on earth.

But defending Pelton is a thankless task. The guy doesn't really care about what he calls "flatulent political correctness," is congenitally arrogant, and expects his work to speak for itself. I suppose I stand up for Pelton because we spent some intense time together, working reasonably hard at not getting killed or kidnapped, and that is the basis of at least one kind of concentrated friendship. Still, I wouldn't travel with him again on a bet. Robert Pelton really does go to dangerous places and he really does do dangerous things. He's not a fraud and for that reason, I worry about him. The jerk.

Collision Course

Nations rise and nations fall. They crest like waves and collapse against the shores of time. Or so Chief Seattle said, not far from here, almost 150 years ago. His words are a meditation, an admonishment, and I intended to think real hard about them if I survived the immediate encounter with a car ferry that was steaming directly at us as my partner and I paddled our kayaks over the calm gray waters of Puget Sound.

The trip was supposed to be a simple exercise in urban wilderness camping and backyard kayaking. I hailed my partner, Joel Rogers, a writer and photographer whose books I blame for much of my original interest in the sport of sea kayaking, which is to say I read him long before I ever met him.

"Joel? Hey, Joel."

"What?"

"I think we're on a collision course here."

"Collision course?" Joel believed, for some reason, that I didn't know a whole hell of a lot about seamanship.

"With that car ferry off to the right."

"Starboard, you mean."

"Starboard."

Joel didn't even have to look. "She should pass in front of us," he said. " 'Bout half a mile."

"Oh."

For the next few minutes, I listened to the sounds our paddles made as they dipped into the sea. Paddling sometimes feels like a religious chant, a prayer offered to sea. It's tiring and repetitive, so that the mind often turns itself off to the clatter of the merely external. In this trancelike state, it's sometimes possible to feel the soul spiral inward upon itself.

But not when you think a huge car ferry is bearing down on you.

I reviewed the one thing I knew about the geometry of collision courses. If, over time, the angle between two moving vessels doesn't change, then they will eventually collide. I didn't see our angle changing at all, and I mentioned this to Joel, with some urgency.

His mind, it seemed, was somewhere off in the mists—perhaps his soul was spiraling somewhere—and he didn't want to listen to me whining about the merely mundane.

"Don't worry about it," he said.

Our destination for the day was just ahead. Blake Island, a half square mile of ridged woodland and shoreline, is located pretty much smack in the middle of Puget Sound. A Washington state park, Blake is thought to be the birthplace of Chief Sealth, or Seattle. That would have been sometime around 1786. In 1855, the chief signed the Port Elliot Treaty between the U.S. government and tribes of the Puget Sound area. He is remembered and revered today largely for an elegant and nearly heartbreaking speech he gave on that occasion.

There are several versions of the speech floating about, not all of them entirely authentic. In one rendition, for instance, Chief Seattle says: "I have seen thousands of rotting buffaloes on the prairie left by the white man who shot them from a passing train." But he saw no such thing. The historical record is clear: Chief Seattle never traveled west of the Cascade Mountains, almost certainly never saw a buffalo, and died before the railroad reached the West Coast. Which doesn't mean that various white men didn't shoot thousands of buffalo from passing trains.

When I glanced up again, the angle between our kayaks and the car ferry didn't seem to be changing in the least. Here was a Native American technology—the kayak—on a collision course with an enormous internal-combustion engine carrying several hundred smaller internal-combustion engines. If the situation hadn't been so intensely personal, I might have been tempted to think of it as metaphor in action.

The late-afternoon sun began a process of sinking into a cloud bank to the west, and the sky looked bruised. The sea, formerly gray, began taking on the colors of the sky above, so that we were dipping our paddles into areas of welts and wounds. As the light began to fail, red-orange water rapidly faded into puddles of black and blue. On the ferry, lights suddenly glittered on the upper decks. Death looked very festive, rushing toward us over the sea of contusions.

Did we paddle for our lives, cross the ferry's bow, and try to beat it to the island?

Joel didn't think so. He said, "Let's stop paddling here."

Which, as far as I could see, would leave us bobbing helplessly dead in the path of the ferry.

"She'll pass about half a mile ahead," Joel said again.

I glanced behind us. The far-off and snowcapped summit of Mount Rainier, which rose nearly three miles above us, caught the last rays of the setting sun, and seemed to glow, as from fires within. At sea level, however, twilight had already failed into night. Only two miles behind us, the lights of Seattle's waterfront glittered in the cold clear night. It was a real pretty place, I thought, to be crushed by a car ferry.

In my vision:

Chief Seattle, a white guy wearing bell bottoms and Birkenstocks, steps out of his VW van to suggest that "all things are connected." It is in the ancient time—somewhere around 1976, I'd guess—and Joni Mitchell is singing about paving paradise and putting up a parking lot, which, in fact, is precisely what is happening in my hometown: the woods where I played as a boy have been felled to make way for Waukesha, Wisconsin's first Kmart. I'm angry about that. I'm angry about a lot of things. There are oil spills and nuclear plant failures and the world is plunging straight to hell in a basket woven of toxic waste.

"Whatever befalls the earth befalls the sons of the earth," Chief Seattle says.

He's here to provide the big picture, and save the earth. His words are emblazoned on posters, and often uttered as a kind of secular prayer to kick off environmental meetings. He is wise; he admonishes; he exhorts; he provides a perspective out of time. His words are both simple and elegant. They would, I imagine, be even more inspirational if the historical Chief Seattle had actually said them.

In fact, the wall-poster version of Chief Seattle's speech, complete with slaughtered buffalo, was actually written in the late 1970s by a screenwriter named Ted Perry for the movie *Home*, which was produced in the United States by the Southern Baptist Convention. Perry was writing a piece of fiction, and never intended that his Chief Seattle be confused with the real one. The writer, I'm told, has spent quite a bit of time in the past few years trying to set the record straight.

Chief Seattle gave the actual speech in the Squamish dialect, and a translation by a Dr. Smith was published in the *Seattle Sunday Star* on October 29, 1887. In this version, Chief Seattle says: "Every part of this soil is sacred in the estimation of my people. Every hillside, every valley, every plain and grove, has been hallowed by some sad or happy event in days long vanished." He assumed, as many whites and many Indians did in those days, that the tribes of America would vanish by the turn of the century. He said: "But why should I mourn at the untimely fate of my people? Tribe follows tribe, and nation follows nation, like the waves of the sea. It is the order of nature, and regret is useless. Your time of decay may be distant, but it will surely come, for even the White Man whose God walked and talked with him as friend to friend, cannot be exempt from the common destiny. We may be brothers after all. We will see."

"In all the earth," Chief Seattle actually said, "there is no place dedicated to solitude."

Together, Joel Rogers and I have spent some time together looking for places on the earth dedicated to solitude. He is known for his photos of remote wilderness areas: great expanses of sea and shore populated by whales and seals and salmon. The two of us have paddled northern Vancouver Island and the Queen Charlotte Islands, paddled for a week at a time without ever seeing another human being. These days, about twice a year, Joel and I call each other and plan kayaking trips to the far corners of the earth. And then we call each other back and complain about money or time or complications in our respective love lives. We don't get out much anymore.

The last time we spoke on the phone, Joel told me he'd recently completed a 150-mile solo kayak trip from the southern tip of Puget Sound all the way north to the San Juan Islands, near the border with Canada. This isn't a typical Joel Rogers expedition: Puget Sound is the site of three busy seaports as well as dozens of cities and towns. Where the hell could you camp?

"There's places," he told me.

"Near Seattle?"

"Damn near in the city limits."

Joel himself lives in Seattle, on the waterfront, actually, and considers Puget Sound his "home waters." In *Watertrail*, a new book of photographs and recollections about his trip, Joel says that in sixteen years of kayaking, he has "largely ignored" Puget Sound, considering it, I imagine, to be not sufficiently remote. The sound, he says, was "a ferry ride to other adventures, a body of water to travel around rather than a destination to be paddled, weathered, understood."

In recent times, Puget Sound had not been a good destination for extended kayaking because appropriate campsites were separated by dozens of miles, and it was impossible to paddle from one to the other in a single day. In 1990, a group of avid kayakers formed the Washington Water Trails Association (phone: 206-545-9161), an organization committed to providing a marine-trail system in the Puget Sound area. In essence, this meant negotiating for campsites with the Washington State Parks and Recreation Commission and the Department of Natural Resources, which owned most of the appropriate land. The goal was to provide overnight camps every five to eight miles all the way from Olympia to the Canadian border.

In January 1993, the initial twenty campsites—only human- and wind-powered beachable crafts permitted—were opened and the Cascadia Marine Trail system was born.

When Joel and I spoke in late February, he suggested paddling a part of the Cascadia Marine Trail, just off Seattle. Solitude, he'd discovered, was not necessarily located in a province far away.

The thing of it was: Joel was real busy. He only had a couple of days. If I could get from my home in Montana to Seattle by tomorrow afternoon, we could be camping on historic Blake Island, in the middle of Puget Sound, that evening.

Easy. Puget Sound is practically in my backyard, and the nearest ocean to those of us who live on the northeastern slope of the Rocky Mountains. It's a mere 736 miles due west, along Interstate 90, where daytime speed limits are 70, or 75, and, in my state, simply "reasonable and prudent," which means, oh, 85 or 90. Still, it was February and there was some snow in the mountain passes. It took twelve hours, and I got to Seattle late, at four that afternoon, parked my truck, and climbed into one of Joel's waiting kayaks.

Which is why we were still paddling at twilight, and why, I imagined, there was a car ferry bearing down on us. As it got closer, however, the angle began to change slightly, then slightly more. Suddenly, it began to change very rapidly indeed until the ferry passed, as Joel had said it would, about half a mile in front of us.

I listened to the engines thrumming into the distance until I was able again to hear the dip and plash of my own paddle in the sea. The irony wasn't lost on me: I'd driven twelve hours, burning about $75 worth of gasoline, precisely so that I could get away from such annoyances as internal-combustion engines. I resented the ferry about as much as I resented myself, which is to say, regretfully, not very much at all. Mine is an ideology of convenient spirituality.

.   .   .

We had paddled along the heavily wooded western edge of Blake Island, moving south toward a wide swath of sand where a Cascadia Marine Trail sign marked the campsite. We beached the kayaks. To the east, I could see an enormous full moon rising over Seattle.

Blake Island is a popular park, and there are over fifty campsites, complete with moorings for power craft. The Marine Trail camp is set about half a mile away from the other sites, which didn't really matter much because there was no one else staying overnight on the island this February evening. I suppose there was a ranger in residence somewhere, but it was as if we had the island all to ourselves. I stood for a moment under the full moon, and stared at the great city glittering in the distance, only three miles away.

Joel burned us a dinner of bean and cheese burritos on his camp stove then wandered off to shoot some time-lapse photographs of the moon over Seattle. It was going to be a strange picture, I thought, with all the planes zipping over the city from Sea-Tac airport. There'd be dozens of radiating rays in the photo, like significance streaks in a cartoon. The image suggested a perspective that was not immediately forthcoming.

Somewhere in the city, I could hear the faint dithering dweep and howl of a police siren, and then I saw the car's blue and red lights flashing as it raced along a hillside, just parallel to the waterfront. Someone in trouble or hurt. It felt strange to be camping, cooking on a camp stove, and watching a live version of *Cops*.

I listened hard, but lost the sound of the siren in a rustle of leaves stirred by a soft breeze. I was camping damn near in the city limits, on the Cascadia Marine Trail, in the place where Chief Seattle was born, and, on this one particular evening, it was a place dedicated to solitude. A small place, a small thing.

I don't know about our time of decay, or nations cresting and collapsing like waves on the sand. I do know this: That white guy Chief Seattle? The one in bell bottoms who was out to save the world all at once? That was me, crashing up against the shores of time.

The Big Muddy

Mud on the banks of the Missouri River will suck you down to midcalf, pull the boots or sandals off your feet, cling tenaciously to your skin, clothes, canoe, ice chest, and every last thing you own, and then accompany you home and distribute itself around your living quarters and deposit a ring around your tub that appears to wash off and then magically reappears for about a week or seven. The enduring and insistent mire is locally called "gumbo" and is sometimes described as "greasy." After a heavy rain, the mud extends out miles from the banks of the river. Most of the roads to and from the Wild and Scenic section of the Missouri—which, to confuse matters, is located entirely in Montana—are gravel or dirt, and it's a simple matter to drop your car axle deep into the gumbo mud, a situation which can be life-threatening along the Missouri at its most Wild and Scenic, an area that is not within walking distance of anywhere. I know, it's happened to me.

That was when I'd first moved to Montana, over two decades ago. I was scouting the Missouri at the time, wondering about the classic float, a trip that was then pretty high up on my Life List of Stuff to Do. I got home that year, enlightened in the matter of mud, and then things began to happen fairly rapidly, two decades galloped by, and when I next checked the to-do list, there it was, "Missouri River Float," undone and staring me in the face like an accusation. I began to dream about it, that float, and the dreams were all bright and sunny, but I was unable to get to the sparkling green water because I was knee- and ankle-deep in mud.

These greasy frustration dreams were unacceptable. My will was stronger than mud, damn it. And so I was on my way to Fort Benton, Montana, the put-in point for the 149-mile-long Wild and Scenic section of what, in any fair and decent world, would be considered the longest river on the planet. The Missouri rises at Three Forks, Montana, at the confluence of the Jefferson, Madison, and Gallatin rivers, flows vaguely north, then turns east through Montana to North Dakota, before dropping south through South Dakota, Nebraska, and Missouri, finally joining the Mississippi at St. Louis. That's 2,546 miles: longer than the upper and lower Mississippi put together.

If the Mississippi is to be considered a continuation of the Missouri—as I'm arguing it should be—the river is 4,220 miles long: longer than the Nile (4,132 miles), the Amazon (4,000), and the Yangtze (3,915). It's a great big huge world-beater of a river, a ribbon of history and geology and wildlife. Along this free-flowing stretch of the Missouri, mule deer and bighorn sheep frolic all over the adjacent geology, mourning doves mourn unseen in the occasional cottonwood, and rattlesnakes hiss from the banks. There are thirteen Lewis and Clark campsites, some of them set amid cliffs that look like toadstools or ancient Greek temples or castles in Spain or defunct comedians; there are dinosaurs, buried in the mud; there is a violent and often grimly amusing history; and there is, of course, the matter of my own greasy river dreams.

Fort Benton, Montana, was one of the truly tough towns of the old West. At the turn of the last century, it was, according to one newspaper, "a scalp market, the home of cutthroats and horse thieves." Armed robberies, gunfights, and lynchings were common, almost daily occurrences. The U.S. Army saw the town as "a whiskey-trading post for hostile Indians." And indeed, there is a recipe for "Indian whiskey" at the local museum: "To muddy Missouri Water add 1 quart of alcohol, 1 pound of rank black chewing tobacco, 1 handful of red peppers, 1 bottle Jamaica ginger and 1 quart black molasses. Mix well and boil until strength is drawn from the tobacco and peppers." Firewater, indeed.

In 1868, irate citizens of Fort Benton lynched their own town marshal in an effort to make the streets safe for extreme drunkenness. It seems someone had been stealing from passed-out inebriates distributed about in the muddy streets of an evening. Townsfolk complained to the marshal, William Hinson, who said (regrettably, he may have thought later), "What our town needs is a half a dozen hangings."

A vigilante sting operation sent out a decoy drunk one night, and it turned out that Hinson himself was the thief. The next day, the citizens told Marshal Hinson they knew who'd been stealing them blind, told him they were going to hang the fellow in half an hour, and asked him to bring a rope. And thus Hinson's last official act was supplying the noose for his own execution. The hanging site is right next to the present-day Episcopal church, and most citizens, I imagine, would be happy to point it out to you. I don't know. I didn't get to stay in Fort Benton very long because I was late. So was everyone else.

Bobbie Gilmore, a kayak guide, had come from Whitefish, Montana, hauling a trailer full of sea kayaks. My old pal photographer Joel Rogers came from Seattle with two of his friends, David Fox and Scott Wellsandt. Linnea Larson and I were driving in from the other direction, and we all got to Fort Benton at about the same time, which was several hours later than we'd planned. It was a graceful little town of shady neighborhoods and old brick buildings fronting the river. The Grand Union Hotel, once the finest accommodation between Minneapolis and Seattle, had been refurbished and looked inviting, especially since the sunset was eminent.

Wise travelers might have checked into the hotel and gotten a leisurely start in the morning. We packed up the kayaks in a frenzy of sweat and started having fun right away. We paddled forty-five minutes into the night then set up our tents, prepared dinner—I don't recall what, it may have been Joel's quesadillas—and sat around the fire, catching our breath. There were no artificial lights anywhere and the stars were bright enough to cast shadows. It was a time for thoughtful comments on the day that had been.

"You know," I said, settling back with a drink in the starlight, "it takes a real moron to forget his sleeping bag."

"You forgot your sleeping bag?" Joel asked.

"Isn't that what I just said?"

The nights were mild, and the others were fools to carry bulky sleeping bags, or so I told myself, paddling the next day. There were a few pelicans downriver, and they rose as we approached. I love the idea of pelicans eight hundred miles away from any ocean, and, quoting from a bird book, told everyone that the birds had a wingspan of eight feet.

"I don't think that one does," David Fox said.

"Probably a juvenile," I said.

"Those two don't," David continued, "or that one either." When David was last in Montana, he'd testified in a Billings courtroom. He'd been working for CNN, covering the Freeman militia standoff outside of Jordan. The Freemen had "confiscated" his video cameras, probably for being too literal about eyewitness evidence, like the wingspan of certain birds.

We passed through Black Bluff Rapids, which is marked at river mile twenty on the BLM Upper Missouri National Wild and Scenic River map. The water was smooth as a mirror—a muddy mirror—and the rapids didn't actually exist.

In point of fact, most of the "rapids" marked on the map are from the steamboat days of the late 1800s. They are gravel bars, or areas that are tricky to navigate upriver in a steamboat. The Missouri trucks along at an easy average of 3.5 miles an hour and there is no whitewater whatsoever. It is a lazy float, appropriate for beginning canoeists or kayakers or rafters. I suppose you could get in trouble on the river, but you'd have to work at it in a fairly assiduous manner.

Bobbie, apparently attempting to raise the adrenaline quotient, said, "Well, in a couple of days we'll hit Deadman Rapid." She let the name sink in. "Women," she added solemnly, "can go through there." At mile twenty-two, we passed the mouth of the Marias River on our left, where Lewis and Clark spent nearly ten days on their upriver trip: June 2 through 10, 1805. They were stuck there in the throes of a navigational quandary. Their mandate from President Thomas Jefferson was to ascend the Missouri, cross the mountains, and descend the Columbia to the Pacific. At this fork in the river, each stream seemed about the same size. Which was the Missouri? (These days, there is little doubt. The Marias, confined by the Tiber Dam, seventy miles upstream, is now little more than a creek at its confluence with the Missouri.)

Most of the men in the Lewis and Clark party thought the north fork, the Marias, was the Missouri; both Lewis and Clark were skeptical. They measured the width of each stream, explored up the banks of each, and inquired locally, always a wise move for any traveler. Bolstered by what the Indians said, they concluded, correctly, that the south fork was the Missouri, and would take them into the mountains.

The river carried us past the Marias. Bobbie was giving Linnea some paddling advice. I was eavesdropping because I can use all the help I can get. "I tell my clients that a woman's center of gravity is lower, so women are more stable in kayaks than men," Bobbie said. "Women are probably more stable in life altogether."

"You mean," I interjected, in all innocence, "because they got fat butts?"

"Said the moron who forgot his sleeping bag."

The character of the Missouri changes abruptly about forty miles into the float. At first it's just as one might expect: a big, slow-moving river, lazing through meanders in a high plain with mountains shining in the far distance. But at the ferry-crossing town of Virgelle, the river changes direction, sweeping almost 90 degrees from northeast to southeast. The Missouri straightens out and floaters find themselves, for the entire rest of the trip, in a canyon several hundred feet deep. It is a relatively new thing, this canyon. The Missouri used to flow north, toward Hudson Bay, but glaciers grinding down from Canada during the ice age blocked the northward run and formed a dam that turned the river south and east. The Missouri spun about in a rage and shot through soft rock to the south, tearing up the land in a fury of frustration. The rocks were and are soft because this area of Montana was once a vast inland sea. Dinosaurs frolicked on its banks, especially to the east, near the final stretch of what is now the classic Wild and Scenic float. When the sea finally receded, 65 million years ago, it left a legacy of sedimentary rocks—clays, sands, silts: a dried-out sea bottom, essentially—and the Missouri, diverted by glaciers, cut through this soft stone like a hot knife through butter.

Meanwhile, tributary streams flowing into the Missouri from either side formed their own small canyons, which cut into the main channel of the river. It is a strange, crumpled landscape, odd and alien and vaguely disturbing. The land seems not at all as it should be; it looks somehow shattered, broken; and anyone who sees it will know immediately why the area is known as the Missouri Breaks.

Ten miles into the canyon, sandstone parapets rose on the riverbanks, and the vertically striated columns stood out like eroded statues in Egyptian temples. The canyon walls—all battlements and spires, resembling broken teeth—enclosed us as we floated farther downriver, eventually camping for the night near Eagle Creek, at the Lewis and Clark campsite of May 31, 1805. "The hills and river Clifts which passed today exhibit a most romantic appearance," Lewis wrote in his journal that day, almost two centuries ago. "The bluffs of the river rise to the hight of from 2 to 300 feet and in most places nearly perpendicular; they are formed of remarkable white sandstone."

I was reading aloud from the journal now, and what we saw in the dusk directly across the river was the exact sandstone wall described by Lewis. "The water in the course of time in decending . . . had trickled down the soft sand clifts and woarn it into a thousand grotesque figures. . . ."

"Exactly," said Scott Wellsandt.

Lewis, with "the help of a little imagination and an oblique view," saw "eligant ranges of lofty freestone buildings, having the parapets well stocked with statuary." He saw "collumns standing almost entire with their pedestals and capitals." He saw stone "in the form of vast pyramids of conic structure bearing a serees of other pyramids on their tops."

"What do you see?" I asked Scott.

"That one, over there, looks like the skinny Laurel and Hardy guy. Stan Laurel."

We declined the opportunity to make fun of Scott's vision. Not only was he a great big huge powerful guy, he was the best cook on the float. This evening he'd made pad Thai on a camp stove and it was delicious. "Stan Laurel," I said, hoping Scott'd cook for the rest of the trip. "Anyone can see it."

"Did the cops question you about it?" I asked Bobbie late the next day.

We were standing just across the river from our campsite, on top of the cliffs, staring numbly at the remains of a formation that was once a familiar landmark to Indians and fur trappers and steamboat captains. What we saw was a pair of inward-curving arms, each about ten feet high, stretched upward, to the sky, as in supplication. The arms had once held and balanced capstones so that the formation was a graceful natural arch, eleven feet high, a national landmark called the Eye of the Needle.

"We talked to the BLM and the local cops. We were the last people to see it before . . ."

Sometime between May 25 and May 26, 1997, vandals pried the capstones off the top of the arch, then pushed them over the cliff.

"I was guiding a group," Bobbie said. "We were the last people to see it intact. Climbed up here on the Memorial Day weekend. It was rainy and slick and it poured rain all the next few days." The steep climb winds its way up through a narrow chute, and it is necessary to move carefully, three points on rock at all times. Bobbie carries a climbing rope because a sudden rain can turn the chute into a water slide. "The next group to come through reported it down. Some folks think it may have collapsed on its own, but the cops told me they found the marks of a metal bar on the rocks that had been kicked over the cliff."

The FBI was called in, Bobbie and her group submitted their snapshots—the last photographs ever taken of the intact formation—and then the years began to gently drift along, no arrests were ever made, and the remains of the Eye stand sentinel over the river, testament to a certain virulent variety of human disfigurement.

Late that afternoon, we climbed back into the cliffs behind our campsite. The rock walls closed in around us, forming a water-carved, keyhole-shaped passage of the sort found in caves. Several fallen boulders the size of trucks or houses blocked the way, but Bobbie led us scrambling up over them, insisting that she had something to show us. And, indeed, when we topped out, we immediately saw another Eye of the Needle—an arch of about the same size, wind-scoured and smooth as gritty marble. I climbed up to get slightly above this peculiar eye, and when I looked through it, there, below, stretching out for over a mile, was a maze of canyon and tortured rock, perfectly framed: an invitation to commit poetry or philosophy or any number of the higher aesthetic or contemplative crimes. I imagined there were other Eyes, in other drainages, none of them actually on the river, but all probably worth a climb—isolated instances of beauty and in no urgent need of beholders.

We floated through the White Cliffs, past Citadel Rock, a distinctive crag leaning out over the river and, at a guess, about two hundred feet high. The citadel is an igneous intrusion, which is a pleasantly onomatopoetic way of saying that hot magma rose up into the cracks of the White Cliff sandstone in hard, vertical blades called dikes. As the softer sandstone falls away, the dikes remain: towers of odd and idiosyncratic rock.

In 1805, Lewis and Clark took note of this particular rock, and on August 16, 1833, a Swiss artist named Karl Bodmer sketched the most famous depiction of the Citadel. Bodmer was traveling with Prince Maximillian of Wied, a German aristocrat with an interest in indigenous American peoples. He'd hired Bodmer to document the journey. The artist's work was accurate and evocative. His drawings and watercolors underscore, I think, one of the few faults of the Lewis and Clark expedition: their failure to bring along an artist like Bodmer to record their trip.

Somewhat farther down the river is another igneous intrusion, a relatively thin blade of rock standing at right angles to the course of the river. From upriver, we could see—at the summit of that rock—a large roundish hole through which blue sky was visible. This was the Hole in the Wall.

We saw two canoes on the bank, and there were two older gentlemen sitting in lawn chairs and fishing for Missouri River sturgeon where we pulled over to climb up. "Uh, our wives are up there," one of the fishermen said, pointing toward the canyons and gullies that led up to the Hole. He held out a mobile phone. "They said they're stuck."

"Probably not so bad," the other fellow said.

"You might give them a hand on your way up," the first man said in a paroxysm of chivalry.

One of the women was frozen at a tricky down-climb and her friend wouldn't leave her. Bobbie climbed up to their position, deployed the rope, and sent the women back to their husbands, who were talking about sturgeon on the riverbank far below.

The Hole in the Wall is about three hundred feet above the river, standing above a ridge that drops to a sloping grassy hillside. We moved through the grass, wary of snakes. Prairie rattlers, up to six feet long, make their homes along the Missouri. We'd seen no rattlers, but the campsites were full of bull snakes slithering along on their reptilian business. They are bigger than rattlers and essentially harmless to humans. It is a tenant of Montana folk wisdom that when the bull snakes are plentiful, rattlers are scarce. Still, it is disconcerting to nearly step on a seven-foot-long snake. Bulls will hiss, and they can bite, but are not venomous.

As we moved through the grass, Scott hissed, snakelike. Linnea froze with a foot in the air, and we all laughed—ha, ha, ha—about how funny our best chef was today, and nobody snuck up from behind to bean him with a rock.

The view was 320 degrees of palaces and turrets and spires. We could hear the wind whistling and booming through the Hole as we crawled up the backside of the formation, past initials and names and dates carved into the rock. None of them said: "Meriwether Lewis, 1805."

And then we were back on the river, paddling past piles of columned rocks standing alone on the sage-littered hillsides that looked like Greek temples.

"That one," I said, paddling beside Scott, "looks like the Acropolis."

"I see a Buddha," he said.

"You're right," I said, staring at the Acropolis. "Spitting image of the Buddha."

We camped near a place called Steamboat Rock, because it looks like a steamboat, though it is likely Scott saw other images. No one asked him. I climbed a dry drainage and found a big-game trail leading up to the summit of a ridge overlooking a hillside that dropped down to the river. The slope was crowded with closely spaced but individual pillars that looked, to me, like the rows upon rows of terra-cotta soldiers at Xi'an, in China.

Back at camp, as Scott cooked, Joel and I argued a bit about cows. Very occasionally, we saw a few of the animals on a distant hillside. Once we found a dozen standing in the water. Joel is one of those folks who would like to see the federal government deny grazing leases and buy up—or merely confiscate—millions of acres to save the land from the depredations of ranchers. I, on the other hand, live in Montana, know many ranchers, and believe that they are often conscientious stewards of the land.

The BLM manages the Upper Missouri Wild and Scenic River with the stated purpose of ensuring "that the river will retain its essentially wild and pristine nature." The BLM asks floaters to do their part in protecting this vision, which Joel translated as "destroy all cows."

"Actually," Linnea said, "I floated this stretch fifteen years ago, and there were cows everywhere." Now it was a jolt to see just one, even from a distance.

I thought about that while floating the next day. There was no one else on the river at all, and when I blasted out ahead of the others, paddling like a bastard, it was easy to imagine that I was the first person on the river, the first to see this stretch.

There is a bridge over the Missouri where the Judith River empties into it from the south, and a BLM campsite at what is called Judith Landing. It was a weekend and there was a dirt bike competition on a track just up from the river. The bikes roared over various jumps in phalanxes of four and five.

"Nice place," I said to Joel, shouting over the howl of dirt machines. "No cows."

About a half mile down, we lost the sound of the dirt bikes and set up camp on the grassy banks of the river. There weren't a lot of trees, not as many as one would expect, anyway, and that is partially the legacy of steamboats that brought trappers and traders and pioneers up the river for the entire last half of the nineteenth century. A steamboat burned about thirty cords of wood a day, and, in the years between 1860 and 1888, there were four hundred steamboats operating on the Missouri in Montana. Wood was purchased from enterprising businessmen called woodhawks, who, naturally, cut down the most convenient trees available, the cottonwoods on the riverbank. The cottonwoods have not come back in force. They need an occasional flood to propagate properly, and a dam above the Wild and Scenic stretch of the river moderates the yearly flood.

"And even if a few do get a start, there are always cows to trample them and such," Joel said.

"You see any cows?" I asked.

"They used to be here."

"How do you know?"

"Because there're no cottonwoods."

And so it went, bickering on about cows all the next day, until, once again, I paddled out far ahead, then drifted down the river in splendid solitude. The White Cliffs had given way to layers of sand and clay called Claggett Shale, the Judith River Formation, and Bearpaw Shale.

Shale means badlands: those areas of tortured, eroded hills and cliffs unsuitable for ranching or farming. Badlands are seldom inhabited by humans (or cows), which is why they are generally alive with wildlife of almost every description. We saw golden eagles, bald eagles, osprey, mule deer, antelope, foxes.

At our campsite that night, we watched the sun set on some bighorn sheep up in the notch of a ridgeline above. I thought it might be possible to climb up on the notch, but Joel said it couldn't be done.

Which is why, the next day, David Fox, Bobbie Gilmore, and I were laboring up a hillside of crumbling black mud: just about what you'd expect from an old, dried-out seabed. Near the top I found myself in trouble. There was no going down—too crumbly—and the last few moves were pretty much impossible, just as Joel had said. What was I doing up here, anyway? Trying to prove something to Joel about cows?

Bobbie and David were already standing on top, just above me, watching my struggles.

"You know," Bobbie said, "if you got your weight out over your feet, you'd be right up here. You climb like a reptile."

True enough, but I managed to find a handhold and lever myself up over the top. It was a fine view all around, especially directly below, where the bighorn sheep were staring up at us with an air of incredulous curiosity. I waved down at the camp, signaling Joel in a gesture that I hoped expressed the oxymoronic concept of bovine nobility.

The last ten miles of the float were in the Charles M. Russell National Wildlife Refuge, a million acres of native prairies and forests in the groins of the hills, and otherwise all badlands and river bottom. The mud was about as bad as it gets here, and there was no way to stop for lunch anywhere along any bank without sinking into the greasy muck up to the knee. And there was no way to scrape the mud off legs or sandals without simply spreading it around, distributing it more evenly about the body.

So we were filthy when we took out at the Fred Robinson Bridge on Montana Highway 191. We washed Bobbie's kayaks a number of times, but every time they dried, we could still see the same thin skim of Missouri mud on them. Everyone embraced everyone else—spreading more gumbo mud about—and I mentally ticked "Missouri River Float" off the Life List but noticed that, almost immediately, it migrated directly into the "Do Yearly" column. Missouri mud does not want to let you go. It clutches at you across time and space. It lives in dreams, in the heart, and in the soul, and I was still washing little bits of it out of my bathtub three days later.

Professor Cahill's Travel 101

I've been writing about travel for twenty years now. I get interviewed about it a lot, and the articles that result always have excruciating titles, like "A Travel Pro's Advice for Hapless Innocents."

But travel advice, on the whole, is a fairly straightforward affair. It's all pretty obvious: Make sure you have a current passport and a visa, if necessary. Pack half the clothes you think you'll need, and take twice the money. Get the proper shots, carry the appropriate medications, consult your doctor or the Centers for Disease Control. Purify drinking water in cholera-ridden areas. Study up on the festering political and cultural animosities so that you don't do something to create a situation in which already angry or zealous people feel obligated to march on your campsite with pitchforks and torches. That sort of thing.

On guided expeditions, a lot of this is taken care of for you. Of course, there are those who believe that commercial adventure travel lacks any semblance of actual adventure, in that your chances of being killed in the field are substantially diminished in the presence of competent guides. This may be true, but a guided trip is still the best way to learn the ropes and calibrate your own tolerance for peril. You alone get to decide if the trip was an "adventure." That's the rule.

What follows is a personal list of somewhat less-evident rules, which can be used whether you're traveling on your own or on a guided trip. A few are entirely idiosyncratic. Like . . .

Rule 1: Avoid psychotic travel companions. Here's the nightmare: It's two in the morning. You are sitting around the campfire speaking slowly, with exaggerated calm, enunciating each word very, very carefully. You are saying, "Give me the *gun*, Laszlo. Give *me* the gun, Laszlo. *Give* me the gun, Laszlo."

Rule 1, corollary 1: The most carefully chosen travel companions become the most psychotic.

Rule 1, corollary 2: Psychosis is contagious.

Rule 2: Have a quest. The quest is the most significant and consequential of all travel plans. What you really want to do is meet indigenous folks, understand their concerns, find out how things work, make friends. You don't do this in the company of traveling English-speakers. So have a quest, some bit of business that will shove you into the cultural maelstrom. Perhaps you have distant relatives in the country. Look them up. That's your quest. It will force you to use the phone book (people in Iceland, you'll note, are listed by their first rather than last names) and to arrange transportation to an area of the country that is not likely a tourist destination. Perhaps you're interested in trains, or motorcycle clubs, or ecological issues. Find locals who share your passion. You'll make friends.

Rule 3: Exercise ordinary caution. Never, never, never put a marshmallow in your mouth and try to feed it to a bear.

Rule 4: You are the protagonist. There is a variety of travel book currently in vogue. The writer, a man or woman broken by a bad relationship, sets off on a journey designed to heal the soul. By the end of the book, the formerly tortured scribe is figuratively knocking back margaritas in an orgy of cleansing regeneration.

Used to be, we sent mythical or fictional characters on such journeys. Gilgamesh searching for the answer to death; Odysseus on a ten-year voyage of discovery; Dante and Orpheus in hell; Huck Finn on the Mississippi. These days, we tend to be more democratic in our mythology. You get to be the driving force. Make your myth a good one.

Rule 5: Boredom greases the cogs in the machinery of marvels.

In *The Immense Journey,* the anthropologist and naturalist Loren Eiseley says,

> It is a commonplace of all religious thought, even the most primitive, that the man seeking visions and insight must go apart from his fellows and live for a time in the wilderness. If he is of the proper sort, he will return with a message. It may not be a message from the god he set out to seek, but even if he has failed in that particular, he will have had a vision or seen a marvel, and these are always worth listening to and thinking about.

What Eiseley doesn't say is that, on your quest for marvels and insights, you will be bored. Oh, God, will you be bored. The three days waiting for an Indonesian bureaucrat to issue you a travel permit; the rock slide in Costa Rica that caused a twenty-three-hour traffic jam; the five-day wait for the Congo River passenger barge; the eight sweaty hours spent in the transit lounge of the Bujumbura airport, waiting for crews to clean up the wreckage of the last plane that tried to land in Kigali. Boring.

Bring along a big book. This is your chance to finally finish *War and Peace.* And remember—while you're plowing through Andrey's interminable conversations with Karatayev—that boredom is often the price we pay for marvels.

Rule 6: Stop whining. If you're cold and wet, it's a good bet that everyone else in your party is too. Why should they listen to you talk about what they already know? Travel is boring enough as it is.

Rule 6, corollary 1: This can't be stressed strongly enough: No one wants to hear about your last bowel movement.

Rule 7: Read guidebooks. Guidebooks, books on the country, and books by local authors can all help you refine the nature of your quest.

Rule 7, corollary 1: Expect the books to be wrong or out of date.

Rule 8: It ain't about money. There are guidebooks for backpackers and budget travelers that say that in most Third World countries, there's a three-tiered price system. The first price is for stupid, rich outsiders. The second is for citizens who are not local. And the third is for locals. Strive, the books tell you, for the third price. This, they say, will increase your interpersonal skills and tell you much about the country.

Okay, true enough. There are places where you are expected to bargain and sharpies who want to take advantage of you. Unfortunately, too many people who think of themselves as "world travelers" become obsessed with money. It's loathsome to see some young trekker arguing for an hour with an elderly woman over a fifteen-cent charge for an afternoon of washing clothes.

Too often money, and the process of saving money, becomes the entire point of traveling. If the nature of your quest is financial, stay home and get into arbitrage.

Rule 8, corollary 1: Similarly, don't listen to fellow travelers who espouse this philosophy: "Don't spoil the natives" is the way it is often put. Screw these people. Spend what you need to in order to accomplish your quest.

Rule 8, corollary 2: Thinking of your hosts as "natives" who can be "spoiled" dehumanizes people and creates the kind of abyss that is impossible to bridge with friendship.

Rule 9: Don't worry too much about gear. Unless you're going to climb a mountain or scuba-dive on your own, bringing too much of your own equipment can be a problem. Do people live where you're going? Have they lived there for centuries? For a millennium? Maybe they know something about survival in the place where they live. Why spend three days trying to find a machete in Denver when you can buy a better one for a quarter of the price in Honduras?

My own kit is fairly standard: diarrhea medicine, a dry pad to sit on, hot sauce for bland meals, dental floss to use as sewing thread, a Leatherman tool, something to read, and duct tape, which the Bambenjele pygmies of the northern Congo told me represents the high point of my culture.

Rule 10: Don't follow rules. This is probably the most important rule.

Rule 11: Try the local foods. Eat what is put in front of you. They are not making fun of you. The rooster's head floating in the soup really is given to the honored guest. It is impolite not to eat it. If you're a picky eater, stay home.

Rule 11, corollary 1: Take the usual precautions, but expect to get sick anyway.

Rule 11, corollary 2: See Rule 6, corollary 1.

Rule 12: Learn the rudiments of the local language. It's important to be able to say: I'm sorry; excuse me; I didn't know; I'm not from around here; where's the bathroom; thank you; how much is a beer; I beg your pardon; I'll pay for it; call a doctor; call the police; don't call the police.

Rule 12, corollary 1: Intimate relations fuel idiomatic fluency. The colonial Dutch had a saying that holds true to this day: "The best way to learn a language is under the mosquito net."

Rule 13: You are the foreigner, dickweed.

Once, in Costa Rica, I saw an older gentleman in Bermuda shorts and black shoes upbraid a waiter who didn't understand the word "ticket," as used to mean "bill."

"Gimme my ticket."

"Your ticket, sir?"

"Yeah, my ticket. What's wrong with you?"

"I don't understand this word, 'ticket.' "

"How old are you?" the American asked.

"I have twenty-nine years, sir."

"Well, goddamn it," the man said, "you're old enough to know English by now."

This is why people burn flags.

Rule 14: The "natives" have their pride. One thing an American traveler hears quite often is "You Americans have a great nation, and much power, but we [Peruvians, Mongolians, Egyptians, Congolese, Bolivians, Turks] have the great soul." Don't argue with these folks, Miles Davis and Smokey Robinson notwithstanding. Instead, inquire about the nature of the national soul. You could learn something.

Rule 15: Schedule a rest day every now and then. Contrary to what you read, sudden insights seldom happen at the summit of a mountain, at the moment the whale is sighted, or in the face of some overwhelming bit of landscape. You haven't yet assimilated the experience. Look for epiphanies on those days when you're lying on your back, watching the ceiling fan push dust motes through a shaft of light falling through a grimy window. Exhaustion seldom engenders insight.

Rule 16: Don't drink too much in a little basement bar just off a street called Florida in Buenos Aires . . . because you'll find yourself involuntarily surrounded by *coperas,* or what we would call B-girls, and three bartenders will all be opening bottles of "champagne" that you didn't order and that cost $60 apiece, and you'll have to fight your way up the stairs to the exit, throwing money at the bouncers, and the *coperas* will run out into the street and yell *"Maricón"* at you as you stagger away, thinking, "Geez, I thought they liked me."

Rule 17: Don't become involved with your guide. This is often a cause of heartbreak. Worse, there are situations in which the affair works out. Then you end up married to a guide.

Rule 18: Wait until the last possible moment to punch out disagreeable traveling companions. It's best not to punch out traveling companions during the first two-thirds of a trip. The person may possess skills that could come in handy. It's best to swallow insults, listen to complaints, and nod sympathetically at the vivid description of the last bowel movement. Then, at the moment of greatest annoyance, simply recall your resolve to deck this bozo with a sucker punch. Don't do it, just think about it. In practice, you'll find the idea of a physical comeuppance soothing. And by the end of the trip, you may even find you've developed a grudging respect for the person. You may actually have become friends. But let's say it's time for the last good-bye, and you still think the person would benefit from a physical explanation of his various failings. Don't throw that punch. Think instead about how happy you're going to be when you've seen the last of this slime weasel. The punch is a psychological device, a coping mechanism, and it lives only in your mind.

Rule 19: Mold experience into stories as a mnemonic device.

Travel is a chaos of experience, momentarily memorable and dis-tressing in its capacity to flee the mind and disappear without a trace. Guides, professional travelers, mold the clay of experience into stories. All guides believe their stories are unforgettable. Some of them are.

Here's a typical guide story: Two guides, whom we'll call Big Mike and Medium Mike, are in the midst of a long, boring wait in Punta Arenas, Chile. They're waiting for a freighter that will take them to Antarctica. Medium Mike is telling the story. "So the freighter is being loaded and may leave at any time. One of us has to wait for the departure call. We draw straws. I get to wait. It's Sat-urday night. Big Mike goes to the local house of ill repute. He's there all night. Seven o'clock the next morning I get the call. Boat's leaving in two hours. I run down to the place where Big Mike is, but the door is locked. No one answers my knock. I'm getting fran-tic. The windows are high off the sidewalk, so I'm on a cement block, pounding on a window, yelling for them to open up, c'mon, this is important. About this time, a group of nuns walk by on their way to Mass. One of them stops and says, 'Son, couldn't you wait until after church?' "

Rule 19, corollary 1: You don't have to be a guide to tell guide sto-ries.

Rule 19, corollary 2: All guide stories begin, "No shit, there I was . . ."

Rule 19, corollary 3: The worse the experience, the better the story. Therefore . . .

Rule 20: There are no bad experiences.

The Cowpersons of Tanzania

Two donkeys were missing—and the Masai were not happy. The animals weren't merely lost, the Masai concluded, but had been stolen, probably by Barabaig, a people the Masai call "enemy." Something had to be done. Blood might be shed, even over a couple of donkeys, because here in Tanzania among the various semi-nomadic tribes of East Africa, livestock was treasured: it represented a man's wealth, his self-esteem, his standing in the community.

So the Masai had called a meeting with the Barabaig, and now two groups of men—about twenty on each side—were sitting in separate assemblies under the shade of an immense acacia tree, whose small, flat leaves grew only at the top of the tree, about forty feet up in the air. Everyone knew this was a serious political meeting, and, consequently, everyone was seriously armed, most with spears, a few with bows and poison-tipped arrows.

The Masai didn't exactly frown on donkey theft. They believe that God gave them an exclusive on livestock and that when they take donkeys, cows, or goats that ostensibly belong to another tribe, they are simply "repossessing" them. It's the way a lot of Masai start their herds. The Barabaig were much of the same mind, except that they thought God had given livestock to the Barabaig. So donkey and cattle theft among the two groups was a way of life, and a rite of passage for a young man in his quest to progress from boy to warrior.

This was all understood. What irritated the Masai was that whoever stole their donkeys lived nearby. What was that about? You were supposed to travel far and steal livestock from people you never met. This bush-league move, on the other hand, was entirely unacceptable. The Barabaig, for their part, considered themselves innocent victims of circumstance, if, indeed, any of them had actually stolen the donkeys. Both groups were seminomadic, but the Barabaig had been grazing cattle here first. The Masai had only relocated here in the past few months, driven south from their usual territory by drought. It was not as if the donkeys had been stolen from old friends.

The Masai and Barabaig dressed much alike, in long robes called *shoukas*. The Masai were in red, with muted checks, while the Barabaig's *shoukas* were red or orange or purple.

The convocation began with flowery speeches on both sides.

"This is a good thing," my friend and safari guide Peter Jones assured me. "In the old days, there would have been a lot of killing, and then years of blood feuds." Even in Tanzania, arguably one of the most peaceful nations in Africa, things can degenerate into violence very quickly. In fact, less than twenty years ago, Warangi tribesmen had killed five Barabaig and wounded many more at a conference just like this one.

Peter Jones is the son of a respected English academic and a former Harvard archaeology instructor who himself has lived in Tanzania for almost twenty years. For reasons as simple and convoluted as love, Peter married a friend of mine from Montana whom I used to know as Mimi. These days, she signs her e-mails Margot, and I thought perhaps she'd become pretentious in the manner of silly white persons who live in East Africa. I found soon after I arrived, however, that in Swahili "mimi" means "me, myself." This led to such Swahili sentences as "Hello, I'm me myself." Or: "May I introduce you to my wife, me myself." Margot, her given name, was easier.

Peter and Margot live at Ndarakwai, a former cattle ranch about four thousand feet up the slopes of Mount Kilimanjaro, and, in the past five years, working with their Masai and Chagga neighbors, they have managed to bring back the game that had once been decimated in the name of African beef. There are zebras and baboons and elephants and leopards and giraffes on the ten-thousand-acre ranch, all protected by several highly paid antipoaching rangers. There are, Margot told me, even three lions on the place now. She asked me not to mention that to her Masai neighbors.

The Masai revere all creatures—they call them God's cattle—but lions are exempt from this wide-scale veneration. Lions kill cattle. Indeed, a week before the donkey conference, I spoke with Thomas, the Masai ranch manager at Ndarakwai and he told me a story about the lion he had killed single-handedly. He was staying at his parents' *boma*, a Swahili word that means "fort," when he heard a rustling in the thorns outside. Now, a Masai *boma* is usually surrounded by a ten-foot-high, three-foot-deep fence of thorny branches cut from acacia trees. Another fence inside the outer one—equally high, equally deep—serves as a pen for the livestock. The huts are usually situated in the narrow space between the inner and outer fences, and that was where Thomas heard the lion one night. He stepped outside, barefoot, armed with a flashlight, a knife, and a spear. The lion had penetrated the outer fence, and was standing about fifteen feet away. Thomas hurled the spear and caught the lion in the heart and lungs. It died very quickly.

"I'd killed maybe six lions before," Thomas said, "but always with thirty or forty other men." The lion was fed to the dogs— "we like dogs; we hate lions"—but the big cat's tail was fixed on the end of a long stick. The next morning, Thomas, with his arm painted white, carried the stick and led the village in a kind of skipping run while everyone sang the lion song. Single guys who kill lions, he led us to believe, pretty much have their choice of single women.

The Joneses had invited Thomas to come to the United States, in fact to my hometown in Montana, where Mi . . . uh, Margot still had a house. Thomas was anxious to walk among Montana cows. He'd seen pictures of them and found them astounding. The small, heat-resistant African cattle he knew came up to his chest at the shoulder, and even the fattest of them still showed a faint ridge of rib. "But your cattle," he said, "I don't believe them. I think they are blown up with air. They look like they are going to explode."

Thomas, like most Masai, was tall and slender and immensely dignified. When he went on safari he wore Western clothes: neatly pressed pants, boots, a clean dress shirt. His parents walked naked under their *shoukas* and said that he was now "one of those who fart in their clothes." Thomas, in his fart pants, wouldn't feel at all out of place in any major American city, except for his earlobes, each of which has a dime-sized hole in it. Most Masai (and Barabaig) have such ear loops, and, in the city of Arusha, they're considered the mark of a country bumpkin. Several plastic surgeons there specialize in repairing loops, and Thomas wanted to fix his ears before coming to America. Michael Llewelyn, a photographer from Los Angeles who was along for the trip, told Thomas that he thought the surgery was a bad idea: ear loops would be considered incredibly smart and trendy among the Americans he knew, many of whom only had nipple and nose rings. Still, Thomas was adamant.

At the moment, he was showing off the ranch and the three of us were strolling along an elephant trail not far behind a sizable herd, judging by the number of trees that had been butted down so the beasts could get at the green leaves that grew above the reach of their trunks.

"People say the elephants destroy trees," Thomas said. "I say they plant them, because the elephant eats the seed pod, takes it far from the mother tree, then drops it on the ground in a big pile of fertilizer."

In the space of an hour's walk, we saw guinea fowl, zebras, bushbucks, kudus, impalas, banded mongooses, elephants, giraffes, baboons, and dik-diks, a horned antelope the size of a bunny that I immediately recognized as a jackalope.

Meanwhile, at the main house, Peter worked out the logistics for a three-week walking safari. Margot wouldn't be joining us, because she had to stay home and oil her elephant. It was just a baby, a yearling that Margot and Peter had found wandering about a nearby waterhole, alone and forlorn, apparently lost or abandoned by its mother. The Joneses had built a stockade and gotten permission from the Tanzanian game department to raise the creature until it was old enough to be released into the wild, but the project had turned out to be bigger than they'd ever imagined. Elephants are social animals, and it was necessary to have someone with the animal twenty-four hours a day, so three local men now had full-time jobs for the next several years. In addition, a baby elephant spends a lot of time standing under its mother, in the shade, where it rubs its back on mom's belly, which keeps its skin smooth and supple. Without a mother around, the baby elephant had grown sunburned, and experts had advised rubbing down its cracked skin several times a day with coconut oil, which was Margot's job.

That left me, Michael, Peter, and Gobre, one of Peter's anti-poaching rangers, on the safari, along with several African men we'd meet later. Peter and I had discussed this trip many times over the years. No white person had been where we were going, as far as he knew, not in recent memory, anyway. There would be Masai and Barabaig cattle herders at the beginning of the trip, and then we'd get into Sandawe country. Agriculturists and beekeepers, the Sandawe are generally smaller and less physically imposing than the other two tribes, but they are renowned bow hunters who supplement their crops with game meat, crack archers who are greatly feared in war. The Masai say that you can't hide from a Sandawe arrow: the little bastards can shoot them around corners. When Sandawe come to Arusha or Dar es Salaam, they get jobs as night watchmen, and they are the men you see in the evening sitting outside imposing homes or corporate headquarters or government buildings wearing shorts and holding bows. People in Tanzania don't mess with an armed Sandawe.

And so, as Margot oiled her elephant, we piled into one of Peter's Land Cruisers and started off on the ten-hour drive south to Kalema, where we would begin our foot journey through a region of Tanzania one guidebook called "arid, featureless, and monotonous." We parked in a secure area north of town and began walking. There were now three local Sandawe with us. One was Gele, so named because when he was born, his umbilical cord was buried near a baobab tree, or *gele* in Sandawe. Baobabs look as if they're growing upside down with their roots in the air: a tree that started off life with giant sequoia ambitions got a third of the way there and erupted into an angry tangle of bare, Medusa-like branches. The trees are plentiful in this part of Africa, and, sure enough, a second member of our group was also named Gele (guess where his umbilical cord was buried?), though he asked us to call him Motabo, which means "Thursday," after the day he was born. The third Sandawe was an older man named Ali. He didn't mention his umbilical cord.

We walked on paths that skirted the cornfields, then wound slowly down through towering grasses to the dry bed of a "sand river," where the water runs thirty feet high in the wet season. Now, there was only a wide, winding gully of sand and a few community wells dug ten feet deep into the riverbed.

Gele saw a dead acacia tree that looked as if it had been attacked by Lizzie Borden. "Sandawe," he said. There was food in the dead tree that only his people ate. He demonstrated, whacking at the wood with a heavy, long-handled hatchet called a *hengo*. As chips fell away from the tree, we could see large bore holes, and in these holes were white grubs as long as my index finger and thicker than my thumb. We took a dozen back to our camp and Ali split a stick, arranged the live grubs just so, and placed the stick in the ground, leaning over the fire, so that the unfortunate grubs were roasted alive. In an hour or so, they were done. The grubs had the consistency of roasted marshmallows—crispy on the outside, squishy on the inside—and because they were very fatty, I can only describe the taste as that of "creamy bacon."

The next day, we crossed the sand river and met a Sandawe man who asked us if we were Arabs. We laughed a bit and said we were English and American. The man, a little irritated, said, "How am I supposed to know? I live in the bush." He'd only seen white people going by in cars, on the road. The man wanted to know where we were going. Kwa Mtoro, we said, a town about a week's walk away. "On those feet?" the man asked. He seemed astonished. It was our first encounter with the African perception that white men can't walk.

Actually, aside from the dust and midafternoon heat, it was a pleasant stroll for all of us. Peter had hired a couple of donkeys and no one carried a particularly heavy pack. We walked east, along ancient trails between water holes, paths that had been used by Arab slave raiders and Victorian-era English explorers. We were in the depths of a valley, ringed by distant mountains, and the ground under our feet was sandy in the dry season. There were golden grasses, calf-high, growing under pleasantly spaced glades of thorny acacia trees so shaped and patterned by the wind (and grazing giraffes) that they looked a bit like a formal topiary garden in a Northern California wine-growing region. Napa. Sonoma.

Occasionally, I stumbled over round, steering wheel–sized holes: an elephant's wet-season passing baked into the trail. We saw antelope of various sorts, the tracks of giraffe, and the chalky-white scat left by hyenas, animals that are able to digest bones. Peter pointed out a place where a cobra had crossed the trail, a long, straight track like that of a smooth-tired motorcycle.

This wasn't the game park experience, where tourists are confined to cars and the animals are all about, all the time. It wasn't Ndarakwai, where rangers protected the game. This was Africa, where people lived, and hunted, and where the animals were anything but naive.

We camped near a community well shared by Barabaig, Sandawe, and a few clans of Masai. A young Barabaig boy herding cattle passed by just before sundown, and Gobre spoke to him urgently in his own language. It was important that the cattle be moved immediately, and the boy ran them off into the tall grass. Apparently, Gobre's warning came too late, however, because minutes later a Barabaig man, presumably the boy's father, arrived waving his stick and yelling at Gobre. The two passed angry words, until the stick man left, muttering darkly.

Our camp was a mishmash of tribes—Sandawe, Warangi, Hehe, white guys—and no one understood what had just happened.

Gobre explained that one Barabaig may not see another's cattle. He could curse the cows out of sheer jealousy. It happened all the time. Some clans were famous for sorcery, and the talent for witchery was passed down from father to son. Since "we Barabaig aren't particular about who sleeps with our wives," any man might have the talent. You couldn't trust anyone.

"Wait," I said, "you're jealous about cattle but not about your wives?"

"Of course," Gobre said. This, I thought, was animal husbandry taken to a certain extreme.

"Can you curse cattle?" I asked.

"No," Gobre said, "but there are many who can."

The other Africans thought this was all pretty silly—a Barabaig thing—and we began talking about the differences between Tanzanian tribes. There are 120 of them, none of which forms more than 10 percent of the population. Yet the country is not riven with the genocidal tribal wars that have devastated neighboring Burundi, Rwanda, and Zaire. This is largely the accomplishment of the country's first president, Julius Nyerere, who took office after independence in 1961. An erudite man—he is still known as "the Teacher"—Nyerere made Swahili, the traditional idiom of trade, Tanzania's national language. No one tribe was favored and everyone could finally communicate with everyone else. In time, Tanzania became an island of relative peace in the bloody chaos that is contemporary Africa, and, indeed, when then-President Clinton visited Arusha—where the Rwanda war-crimes tribunals were being held—he referred to the city as "the Geneva of Africa."

Whites have always been a small minority in Tanzania: just another tribe with our own odd customs, like the tendency to be more jealous about our wives than our cows. There was a short period of German colonialism before the First World War, and Hendric, our chef, was proud of the fact that his people, the Hehe, had mounted a hard-fought rebellion. After the war, the British claimed Tanzania (then Tanganyika) as a "protectorate," not a colony. Consequently, the vast majority of British subjects in East

Africa preferred to settle in nearby Kenya, an actual colony of the British Empire, upon which the sun would never set. Tanganyika earned its independence in 1961, without a single drop of blood shed. In 1964, it combined with the island of Zanzibar to become Tanzania.

So there wasn't an unpleasant air of anticolonial hatred that whites are sometimes subjected to in Africa; neither was there the equally objectionable fawning that I've sometimes experienced elsewhere on the continent.

Which isn't to say we don't come in for our own share of teasing. In any African tea shop, for instance, the cup is filled absolutely to the brim. Whites, however, prefer and receive a slightly less generous pour. It was Hendric's opinion that we do it that way so we won't burn our long noses.

All in all, the Africans said, as we sat by the fire, it was often easier to talk to whites than it was to Africans of other tribes. This is because many tribes that once warred with one another now have what is called "a teasing relationship." If, for instance, Hendric put his T-shirt on inside out, a Warangi could claim the garment and Hendric would have to give it to him. Should a Sandawe ask to see anything Hendric owned—a pack of cigarettes, a pair of shoes—he had to place the object on the ground. If he just handed it over, the Sandawe would own it. This "teasing" is entirely preferable to war, and the various relationships are even recognized in Tanzania's informal outdoor courts.

One day, we visited the *boma* of a Barabaig man named Kisurumbu, also called John. The interior thornbush corral contained what seemed to be an enormous number of cattle, and there were several dirt-floored huts scattered about, one for John, one for each of his three wives, and another for his unmarried younger brother. The women all wore stiff, beaded cowhide dresses of the type once worn by American Indians, along with white bracelets cut from some PVC piping stolen from a foreign-aid water project. Older women had ceremonial scars about the eyes.

The children were eating *ugali,* which is boiled cornmeal, white as Styrofoam and of about the same consistency. They drank milk as well, enormous quantities of it while the cows bellowed away in the inner corral. As the sun rose higher in the sky, we were assaulted by wave upon wave of flies, great, hateful clouds of them crawling about on our arms and legs and faces.

The flies were particularly attracted to milk, and they covered the mouths of the children and infants in heaving black masses. It looked like a late-night TV commercial urging viewers to save the children, except that these kids were laughing merrily and were as roly-poly as any well-fed American infant. Still, conditioned by commercials, and repelled by the flies, I felt an urge to reach into my pocket and save the children.

That changed about the time John's teenage brother, Hamisi, let the cows out to graze for the day. There were just over four hundred of them, and I knew an average cow would fetch $150 at the market, with the best animals selling for over $200. John also had several donkeys, some sheep, and a herd of goats. He told us he owned more livestock up north. I didn't ask how many more cows he had—this is aggressively impolite, as it is in Montana—but it seemed to me that John and his family had a net worth of somewhere near $100,000. They were well-to-do by almost anyone's standards, and they lived in close proximity to their wealth, which is to say, in the barnyard. The flies were one measure of their affluence.

Hamisi let the cows out of the *boma* to graze and I strolled along with him. The boy was thinking about marriage, and wondered what Americans paid in terms of a bride price.

"Nothing," I said.

"Her father gets nothing?"

"We make the deal with the girl. What do you guys pay?"

Hamisi said that the typical Barabaig gave the father two large rounds of chewing tobacco, four four-gallon cans of honey worth about $40 apiece, and one cow. When the wife becomes pregnant, it cost another cow. It used to be a lot more, as many as ten cows, for instance, but these days women were becoming very undependable, and quite reluctant to follow the unwritten rules. Sometimes—

this was hardly thinkable—if they didn't like you, they'd just go away.

"That's when we pay," I said, out of sad experience.

"When they go away, you pay the father?"

"The woman."

Hamisi shook his head in wonder at the infinite imbecility of the white tribe.

We strolled through the sandy soil under the acacias taking care to avoid the piles of cowflop. It occurred to me that Tanzania's tribes, with their teasing relationships, had a droll and entirely indigenous sense of humor. I meant to explore it.

"So what's the funniest thing that happens out here?" I asked.

"Well," Hamisi replied thoughtfully, "sometimes someone tries to steal the cows."

This did not seem a matter of great hilarity to me. "No," I said, "I mean something even funnier than that."

"Sometimes a calf gets stuck in the birth canal," Hamisi said. "Then you have to call a person who can get it out."

I admitted that must be a real knee-slapper when it happened. "But what I mean," I said, "is something that really makes you laugh every time you think about it. Something so hilarious you can hardly stand it."

Hamisi thought for a long time, then said, "Every once in a while, something scares the cows, and they all run away."

So that was the funniest thing that ever happened out in the fields: a stampede.

We climbed out of the valley into a deciduous woodland at about 4,500 feet. Some local Sandawe hunters took us up to high granite promontories where all kinds of art had been drawn on the rock over the centuries, over the millennium. There were wildebeests, humans, elephants, rhinos, and giraffes pictured in three different sites. One giraffe was brilliantly done—anatomically perfect, from the notch in its lower chest to the hock high up on the back legs. The sites were, Peter thought, anywhere from twenty thousand to forty thousand years old: a major archaeological find, undocumented and perfectly preserved. Peter took a GPS reading. He would come back later, study the art, and perhaps someone would write a scientific paper.

As Peter sketched the ancient giraffe in his notebook, the Sandawe built a smoky fire under a tree. Bees were moving in and out of a large hole in one of the branches and there was honey for the taking. Gele climbed the tree with a smoking branch, thrust it into the hole, and there was the disconcerting sound of angry buzzing bees, the sound of something awful about to happen in a horror film. Gele worked in complete silence, pulling comb after comb out of the hive.

"Are you getting stung?" Peter called.

"Yes, very much," Gele said.

Later, we sat under the giraffe and ate honey, while Ali pulled a dozen white stingers out of Gele's arm.

"Can't those bees kill you?" I asked Ali.

"We try not to let that happen," he said.

Later that day, we trudged through a high marsh beside an actual running river, and the path led down to the dry and dusty town of Kwa Mtoro, where we went to the monthly market. Sandawe people sold millet and honey beer, called scud; cows were auctioned off; batteries and caps and T-shirts and single cigarettes were for sale.

A few days later, we partied with the Barabaig, who had brewed up about sixty gallons of honey beer, made from honey we bought for the tribe from the Sandawe. Barabaig from all over arrived. The women greeted one another fiercely: they stood four steps apart, then came together in a thudding hug. I could hear the cowhide slapping fifty yards away.

Outside the *boma* of a respected elder named Kalish, young men stood together in a group while a like number of women in cowhide dresses stood half a football field away. The men sang and banged their sticks on cowhide shields. Occasionally, one would step in front and leap straight up in the air, sometimes a dozen times or more. It was bad form to bend the knees. The leap came only from the feet and calves, so when two or three men jumped together, in unison, it looked as if gravity had no dominion over them.

The women, for their part, came out jumping in the same manner. The dancing went on for several hours—the young men and women staring at one another, assessing athletic prowess, and deciding, I imagined, who might make for a hot sex partner.

We weren't called on to jump, but Kalish invited me into a hut inside the *boma,* where we drank honey beer out of cow horns and discussed the important matters of the day, as elders and white men who can't jump are wont to do. Sunlight fell in shafts through the poles in the hut, and Peter said that the ceremony was significantly different from Masai dances. It was, he thought, pretty much an anthropologist's wet dream. I drank another horn full of the foaming, yeasty beer: it tasted like a sweet, liquid form of dirt.

"Drink," Kalish said, and I did, spilling plenty a polite quantity down my shirt. The cow horn came around many times, and while I drank, I reflected on what was surely the high point of my trip: the great donkey conference.

Early on, we'd encountered three heavily armed Masai crossing the sand river. They said they were going to a meeting with the Barabaig about some stolen donkeys. We could come and watch, they said, as long as we kept our distance and our mouths shut. Which is how we found ourselves sitting under the spreading acacia tree observing African politics in action. Since the Masai were the complaining party, they got to start. A man stood and said, "We know sometimes a Masai's livestock is stolen by his own son, but we have investigated, and this has not happened. We have also searched the bush, and there are no bones. The donkeys must be in someone else's hands."

A Barabaig man stood to reply: "Either you know who took the donkeys or you don't. You can't just make vague accusations."

Though the Barabaig and Masai each have their own language, everyone was speaking Swahili, which Peter quietly translated. Speakers were polite; tones were reasonable.

"The livestock," a Masai man said, "is in Barabaig hands. There is no point in pretending otherwise. Please, let's work this out. There are no long roads without twists and turns, without sharp corners. Together, we can straighten out this road." The discussion continued apace for four or five hours until the Barabaig asked for time to confer among themselves. They went off down a slope, out of sight. Gobre, our Barabaig pal, wandered after them to eavesdrop. He was dressed in Western clothes, and none of the locals knew he spoke Barabaig.

The men conferred until well after dark. We wandered back to our own camp, where Gobre filled us in on the Barabaig conference. They were going to meet with the Masai again tomorrow. And yes, two of the young men had stolen the damn donkeys. They had already sold them, so they couldn't just give them back. That left only three alternatives, the way the Barabaig saw it: they could rush in and spear as many Masai as possible; they could pack up and move out in the middle of the night, as they had done before in similar situations; or they could find some way to pay the Masai for their donkeys.

"You think there could be violence?" I asked.

Nobody thought so, but then Gobre began telling the infamous story about a small massacre his people had suffered at the hands of the Warangi under similar circumstances about fifteen years ago. The parlay was about—what else?—stolen livestock, with accusations on both sides. Gobre had been at the meeting. There were only about fifty Barabaig, he said, all sitting, waiting for the meeting to begin. In contrast, more than two hundred Warangi showed, and they didn't sit, but rather positioned themselves in such a way that the Barabaig suddenly found themselves surrounded. Gobre had a gift for comic understatement. Everyone was laughing. It finally dawned on me that this was considered an amusing story. It was even funnier than a stampede.

"We were sitting there like a pack of goats," he said, as the other Africans in our party doubled over in laughter. Gobre said the sight of the advancing Warangi made him "uneasy," and so he excused himself to go "dig for medicine," an African euphemism for relieving oneself. More laughter. He was walking through a nearby cornfield when the Warangi began firing their arrows into the sitting Barabaig. "I could hear the screams," Gobre said, "and I ran. Five people died, including my son-in-law."

And then the laughter stopped. Abruptly. East Africans, it seemed, can laugh at death and pay it solemn homage in the space of a single breath. Or maybe the body count just brought home the parallels with a certain other livestock parlay due to commence about a mile away at nine o'clock the next morning.

So it was with a degree of trepidation that we attended the second day of the great donkey dispute. We took a position some distance away from the great acacia tree, so that we could slip away into the bush at the first sign of trouble. The Barabaig, however, did not rush in immediately and spear the Masai. They hadn't left in the night, so perhaps they were going to pay. We moved closer to monitor the debate.

About two-thirty that afternoon, an older Barabaig in a purple *shouka* finally admitted that his son had stolen the donkeys, and the aggrieved Masai said he would be willing to accept the donkeys back, along with two cows in payment for the emotional pain and aggravation he had suffered in searching for his animals. After many eloquent speeches, the thief's father agreed to the payment of two cows only (worth about $300), since the donkeys themselves were, of course, long gone. The Masai thought that was fair if the father threw in 30,000 shillings (about $36), a figure that was negotiated down to about $12.

So, after seventeen hours, the great donkey contretemps was settled without bloodshed. A Masai said, "We knew you Barabaig had the donkeys, but we chose not to steal back from you, because we respect you." The Masai left, but the Barabaig stayed for another several hours. The father had just lost two cows out of a total of ten in his herd. It was suggested that his son pay him back. The son refused, but under intense community pressure changed his mind ten minutes later—a virtual split second in Barabaig political time. Still, he was only going to pay one cow. He hadn't stolen the donkeys alone, and his rustling buddy should pay the other. The second thief stood and declared that he had no cows and no money to boot. An hour of argument ensued, and the second thief was given four days to come up with a cow.

Later I discussed the matter with Gobre. "They gave him four days because . . . ?"

"He has to go somewhere where they don't know him . . ."

"And?"

"Steal one."

My Brother, the Pot Dealer

It was somewhere near three in the morning when Chilero's screams began echoing off the canyon walls. "Oyyyyy-yoy-yoy-yoy-yoy!"

Make that first "Oyyyyy" enormously loud; be sure it's filled with pain and terror and fear.

"Oyyyyy-yoy-yoy-yoy-yoy," Chilero howled again. "Where are you?" he screamed in Spanish. From my position on the ground, I could see his shadow slipping against the starry night sky. Chilero was gliding over the ice, lurching, but never actually falling. He was a graceful man, drunk or sober.

He'd been sleeping in the front seat of my truck, and now, at three in the morning, he was skating over the ice sheet in his slick-soled cowboy boots, looking for his friends. He couldn't see us lying at the base of the canyon wall. We were all trying to sleep, bundled up together in a cocoon of blankets and sleeping bags. The ice below was slowly melting under the heat of our bodies.

"Hace demasiado frío," he screamed in Spanish. *It's too cold.* "Focking cold."

And then it occurred to him that, in this dark night, he was surrounded by the souls and shadows of the Indian people who had populated this river canyon nearly one thousand years ago. He felt their spirits, and he sensed animosity, or so it seemed.

"Indios," he screamed in fear and defiance, "listen to me, *indios,* I am not afraid of you." Chilero had Indian blood. He was proud of it. He just didn't trust people who'd been dead for a thousand years.

We were all awake now, groggy and shivering, all of us watching Chilero rebuild the fire and wishing he'd shut up. There were seven of us on this archaeological outing to the mountains of northern Mexico. The campsite was no doubt beautiful in the summer, but it was the dead of winter, at six thousand feet, and the waterfall that poured over the canyon wall was frozen solid.

We were out camping on this crystalline winter evening so I could learn about my brother's business dealings in Mexico. Presently, these included the semi-ingenious Mormon defense to planned marriage.

Chilero, who was something of a vaquero, crouched by the fire and systematically cursed us all—the focking gringos, the stupid Mexicans, the black guy, everyone. *"Me hablen,"* he screamed. *Talk to me.*

He thought we'd abandoned him to the night and the souls of the dead.

"Where are you!"

I decided to put Chilero out of his misery and fixed our position for him by finally speaking.

"Podríamos matarlo," I muttered to my brother. We could kill him.

This act of kindness was rewarded with a similar gesture on Chilero's part. We'd all been asleep for some hours after assiduously drinking most of the night, and Chilero brought me just what I needed: a gallon jug of water in one of those flimsy clear unlabeled plastic jars. I took a big, thirsty gulp. It never occurred to me that in Mexico, tequila is sold in such unmarked jars. This was an unpleasant surprise, and a real tough way to wake up.

My brother glanced over at me and pulled the sleeping bag over his head. Sure, I was sick, but in a few hours, he was going to have to deal with the whole planned-marriage thing again.

My brother, Rick, is a trader in pots, ceramics, which he buys in Mexico and sells to upscale galleries in the United States. (Yes, yes: he's heard every conceivable variation of the pot-dealer joke.) Rick buys all his fine-arts pots from one dusty village of about three thousand people. The place is called Mata Ortiz, officially, Juan Mata Ortiz. If my Spanish serves me well, I believe the place would be called Juan "Killer" Ortiz in English.

My brother and I drove down to Mata Ortiz from Tucson, discussing the derivation of the name with a man named Alain Isabelle, another Arizona trader along for the ride.

Juan Ortiz earned the nickname "Mata," or "killer," during the Apache wars of one hundred years ago. He was second in command when Chief Victorio was defeated in 1880, apparently participated in a massacre of unarmed Apaches a year later, and was captured by Chief Juh the next year. The Apaches tortured and eventually killed the man known as "Killer."

So, the town's name either celebrates Ortiz the killer, or Ortiz the killed.

"We should stop at that little place for *sotol*," Rick said.

This is a tequilalike drink which is kept in a five-gallon glass jar so you can see the dead rattlesnake floating near the bottom.

"They put the snake in the jar alive," my brother said.

"But it's clearly dead," Alain pointed out.

"Of course it's dead," my brother said. "It's a rattlesnake. It can't breathe underwater."

"So you're telling me Mexicans like to see snakes drown."

"I'm not telling you any such thing. They say the snake pumps out venom when it dies and that the venom is good for your health."

"I don't believe that," said Alain.

"What, you think Macario lies about *sotol*?"

"You probably just didn't understand him, is all."

And so on. I said: "No more bickering."

There was a silence of several seconds. "The Mexicans say we argue a lot," my brother said.

"Yeah," Alain said. "They say we're like an old married couple and that we ought to get married because we fight so much."

"Don't tell him about that," my brother said.

"What about the woman they want you to marry?"

"Don't tell him about that either."

"They want Rick to marry one of the village women," Alain said, to my brother's intense annoyance.

"Any particular one?" I asked.

"I'm not going to get married," Rick said. He's successfully avoided this entanglement for over forty years.

"We'll see," Alain said. "It's hard to say no to Macario and Nena."

And then we were bouncing down a cruel joke of a dirt road, running past apple and peach orchards, moving up into the Sierra Madre Occidental Mountains. The road dove into the Palanganas River—three feet deep at the most—then rose into a high, wind-swept plain. There were cows and cowboys on the land. The snow-capped Sierras rose several thousand feet above, and there, below us, on the banks of the river, was a dusty town of one-story adobe-brick buildings.

It was Mata Ortiz, a village that is to ceramicists what Paris in the 1920s was to writers.

The story is legend: in 1976, Spencer MacCallum, an anthropologist, found three extraordinary handmade pots in a Deming, New Mexico, junk shop called Bob's Swap Shop. The owner said that "some poor people" had traded the pots for clothes. MacCallum bought all three pots for $18 apiece. "To me," MacCallum wrote in *Kiva, the Journal of Southwestern Anthropology and History*, "they showed such integrity of form and design" that "I was determined to find the unknown potter."

The trail took him to Mata Ortiz, a dusty railroad town on the high plains of Chihuahua, several hundred miles due south of Deming. People there worked on the railroad, or picked fruit for about $5 a day. MacCallum's questions led him to Juan Quezada, a man who had dropped out of school in the third grade and who is today regarded as a genius in certain academic circles.

As a teenager, Juan cut firewood for sale to the village. The mountain slopes where he worked were littered with lustrous shards of ancient polychrome pottery. The Indian culture is called Paquime, or Casas Grandes, and it flourished near Mata Ortiz around the year A.D. 1000. Juan, an artist by temperament, felt driven by some internal obsession to re-create these pots. The raw materials—clay, minerals for paints—were locally available, and—a major consideration for an impoverished artist—they would be free for the taking.

Juan had never seen anyone make a pot, never read any books on the subject, but he re-created the ancient techniques through a process of trial and error that took fifteen years to perfect. MacCallum subsidized Juan for a while, encouraging him to follow his creative muse and produce his best work.

Juan eventually quit his railroad job and taught his family the techniques he'd discovered. Today, a Juan Quezada pot sells for thousands of dollars. He teaches pottery classes both in Mexico and the United States. His work is on display in museums around the world.

In the early 1980s, other families in the village, noting the Quezadas' success, began making pots. Most learned the techniques from Juan.

The first book written about the Mata Ortiz phenomenon was *The Story of Casas Grandes Pottery* (1991, Western Imports, Box 12591, Tucson, AZ 85732). The author is Rick Cahill, my brother, and he does a thorough job explaining the mechanics of the technique: how the clay is sifted; how the pots are formed by hand, without use of a potter's wheel; how these intricate works of art are painted with a human hair, generally plucked from a child's head; how the pots are fired one at a time, under a fire of dried cow chips. The book is on sale at various galleries that sell Mata Ortiz pots, as well as tourist shops throughout the Southwest.

Rick's book brought many buyers to Mata Ortiz, and, I believe, helped prices rise to current levels. The village is beginning to prosper. Today there are over three hundred potters making a living in Mata Ortiz. Bill Gilbert, a guest curator at the New Mexico Museum of Art, says that while the forms and designs utilized in the early part of the revival derived directly from the prehistoric Casas Grandes style, "aspects of what is taking place . . . appear more closely related to highly energized studios or movements in contemporary art."

This is what has been called the Miracle of Mata Ortiz.

In Mata Ortiz, my brother generally stays with Macario and Nena Ortiz, who call him *primo*, cousin. Macario is one of the world-class potters in the village, a big, hearty man who stands well over six feet tall. He has built the only two-story house in the village and it is painted in colors I imagine a decorator would call "teal and blush." Both Macario and Nena make intricately designed pots, though the interior of their home looks more like a Montana rancher's home than that of internationally known artists.

The kitchen cabinets are built in, there is a gas stove, and a woodstove for warmth and tortillas. A few nice works of art adorn the walls, but the major decorations are framed photos of various family members, a framed print of the Last Supper, and a bas-relief wooden sculpture of a nude young woman standing on her tiptoes and reaching up, as if to pick an apple. The woman has the type of body only seen on chrome mud flaps.

We sat at the dining room table, eating chicken mole, with a family friend named Chilero. When he was a kid, Chilero had sold chiles on the street corners of Mata Ortiz, hence the name. These days, Chilero works for Macario, growing chiles and wrangling cows on one of Macario's properties. I had the impression that Macario employed any number of neighbors and friends, and that he essentially supported several less fortunate families.

"Did you know your brother is getting married?" Macario asked me.

"Let's talk about business," Rick said.

"Your brother should have children," Macario said.

"Children are a blessing," Chilero pointed out.

"I'm only here two weeks out of the month," Rick countered. "How can I have children?"

"The village will help," Nena said.

"Somebody wrote a book about that," I said. And indeed, neighbor children were always running in and out of the Ortiz house.

"There is a woman in Tucson who I'm serious about," Rick said.

Macario shrugged off the comment. "First, of course, you need to buy a house."

"Macario, I don't have money for a house, or for a wife, or for children."

Macario knew how to fix that. Rick should just buy a lot of Macario Ortiz pots, sell them in the United States, bring the money back, and buy a house that—it just so happened—Macario owned and wanted to sell. A bottle of tequila was brought out, opened, and the cap thrown in the trash, as is the custom.

And then, sometime later, we were knocking on the door of an adobe-brick house with apple and peach trees in the yard. The place had electricity, running water, a wood-fired hot-water heater, and a genuine sit-down toilet. Macario's married son lived there. Macario wanted to build him a new house. But he needed to sell the old one first.

A price was mentioned. It was too much. Rick didn't have the money. That was all right with Macario. Rick could write a check for the whole amount, and then, when the check was good, Macario would cash it.

"So," Rick told me later, "I wrote him the check so we could finally stop talking about it. I can always change my mind later."

"I think you just bought a house," I said.

"Macario—you've got to know Macario—thinks I'll be happy here. And I am happy here. In his mind, he does this stuff for my own good. He's my best friend."

As far as I could see, the deal was supposed to go like this: My brother would give Macario a lot of money for his pots, which Rick would sell for a profit, that profit to be spent on a house Macario owned. As a homeowner, Rick would be in a position to marry someone and support her family. A family, I thought, probably presently being supported by Macario Ortiz.

Then, of course, if my brother were to marry in Mata Ortiz, there would be a big fiesta, and Rick would have to buy some cows to slaughter for the wedding celebration. Macario, as it happened, has a nice herd of cattle.

"But," Rick told me, "I'm not getting married."

.   .   .

In honor of my visit, we drove my truck up into the Sierra Madres, to a place where the Piedras Verdes River intersects with the Arroyo Casa Blanca. The place looked a little like the canyonlands of Utah. Not that we were able to see it that first night.

It took most of an afternoon to gather up all the people who wanted to come, and we didn't get started on the four-hour drive through the mountains until after dark, which is how we came to camp on a sheet of ice beneath a frozen waterfall.

Then Chilero stumbled out of the truck about three in the morning, screaming and cursing. When everyone was thoroughly awake, he began playing his guitar and singing. For hours.

"Debemos matarlo," I said. *We must kill him.*

Just after dawn, we walked up the hill to a cave set high in the canyon wall. The Cave of the Pot was a Paquime habitation site about A.D. 1000. Set in the center of the cave was a large granary, perhaps twelve feet high, shaped rather like a child's top or a pot. There was a series of low, tumble-down walls, with the distinctive T-shaped doors the Paquime culture favored.

I sat near the granary, and looked out across the valley of the Piedras Verdes, thinking. During my stay in Mata Ortiz, I had watched Macario work. He sometimes put in sixteen-hour days, and several of his new pots echoed the shape of the granary in the Cave of the Pot.

Rick and Macario were sitting beside me.

"The thing is," Rick told Macario, "my brother and I were raised Mormon."

It took a moment to digest the blatant lie, but then I saw where this was heading.

"The Mormon religion," I said, nodding in an imbecilic manner.

"So," Rick said, "I couldn't really get married in the Catholic Church."

"But you don't go to the temple," Macario said.

"I'm an agnostic Mormon."

"Jack Mormon," I said.

"That's right," Rick said. "Jack Mormon."

"Well, then, no, you couldn't be married in the Catholic Church."

Macario seemed to dismiss the entire idea. He turned to study the granary. I imagined that he was planning a new variation on the shape. Some fine new pot. A museum-quality piece of work.

"But isn't it true," my brother's best friend asked him finally, "that Mormons can have several wives?"

I was, it occurred to me, watching a truly great artist at work.

Dirty Money

It was a money-laundering scheme for rapacious dimwits and hoggish simpletons. There was $2 million in it, all told, and if I played my cards right, I'd walk out of Bamako, in the West African country of Mali, with a sizable chunk of that cash, bundled up in limp $20 and $50 and $100 bills.

I don't know how my potential benefactor picked me to share in the bonanza. I was working out, after a fashion, which is to say I was attempting to balance a rickety hotel lawn chair on a lumpy grass bank overlooking the Niger River. I was alone, and my flight home was to leave the next evening. The entire plan for the rest of the day consisted of watching the sunset. The orb in question seemed to be taking its time in this endeavor, and I was bored.

"Ah," a voice behind me said. "You speak English."

I turned to the man behind me. He was dressed in a kind of green jumpsuit with wide lapels, which he wore over a white silk shirt. The shirt was open to the sternum, and dangling from a gold chain around his neck he wore what appeared to be an enormous gold nugget. It was a style I'd describe as "street pimp, '79."

"How do you know I speak English?"

He pointed at the two-month-old issue of a weekly newsmagazine on my lap.

"*Newsweek,*" he said. The man gestured a question at the lawn chair near mine.

"Please," I said.

"I am tired of speaking in French," my new friend announced, "and I am very bored."

"Where is the joy of life?" I asked in French, which pretty much depleted my vocabulary in that language.

The man stared at me blankly and fingered the nugget at his chest. "I am a guest in this hotel," he said abruptly.

"Good restaurant," I said.

"They speak French."

"Yes."

"I am from Liberia. In Liberia, we speak English." He extended a hand for me to shake in the gentle, palm-against-palm, African slide-away style. "My name is Fabrice."

I shook his hand and told him my name.

"Tim," Fabrice said, "we have a deal, you and I."

"What's that?"

"We will speak English tonight, and we will not be bored."

The prospect of some conversation had its merits.

"Yes," I agreed. "We will speak English."

"Speaking English," Fabrice said. "It is good."

We sat together in mutual contemplation of the inherent excellence of the English language. Neither of us had anything to say.

"Uh, is the fighting over in Liberia?" I asked.

"Oh, yes." Fabrice brightened up a bit. Now we were speaking English.

"Whom did you support?"

"I fought with Charles Taylor."

Taylor had headed up one of the guerrilla groups that opposed former president Samuel Doe. Taylor's troops had fought in the back country. Another guerrilla faction, centered near the capital of Monrovia and led by a man named Prince Johnson, had arranged to meet Doe under the supervision of a West African peacekeeping force. Instead the group overwhelmed the peacekeepers, kidnapped Doe, and tortured and executed him. The initial stages of the process were recorded for posterity on videotape—Doe bleeding from the places where his ears had been—and were played on television. This was in 1990. There has been bloody factional fighting since.

"They say," I observed, "that Charles Taylor was once in jail in the United States."

"Ha!" Fabrice was having none of it. "How did he escape jail? He says he bribed a guard with thirty thousand dollars. In the United States. Do you believe that?"

"I guess not."

"Here," he said, reaching inside his jacket. "Here is my passport."

I looked at the document. It seemed to be a genuine Liberian passport. There was a picture of Fabrice, and underneath it was his signature: Fabrice Clark. He was one of those people who like a wide-nibbed pen, almost like a crayon, and he formed his signature one laborious letter at a time, as if printing. Fabrice was twenty-nine years old and lived in Monrovia.

"So," he said, "you see I am who I say I am."

"I never doubted it."

"I am a businessman."

"How's business?"

Fabrice stared off across the Niger, where the sun was just beginning to set and the sky was gaudy. "I have," Fabrice said in a confiding tone, "a liquidity problem."

I often travel alone and most often in developing countries. In these places it is generally wise to get to the capital city some days before your flight home. Things can happen.

And it is in the capitals of such places that expat Brits and Americans and Australians—all manner of people not native to the country—sit drinking in bars and dreaming of how they might play on government stupidity or individual greed and end up flying out with a satchel of cash in hand.

On occasion, in these joints, some friendly, slightly seedy type will throw an arm over my shoulder and let me in on his latest fast deal. It makes me wonder: Does this stuff happen to everyone who travels alone? Or am I just lucky?

Why did the American expats in Belize, for instance, think I'd want to get involved in their scheme to poison fish on the reefs and sell the surviving but seriously ill tropicals to pet stores across the United States?

Or: Why on earth would I want to get involved in a scheme to steal Balinese house dogs? Distinctive animals, the guy said. Damn things would go for a fortune in the States. We'd sell them through *Dog World* magazine. Call 'em Balinese Hindu hounds, something like that. Besides, you see the way people treat them. Where are they going to have a better life?

And it really wouldn't cost me that much to get in on the ground floor.

I listen to each pitch with sheer astonishment. I collect them. And okay, maybe someday I'll be the guy flying out of Siberia with a suitcase full of money. It could happen. But chatting with Fabrice, I perceived that he thought of me as a mark, either stupid or greedy. I wondered which.

"Everyone," I informed Fabrice, "has a liquidity problem."

Fabrice, for his part, glanced about in the manner of a man selling genuine Rolex watches on the street corner. He reached inside his jacket and produced a letter. The thing had been typed on thick white paper that was now a dingy gray, as if it had been dunked in water or stored in a very humid, tropical climate.

It seemed about as official as any letter in Liberia could possibly be. There was an embossed Liberian flag on the upper left-hand corner and an embossed American flag on the right. On the left side of the paper was a large Firestone logo. The rubber company had been one of the largest foreign corporations in Liberia before the recent troubles. Offsetting the Firestone logo was the seal of the U.S. Treasury.

The document had been written on a manual typewriter, and the enclosed portion of every *e* and every *a* was black. The letter was in English, and the first line said, "This safe contains $2 million. . . ."

The sun now lay across the Niger in a long, undulating orange streak. In the gathering darkness, Fabrice said, "My father . . . this is my father's gift."

As I tried to read the letter, Fabrice filled me in on the emotional mechanics of a country in revolution. His father had been a high official in the Samuel Doe government, in charge of finances. When it became clear that the Doe government could not survive its various challenges, his father had embezzled a sizable fortune, which was put into a safe and hidden where no one could find it.

Family ties, Fabrice explained, were blood-thick, and even though Fabrice fought on the side of the rebels, his father had gotten word to him about the money and the place where it was hidden. When the fighting cooled down, Fabrice went to that place, found the safe, and opened it with the combination his father had given him. Now he was a very rich man.

"So what's your liquidity problem?" I asked.

"Read the letter, please."

"It's too dark."

"Then, Tim, please, come to my room."

He lived five doors down from me in the hotel, and our rooms were similar: an off-brand TV that got CNN International, a telephone, a long, narrow bed, a ceiling fan, a wooden table, and two monastic chairs.

Fluorescent lights made the room seem bleak. The letter was written in ersatz legalese, with a lot of "wheretofores" in regard to parties of the first, second, and third part. It said, in essence, that if the two million American dollars in this safe should ever become discolored in the tropical heat and humidity where it was being kept, such money would become worthless if it was ever cleaned with a money-laundering compound not approved by the U.S. government.

The letter was signed by "Floyd Benson," who identified himself as the U.S. secretary of the treasury. Floyd used a wide-nibbed, crayonlike pen to sign his name, and he seemed to draw his signature one laborious letter at a time.

I had several questions at this point.

"So, uh, Fabrice. You've got the money, but I gather it's discolored."

"Yes. Worthless."

"This letter doesn't say which cleaning compounds are, in fact, approved by the U.S. government."

"There is only one. It is called TQ4."

"And, Fabrice, excuse me, but here's where I'm having a lot of trouble. I mean, how did the secretary of the treasury know that your father was going to, uh, appropriate all this money? And why would he write him a letter? What does Floyd Benson care if some stolen money in Liberia rots away in a hidden safe?"

"This," Fabrice said reasonably, "is not the real letter."

"Because," I said, "there was a treasury secretary named Lloyd Bentsen."

"The letter is not important," Fabrice said. "When you see what I have to show you, then you'll believe me."

Rooting around in a canvas duffel, Fabrice came up with an envelope, some cotton swabs, and a small bottle full of clear liquid. The envelope contained several brown sheets of flimsy paper the size of dollar bills. Fabrice put one on the table, poured a tiny amount of the clear liquid on a bit of cotton, and began swabbing one of the papers. In a matter of thirty seconds, he had cleaned one half of one side of what appeared to be a genuine U.S. $50 bill.

"That," I said, "is incredible."

"I told you: when you see it, you believe it."

"I believe it," I said. "But what's the problem here? You just go out, get some TQ4, and you're a rich man."

"It's my liquidity situation," Fabrice said. "TQ4 is very expensive. I have no money to do this."

"What's it cost?"

"One liter is fifty thousand dollars, American."

"Oh," I said. My expression told Fabrice that this was way out of my range. Still, I asked, "How much will a liter of TQ4 clean?"

"Maybe half the money."

"A million dollars."

"Maybe more, maybe less. The money is in twenties, fifties, and hundreds. You can't tell what they are. You might end up cleaning all twenties."

"Can you buy TQ4 in Bamako?"

"Oh, yes. A man I know. But it is not legal."

"No," I said. "I suppose not. But, Fabrice, what is the smallest amount of TQ4 you could buy? If you had the money."

Fabrice looked me up and down in an appraising manner.

"I think perhaps two thousand dollars' worth."

"I might be able to get that much," I said. "I could have it wired to the Central Bank downtown by noon. But I want to figure something out first."

I took out my pen and notebook and scribbled away for a time. "Look here, Fabrice," I said finally. "Let's say you buy a liter of TQ4 and, through the luck of the draw, manage to clean a million dollars. If we buy two thousand dollars' worth of TQ4, and have the same luck, we'll end with forty thousand dollars."

"Yes," he said. "It could work that way."

"So here's what I propose. I'll have two thousand dollars wired to me tomorrow at the Central Bank. We use that money to buy TQ4. Let's say we clean forty thousand. I walk away with thirty-eight thousand. You take two thousand."

"But that's not fair," Fabrice said. He stamped his foot like a petulant child. "Damn it! Damn it all. It is not good. We should split the money."

"Fabrice," I said. "Fabrice, Fabrice, Fabrice. Look at me. Do I look like I just fell off the turnip truck?"

"I don't understand."

"You understand this. You've got two million dollars to be cleaned. You have a liquidity problem. I can help. All I want is thirty-eight thousand out of forty thousand. You take the other two thousand and go buy more TQ4. You get forty thousand out of that. You buy more TQ4. Clean more money. You end up with . . ." I checked my calculations. "You end up with 1,962,000 dollars, minus about ninety-eight thousand in TQ4 costs. I get a flat thirty-eight thousand. Now who gets the better deal? Hmmm?"

Fabrice grabbed the notebook from my hand, checked my figures, and flopped down on the hard, narrow bed, his eyes squeezed shut.

"Americans," he said, "are very smart."

"Some of us."

"Tim," he said. "You have the money tomorrow. It is two thousand dollars. No less. I will meet you outside the Central Bank at noon."

"And then," I said, "we'll go buy the TQ4 together."

Fabrice, having been beaten in the deal, raised his hands to his face and rubbed his eyes, as if he were suffering from a migraine. "No, Tim. No, no, no. You cannot buy the TQ4 with me. It is illegal. It can only be sold to special people in the United States."

"I suppose we could get in trouble with Floyd Benson."

"There will be guns. You don't buy TQ4 in Bamako and not have a gun."

"So I just give the money to you?"

"Trust me for two thousand. Two hours later you have thirty-eight thousand."

"And you wouldn't just walk away with my money?"

Fabrice opened his eyes and regarded me with a kind of bludgeoning sincerity. "Tim," he said sadly. "Tim, please, is that what you think of me?"

And so we made an agreement to meet on the steps of the bank at noon the next day. I went back to my room, looked in the mirror, sat in a chair for an hour or so, and then shifted to the bed and stared up at the ceiling fan. About three hours later the bedside phone rang. Only one person on earth knew where I was.

"Hello, Fabrice," I said.

"Tim," Fabrice said, "I have been thinking."

"Yes?"

"You will not be on the steps of the bank at noon."

"Well, no, Fabrice, of course not."

"You were just speaking English, then."

"We both were, Fabrice. We were bored. It's like color TV."

"Tim. Now I don't think you are very smart. You have a stupid face."

Which answered my only unresolved question. There was a brief choking sound I took to be a chuckle. "You have such a stupid face," Fabrice said again. "But I enjoyed speaking English with you."

"Me too, Fabrice," I said. "It passed the time."

Panic

I can't remember the host's name, only that the show was a pilot for ABC television, and that it was to be called *Stories*. I was a guest on the program. During each and every commercial break I got up and vomited in a wastebasket set discreetly off camera for the purpose.

Worst case of stage fright in television history, probably.

It was a talk show–type format, but rather formal, with four of us sitting around a coffee table, complete with little cups of coffee, all of us wearing coats and ties.

I have never worn a tie since. It's been over ten years now.

The show was filmed at seven in the morning, but we were to look as if we'd just finished dinner and were having a spontaneous discussion. My impression was that some network exec had attended a dinner party in which the conversation had been about something other than television and had thought: "Hey, wow, good television."

The host said that one of the best episodes they'd filmed so far had to do with people who had seen or had contact with flying saucers. These folks told good stories.

There were two other guests at the coffee table. One was Hugh Downs, the distinguished ABC commentator, a gentleman adventurer who once dove in a cage while great white sharks cruised by outside. The other interviewee was Dick Bass, who, at the time, was the oldest man to climb Mount Everest. We were to tell hair-raising stories of manly courage, or so I gathered. My job was to blather on about various adventures I'd written about in the past, before a sudden and vividly loathsome awareness of personal extinction had confined me to my own house for two months with a condition subsequently diagnosed as panic disorder.

Now, the entire concept of a fearless adventurer suffering panic for no reason at all is High Comedy on the face of it. I knew that. There was a part of me, just observing, that thought: "This is actually the story of *Stories,* happening right here on camera: big-adventure guy paralyzed by fear, for no apparent reason."

Sometime after the second commercial break, when it became achingly obvious that I was suffering a bout of intense emotional torment, Hugh Downs, a nice guy who is as calm and reassuring in person as he has always been on the small screen, sought to hearten and comfort me. "You know," he said, "the great Ethel Merman once said, 'Stage fright's a waste of time. What can they do, kill me?' "

I thought: "Thank you, Hugh, you blithering simpleton. Ethel Merman is *dead.* Does that tell you something, anything at all?"

A stagehand counted down from ten and the filming started again. The host asked: "What would you say your closest call was? Tim? Dick?"

He meant: Tell me a tale about how you came face-to-face with death and spit in its vile face. I could taste the bile rising in the back of my throat. Steel bands tightened around my chest, and I was possessed by a sense of vertigo so intense I could barely catch my breath. I was going to die, perhaps right then and there, but if not then, sometime, sooner or later. The perception wasn't simply academic. It was visceral. Death was nigh, and, contrary to Doctor Johnson's smug prediction, it did not concentrate the mind wonderfully.

Panic disorder strikes at least 1.6 percent of the population. It is characterized by feelings of intense terror, impending death, a pounding heart, and a shadowy sense of unreality. My own version featured several daily attacks of ten to thirty minutes in which I felt smothered and unable to catch my breath. There were chest pains, flushes, and chills, along with a looming sense of imminent insanity. The attacks struck randomly, like lightning out of a clear blue sky. The idea that people might see me in this state of helpless terror was unacceptable. I stayed home, cowering in my own privacy, unable to read, or concentrate, or write, or even watch television. My overwhelming conviction was that I was going batshit.

So when the producer called from ABC and asked me if I wanted to tell hairy-chested stories of virile derring-do, I said, "You bet." I thought: "This terror thing has gone on long enough. I'm going to stroll right over to the abyss and stare directly into it. And I'm going to do it on national TV. Face the fear, boyo."

The producer had seen a picture of me climbing El Capitan, in Yosemite, on a single rope. It looked pretty scary. Could I talk about that?

No problem.

El Cap, I explained, is shaped rather like the prow of a ship, and my companions had anchored a mile-long rope in half a dozen places up top and tossed it over a rubber roller positioned at the bow of the formation so that it fell free for 2,600 feet. A half-mile drop.

We were all cavers. The rope-walking and rappelling techniques we used are common in this dirty, underground sport. Caves generally follow the course of underground rivers, and sometimes these rivers form waterfalls. Over a millennium, the rivers sink deeper into the earth, and the waterfalls become mostly dry pits, sometime hundreds of feet deep. Many cavers like to "yo-yo the pits," which is to say, drop a rope, rappel down, and climb back up solely for the sport of it, never mind the exploration aspect.

That's what we were doing at Yosemite: we were going to yo-yo El Cap.

I recall standing on the talus slope at the bottom of the vertical granite wall with my climbing companion, photographer Nick Nichols. We calculated that the climb would take us five to six hours. Aside from a cruel weight of cameras that Nick carried, our backpacks contained some bits of spare climbing gear, a few sandwiches, and only two quarts of water. We intended to hydrate big-time before we started, and each of us choked down a gallon of water as we contemplated the cliff face.

Nick wanted me to follow him on the rope, for photographic reasons. His professional sense of the situation told him that the better picture was shooting down at my terrified face, with the world dropping out forever below. The alternative was six hours of my butt against the sky.

And so we strapped on our gear—seat harnesses, Gibbs ascenders on our feet, a chest roller that held us tight to the rope, a top jumar for safety—and proceeded to climb the rope. There was a goodly crowd of people watching us from the road. Some of them had binoculars.

About an hour into the climb, Nick called down that he had some bad news. The water we had drunk earlier had gone directly to his bladder. I contemplated the mechanics of the situation and shouted up: "Can't you hold it?"

"Four more hours?" he whined. "No way."

"Why didn't you think of this before we started?" I said. I sounded like my father discussing the same matter with me as a child on a long road trip.

In time, we devised a solution that might keep me dry. I climbed up to Nick, unclipped my top jumar, popped the rope out of my chest roller, and climbed above the ascenders he wore on his feet before clipping back into the rope. In that position—with me directly behind Nick, my arms wrapped tightly around his chest—he unzipped and did what he had to do. It took an inordinately long time to void a gallon of water. The rope was spinning ever so slowly so that, in the fullness of time, we were facing the road, and the crowd, and the people with binoculars. I feared an eventual arrest for public lewdness.

The television producer listened to the story and suggested the spinning-yellow-fountain aspect of the El Cap climb wasn't precisely what a family audience might want to hear. She wondered if there was any time during the ascent in which the choice was life or death.

Well, yes, in fact, a certain lack of foresight on my part had presented me with a number of unsatisfactory choices. I explained that, as Nick and I climbed, the wind came up and blew us back and forth in exciting, seventy-foot pendulum swings. This went on for some hours.

Had we simply dropped the rope off the prow of El Cap, the sharp, granite rock would have sawed it in half, snap bang splat, like that. Instead, the rope was draped over a long, solid rubber tube anchored to the edge of the cliff wall. The final obstacle on the climb was to muscle up over the roller. This was tricky. The rope itself weighed several hundred pounds, and was impossible to drag over the roller. Instead, there was another rope, a short one, anchored above and dangled over the rubber. It was necessary to unclip from the long rope and clip into the short one in order to make the summit.

It was a maneuver I had neglected to consider when I had clipped into the long rope on the talus slope five hours before. I had been contemplating the climb, not the summit, and was concerned with a danger peculiar to this type of climbing. If, for some reason, a climber lost his top jumar and his chest roller, he'd fall backward, and end up hanging from the ascenders on his feet. There is no way to recover from this calamity. You simply hang there, upside down, until you freeze to death. Popsicle on a rope.

With this in mind, I'd run the long rope through the caribiner that held my seat harness together, reasoning that, in the bad, upside-down emergency, I might still be able to pull myself erect. What this rig meant at the summit, however, was that I was going to have to unclip my seat harness to get off the long rope and onto the short one.

But . . . a seat harness, as every climber knows, is the essential contrivance that marries one to the rope. Unclipping wasn't certain death, but the probabilities weren't good. I assessed my chances for over an hour. It was getting cold and late. The half-mile drop yawning below was sinking into darkness as the sky above burst into flame. This sunset, I understood, might well be my last, and I followed its progress as I would that of a bad bruise on my thigh:

at first the sky seemed vividly wounded—all bright, bloody reds that eventually began healing into pastel oranges and pinks, which eventually purpled down into blue-black night. The temperature dropped. My sweat-soaked shirt was beginning to freeze to my body. I would have to do something.

Stories never made it to air. Not the adventure segment or even the one about flying saucers, which proves that sometimes the most fervent of our prayers are actually answered. Hugh Downs has retired from ABC, and Dick Bass is no longer the oldest man to have climbed Mount Everest. That honor now belongs to Georgian mountaineer Lev Sarkisov, who in 1999 reached the summit at age 60 years and 161 days.

And me? I haven't had a panic attack in ten years, knock wood. My doctor recognized the symptoms straight away and prescribed certain medications that had an almost immediate, ameliorative effect. He suggested therapy as well, but a pamphlet he gave me about panic disorder was pretty much all I needed. There were others, I learned, who have had to deal with uncontrolled anxiety. They included scientists such as Charles Darwin and Isaac Newton; actors Sir Laurence Olivier, Sally Field, and James Garner; writers Isaac Asimov, Anne Tyler, and Alfred, Lord Tennyson. Barbra Streisand and Sigmund Freud (natch) were on the list, along with the Norwegian Expressionist Edvard Munch, whose rendition of a panic attack is immortalized in a painting called *The Scream*.

The idea that I wasn't suffering alone—that the malady had a name—was strangely reassuring. Panic disorder feels like standing on the gallows, the rough rope on your neck, waiting, waiting, waiting for the floor to fall away into the never-ending night. But there is no rope, and no immediate threat. None at all. For some of us, these feelings are just another obstacle on the road of excess that the poet William Blake assured us leads to the palace of wisdom.

This is surely something to contemplate, but it doesn't get the grocery shopping done. In my experience, fear of collapsing into a puddle of terror at the mini-mart—agoraphobia—feels precisely the same as real, physical fear in the face of an actual threat. The difference is this: there is almost always something you can do when confronted with an authentic life-or-death situation.

At the summit of El Cap, for instance, my companions rigged up a pair of loops made of webbing, anchored them off, and dropped them over the rubber roller. I placed my feet in the loops, and laboriously muscled the heavy, long rope up over the roller: a triumph of brute strength over clear thinking.

There was no thinking at all, really, not in the ordinary sense of brooding contemplation. Risk sets its own rules, and one reacts to them instinctively, with an empty mind, in a state that some psychologists believe is akin to meditation. And, like the meditative state, risk takers sometimes feel they've caught a glimpse into eternity, into the wisdom of the Universe, and into the curve of blinding light itself. Just a glimpse.

We didn't talk about that on *Stories*. Sitting there sweating, waiting to vomit during the commercials, I was incapable of saying what I felt: that the stories we tell are the way we organize our experiences in order to understand our lives. I didn't say that risk is always a story about mortality, and that mortality is the naked and essential human condition. We put these stories together—in poems and essays and novels and in after-dinner conversations—in an effort to crowbar some meaning out of the pure terror of our existence.

The stories are prisms through which we perceive the world. They are like the lenses we look through in the optometrist's office: put them together incorrectly, and it's all a blur. But drop in the correct stories, turn them this way and that, and—all at once—there is a sudden clarity.

Call it enlightenment and admit that none of us ever gets all the way there. We only see glimpses of it in a flashbulb moment when certain selected stories fall together just right. That's all. In my own case, I know that fear always feels the same, that it is about perceived mortality, and that while courage continually escapes me, appearing on one silly, unaired television show remains the purest and the bravest thing I've ever done.

Trusty and Grace

Grace attends me on my jaunts into the steep mountainside wilderness above my cabin. Sometimes I believe I can actually see flashes of Grace in the slanting light that falls through the tall pines in this cathedral of forest. I am led, by Grace, up the steep hillsides, through areas of deadfall and over mossy logs that cross the constantly roaring whitewater of Falls Creek. Grace leads me through the bear and moose scat, over the forest floor, under a canopy alive with scolding squirrels, through beds of alpine wildflowers— mountain bluebells and clematis and pink twinflower—and in the evening, Grace accompanies me to bed, where she tends to fart a lot.

Everyone should have a little Grace in his or her life, and my Grace is a four-year-old, forty-pound Brittany spaniel whose august and noble soul is made apparent in a metabolism that operates on two speeds: hysterical and off. A faultless athlete, entirely innocent of tranquillity, Grace runs at speeds in excess of 25 miles an hour. The phrase "leaps and bounds" was coined to describe the breakneck rhythm of her passage through the forest. She sails over deadfall in ten-foot-long broad jumps, has no trouble swimming the creek that is too high and too treacherous for humans to cross, and streaks, at top speed, down a certain rocky hillside that most folks would describe as a cliff face.

Sometimes, when Grace leads me through the forest, she maketh me to fall down beside running water, if not into the running water itself. Better to find my own way through the wilderness—it is the Absaroka-Beartooth Wilderness that rises behind my cabin in Montana—and I know that Grace will follow, appearing now and again in a jingle of dog tags, or seen as a brown and white blur racing over the mossy forest floor, or chasing one of the black bears that periodically lumber past my cabin in search of the garbage I never put out. This little drama is played out in snatches of color barely perceived through the trees: a lardy, cinnamon-colored butt waddling up the hill, some young, garbage-obsessed bear harassed by a yipping brown-and-white streak that is the miracle of Grace.

Just lately, Grace and I have been accompanied on our walks by another dog. Trusty is an older golden retriever "type," who trudges heavily up the mountain, content to stay at my heel. Her eyebrows have gone a little white, so she has the look of a wise and aging scholar, a kind of Bertrand Russell of golden retriever types. This is well and fit, because Trusty is a dog who thinks a lot. Trusty thinks about leaves. Not leaves in mass, not forests, not sun-dappled meadows full of wildflowers. Trusty thinks about individual leaves, one at a time, and she thinks about these single leaves for hours, frowning and contemplating both stalk and blade.

Dry leaves are apparently as complex and revelatory as ones fresh from a bush or tree. The dog carries the chosen leaf gently in its mouth to a shady area, out of the sun, flops down onto her belly, and drops the green or brown object between her paws. Then she stares at it, intently, sometimes for over an hour, her patrician English logician's face crumpled in concentration. William Blake wrote the memorable opening stanza of "Auguries of Innocence" for Trusty:

> To see a World in a Grain of Sand
> And a Heaven in a Wild Flower,
> Hold Infinity in the palm of your hand
> And Eternity in an hour.

Presently, after an Eternity, or an hour, some concept great or small will occur to Trusty, some link to the final meaning of it all. She'll snort, a brief "harrumph," which is her canine version of "Eureka!" And the breath expelled through her muzzle will lift the leaf and set it atremble, as if to modify the physics of the entire situation and perhaps alter the very meaning of life, if not the physical state of the Universe, as we know it. Something to think about for another hour, anyway.

I have been watching Trusty contemplate leaves for the last several days. She's not my dog. She belongs to a family that lives in my town, the Liskas, whom Linnea and I count as among our best friends on earth. The father, Jim, once told me about the dog his kids love. The family was having a yard sale, and the dog, penned up in the backyard, longed to be out front. She attempted to climb the fence. Jim heard some strange, strangled sounds and ran out back to investigate. Trusty had gotten stuck between the house and the fence in such a way that she had strangled herself. The future canine philosopher was not breathing. Jim moved fast, hoisting the dog off the fence, and clamping her nose and mouth in such a way that he could give Trusty mouth-to-mouth resuscitation. Thus the dog's life was saved.

"So," I said to Jim, "your lips touched dog lips."

"And I don't even like that dog," he lied.

"She started staring at leaves after that?"

"Brain damage, probably."

Personally, I think it was Trusty's near-death experience that turned her into a canine metaphysician. She sees the world, heaven, infinity, and eternity all in the turn of a leaf.

Linnea and I are keeping Trusty for a few weeks because Jim and his family are one thousand miles away, out east, in Minneapolis, where his young daughter will be undergoing serious and perhaps life-threatening surgery. Her name is Courtney, and she's awfully tired of being called "a brave little girl." She's not a little girl, she just turned fifteen and—like many young women her age—loves horses. Unlike most, she rides like an angel, and competes against adults in the sport and art of dressage.

The doctor, at least, treated her as an adult, fully capable of making her own decisions based on the best and most honest information he could give her.

"Am I going to die?" Courtney asked.

"I don't think so," the doctor said.

"Will I be paralyzed?"

Once again, the doctor didn't think so. What Courtney knew, what the whole family knew was this: her spine needed to be rebuilt. If she did not have the operation, she would surely be paralyzed, probably in less than a year, and that paralysis could easily lead to death.

"Will there be a lot of pain?"

The doctor was candid: yes, for several weeks after the operation, Courtney would be in serious pain.

"And afterwards, will I be able to ride a horse?"

The doctor said that, if everything went well, it was a distinct and very real possibility. But there were no guarantees in a surgery as prolonged and complex as hers.

Courtney and her mother, Gerri, flew to Minneapolis, while Jim and his twelve-year-old son, Daniel, drove out to save money. Linnea and I took Trusty. The operation was scheduled for July 5.

Our little town's seventy-fifth annual Fourth of July parade featured classic cars, and all the town's several fire engines, as well as floats based on the theme "75 years of Ridin', Ropin', and Wranglin'." The Rodeo Queen contestants rode fine mounts and waved imperiously. The marching bagpipe band was, as always, a big hit, as were the miniature horses and the gaited pasafinos, and the mule train, and the cowboy band called the Ringling Five, playing on the back of a flatbed truck emblazoned with their brutally honest motto: "It ain't music."

Last year, some dimwit from Portland, Oregon, traveling through the West, caught our parade and wrote an angry letter to the local newspaper, criticizing the order of march. He was incensed that a float featuring a Marilyn Monroe impersonator was positioned ahead of one featuring a man dressed as Uncle Sam. I was idiotically enraged by the letter, and fired off one of my own, suggesting that next year this patriotic imbecile could march behind Mickey Mouse and ahead of the street sweeper.

The parade is one of my favorite events of the year, a chance to see most of my neighbors, and to cheer for floats my friends and their kids have spent days and sometimes weeks constructing. I like to applaud and acclaim those organizations that I support and think do good work in the community.

"Hurray for the Big Brothers and Sisters," I holler, my hands cupped to my face like a megaphone.

"Hurray for the Rural Volunteer Fire Department!"

This year, the Shriners, a fraternal group I used to find faintly ridiculous, with their secret handshakes and Grand Poo-bahs and distinctive red fez hats, were a large presence in the parade. Many of this year's Shriners were great big men in absurd clown costumes, wearing bulbous noses like neon lightbulbs and huge, floppy red shoes. They rode tiny motorized tricycles in looping circles and blew amplified ooogahh horns. Later, after the parade, a few of them would get drunk, and, somewhere, in one of the downtown bars, some sentimental clown with booze on his breath would tell me, once again, that the Shrine is a philanthropic organization operating a network of twenty-two hospitals that provide expert, no-cost orthopedic and burn care to children under eighteen. At this point, the drunken clowns usually have tears in their eyes and look like a bad painting on black velvet.

"Hurray for the Shriners," I shouted at the top of my lungs.

"What a bunch of bozos," a friend standing by my side said.

I could feel my fists clenching at my sides. My forearms swelled and the muscles corded in my upper arms.

"What?" the guy asked.

"You know Courtney Liska?"

"Having that operation? Brave little girl."

"The Shriners are paying for it."

"Hurray for the Shriners," my friend hollered. "Hurray for the Shriners!"

Grace, from a Christian viewpoint, is the love and mercy God visits upon sinners. The doctrine further holds that we are all sinners by simple virtue of our humanity. That is to say, grace is unmerited, which is why it is celebrated as being amazing. Great theological battles have been fought over the concept of grace and the idea that it is there for the taking, entirely unearned.

My own background is Catholic. I suppose my current status in that Church can best be described as long-lapsed. Even so, no one who has suffered a Catholic education is ever entirely free of the belief, or at least the discipline. Quaint notions, punitive and medieval, color my perception of the physical world. I tend to see the wilderness through the broken prism of my faith.

About a twenty-minute walk above my cabin, there is a place where the Falls Creek forks. Over the years, I've tracked a bit of a trail to that location, but it still requires a little bushwhacking to get there. In early July, the runoff is just beginning as snow melts on the mountains above. The creek is only ten yards wide, but the slope is so steep that whole trees, seventy feet high, are carried down the mountain and battered into slivers against protruding rocks. There is the sound of rushing water, constant and unrelenting, and something deeper, a contrapuntal rumbling that can be felt in the ground itself and which is the sound of large boulders being rolled down the streambed by the sheer and savage fervor of rushing water.

At the exact point where the creek divides, there is a rocky, moss-covered triangle of earth nudging out into the rushing water. It is where I sit when I visit the Fork. A constant mist, thrown up by the creek, makes the spot 10 degrees cooler than the rest of the forest. At dawn and dusk, when the sun is low in the sky, the slanting pillars of light that fall through the mist shimmer with a rainbow's color and look precisely like the light falling through stained-glass windows in a cathedral.

This place, the Fork on Falls Creek, is where I would go to pray, if I could pray, or if I thought that it would do any good at all.

Instead, on the day before Courtney's surgery, I walked up the hill with Grace and Trusty. We arrived at the Fork, and Trusty contemplated a leaf, while Grace appeared now and again, first on this side of the creek, then on that. Any ordinary dog would surely die attempting to cross Falls Creek during the runoff, but this was Grace, and Grace is amazing.

. . .

Courtney went into surgery on the morning of July 5. As they were wheeling her into the operating room, lightly tranquilized, she calmly asked her mother a favor. If she died, would it be possible for Gerri and Jim to put up a memorial to her in the little park down the street from their house? It didn't have to be expensive or anything, but she'd like a little horse that little kids could play on. Before they grew up and could ride a real horse.

The surgery was scheduled for nine that morning, and would take between seven and eight hours. It would be done around five Minneapolis time, four my time.

The day was hectic, and I was on the phone, on and off, for hours, conducting my business, such as it was. About three-thirty I stopped making or taking calls. We waited for word about Courtney from Gerri. Linnea had a list of folks to call, who all had lists themselves. There were dozens of people across the country who, like us, had spent the day worrying about Courtney. Trusty lay on the kitchen floor, studying a leaf I'd provided for the purpose. Linnea and I watched our respective telephones with the same intensity.

At four-twenty, Gerri called. Her voice sounded exhausted, slow and unsteady, as if each of her words had an anvil's worth of weight to it. I listened carefully and didn't hear grief.

"You sound good," I told Gerri, which was a lie on the face of it.

Linnea picked up the extension phone.

"Courtney's out of surgery," Gerri said. "They tell me I can see her in an hour."

The brave little girl had made it. Young lady. Brave woman.

"The nurses tell me she can wriggle her toes."

Not paralyzed.

It had not yet occurred to Gerri that she was relieved or happy, or overcome with joy. Linnea promised to call the half dozen people on her list.

I listened from my position at my desk. Trusty lay near Linnea's feet, staring at a new green leaf. She snorted briefly, the leaf jumped slightly, and the entire Universe tilted on its metaphysical axis.

Three days later, Gerri called and said that the surgery had gone so well that Courtney's therapist thought she could be up on horseback in about thirty days.

I called the dogs and together we started walking up the hill. I hadn't actually prayed at the Fork, and now I was walking up there to not actually give thanks. The dogs were happy, anyway. I had Trusty at my heel and Grace abounding.

ABOUT THE AUTHOR

TIM CAHILL is the author of six previous books, including *A Wolverine Is Eating My Leg, Jaguars Ripped My Flesh,* and *Pass the Butterworms.* He is an editor at large for *Outside* magazine, and his work appears in *National Geographic Adventure, The New York Times Book Review,* and other national publications. He lives in Montana.